CHAOS

in

COLOR

A MEMOIR of
CHILDHOOD TRAUMA
and FORGIVENESS

R. LAYLA SALEK, PhD

RIVER GROVE
BOOKS

The names and identifying characteristics of some persons referenced in this book have been changed to protect their privacy.

Published by River Grove Books
Austin, TX
www.rivergrovebooks.com

Distributed by River Grove Books

Design and composition by Greenleaf Book Group and Kim Lance
Cover design by Greenleaf Book Group and Kim Lance

Publisher's Cataloging-in-Publication data is available.

Print ISBN: 978-1-63299-702-9

eBook ISBN: 978-1-63299-703-6

First Edition

TO FIVE WOMEN:

SHERI, FOR GIVING ME LIFE;

KAREN, FOR SAVING MY LIFE;

BARBARA AND DANETTE, FOR UNVEILING MY LIFE;

AND HERIS, FOR BEING MY LIFE.

Contents

PROLOGUE   *1*

1. MOTHERED   *3*

2. FATHERED   *15*

3. IGNORED   *27*

4. ADORED   *47*

5. DISPLACED   *63*

6. LOVED   *85*

7. VISITED   *97*

8. DIAGNOSED   *99*

9. DISTURBED   *115*

10. FAILED   *129*

11. ISOLATED   *145*

12. ADOPTED   *165*

13. COLLAPSED   183

14. FREED   199

15. MARRIED   223

16. DUPED   245

17. BIRTHED   249

18. POLARIZED   267

19. REATTACHED   269

20. UNTETHERED   285

    EPILOGUE   295

    ABOUT *the* AUTHOR   301

Prologue

Chaos in Color: A Memoir of Childhood Trauma and Forgiveness is a collection of stories from my life between 1972 and 2019. All these years, they have lived in my mind. I have told and retold them a thousand times. Each story is told as I understood, experienced, and processed events in real time, which is how I've carried them with me throughout my life.

To maintain my authentic experience, I did not research or corroborate with others who played a part in these stories. However, after I finished each chapter, I allowed the main characters to read it if I was still in contact with them.

As I aged, I discovered growing up with a mentally ill parent who lived in a distorted reality had, in essence, distorted mine. This distortion, also known as trauma, complicated how my brain stored some of these painful memories. Some are inflated. Others are deflated. Some are crystal clear. Others are lost in the ether.

For a bit of clarification, I want to take a moment and address my odd ability to see some people in colors, which you will notice throughout the book. It automatically occurs without thought. This has happened for me since childhood. You'll see I grew up with a green dad and a brown mom. This is not referring to their skin, but my experience with them, as well as their aura and my memories of them.

However, not everyone I encounter has a color, and there is no reason or pattern for who does or does not have one. Many people who I love dearly do not come with a color attached. I apologize in advance if some people having a color and others not having one is off-putting. I debated whether to include this part of my life, but ultimately, whether it is a distortion or a unique quality of mine, it is a profound personal experience that needs to be part of my narrative. When words fail, colors speak.

As I've acquired new knowledge of some events, my understanding of the details have also changed. Though I did not alter the stories of my own experience, I have included these changes in the epilogue. Facts should be clarified, but I still wanted the audience to read the stories as they unfolded for me in real time, how they were stored in my mind, how they shaped my childhood and adulthood, and how I've carried them with me all these years. No matter how difficult, I stay true to my memories because I want to help others who have also been raised by a mentally ill parent.

The more I search and study, the more I realize I must let go of my attachment to these stories since the present moment is what matters. The very "nowness" of this realization has helped me see that none of these stories are who I am—they are mere glimpses into a faded past. Today, I am only concerned with my present joy. My present shadows. The present breeze on my cheeks. Everything else, I have released.

The characters in this book are real people who continue to share and sculpt my life, and I will be forever grateful to them. Sharing space with someone battling mental illness is a hard but rewarding journey. To all the children of mental illness and all the caregivers for it, I wish you compassion, awareness, and peace in the present moment.

1

Mothered

The trouble was, I had been inadequate all along.
I simply hadn't thought about it.

—SYLVIA PLATH, *THE BELL JAR*

Wicked. Gorgeous. Brown. Strong. Cunning. Sensitive. Broken. Stubborn. Manipulative. Wild. Shrewd. Sharp. Survivor. Depressed. Vengeful. Scrappy. Dark. Manic. Secretive. Aggressive. Unruly. Sexual. Mad. Smart. Cool. Sarcastic. Mean. Impulsive. Moody. Fearful. Ignorant. Lost. Scary. Hysterical. Fun. Paranoid. Witty. Selfish. Clever. Resourceful.

Ill.

The very thought of discussing my mom causes panic. It's as if I am exposing her. Ratting her out. Telling our family secrets. By family, I mean Mom and me.

As I type, I do so with trepidation. Afraid my words will call her into existence. Bring her forth. Send her into a rage. End with a beating. A ball from my gut moves to my throat until tears fall. I stop typing. I breathe deep. I take a moment to comfort myself. *She is gone. Out of reach. Out of touch. She is lost in the world. Lost in her mind. She cannot hurt me. Cannot touch me. Cannot find me.*

Well, she could. I am certain she knows where I am. I am certain the old Sheri could and would hunt me down. But she is too old. Too ill. Too gone. These facts, however, do not suppress my fears. The sound of her name—*Sheri*—evokes anxiety within me, triggering my fight-or-flight reaction. My palms sweat. My heart races. My nostrils widen. My pupils dilate. My hairs stand on end. I want to scream, "I'm sorry, Mom. I didn't mean to. I'll stop writing. I'll stop now. I haven't said anything. Don't hit me! Please! I'm sorry! Stop!"

I often wonder what happened to us. *How did love morph into fear and then hate? What happened to her? What bred her anger? When did violence become normal—an option? When did I become afraid of my mom? At what point in her history did madness take root, gain control of her being, and dictate her senses? When did her beauty turn dark and ugly? Why was suicide a viable solution for her and eventually me?*

I need to know these answers. I must remember the beginning, middle, and end. I want to remember the sane years—the years stuffed with love and hope. I remember loving her until I was five, and I remember being loved by her. I was proud of my petite, feminine mom, shyly seated on the edge of the room. She added to the ambience everywhere she went but was unaware of her effect on others. Unaware her beauty permeated everything and pulled all the attention her way. She was the one they all wanted.

Like all babies with their moms, she was definitely the one I wanted. No one else mattered. I wanted to stare at her for hours. I wanted to swim in those big, black eyes that held my gaze. They were framed by spidery lashes. Lashes I wanted to touch. Shrouded by her long, jet-black hair. I wanted to play with her. I wanted her attention and affection. I wanted to burrow in her brown skin. Her brown energy. Her brown light.

I stared, anticipating her smile. When it finally came, a uniquely imperfect, perfect gap in her teeth was an invitation to pull up a chair.

An invitation to join in the fun. An invitation to stay awhile. She possessed the ability to transform the mundane into an adventure, even if no adventure was to be had. Where in one moment she might be shy, in another she was the life of the party. Her adventures either had no rules or her rules. In both, she was ready to buck authority, play, dance, sing, and enjoy life. She was ready to be my mom. And I was ready to be her daughter.

As a young mom with just me, an only child, our playtime had no concept of time. We played an endless game of hide-and-seek in the front yard. I hid in the same spot behind the same tree every time. I did it on purpose to make her laugh ring out. Her eyes sparkled with happiness, illuminating her brown. In the evenings when we were alone, we giggled and tickled until we were sleepy, falling asleep in the same bed. I was wrapped in adoration, cozy in motherly love. Each night ended identical to the one before.

"Gimme your leg," she'd say. At that, I curled my leg over my mom's side. We both slipped into slumber.

With love and time came trust. I believed her words. I held her beliefs. I trusted her intentions. I believed anything she concocted. Like all parents, she was molding my mind and my world. I was her experiment. I was her amusement. Unfortunately, it was to my detriment and embarrassment. When I was learning to talk, my mom often jumbled words and meanings without ever telling me. She taught me oranges were called moons and the moon was called an orange. Numerous times, I asked for a moon to eat outside of home. Numerous times, I was mocked. Little did I know, much of my world was deliberately twisted because of my mom's twisted mind.

After my first day of daycare, the administrator requested a parent meeting. He wanted to suggest I get my hearing checked.

"Why? She can hear just fine."

"She isn't orienting to her name," said the administrator.

"What name are you calling her?" she snapped back.

The administrator ruffled the papers from my file.

"Roni Reese. The name on her application."

My mom grinned, rose to her feet, and grabbed my hand.

"There is nothing wrong with her ears. She goes by Susie McGillicuddy."

That's how I learned my name was Roni. Younger than five, my sense of identity was faulty. My foundation was already shaky. It didn't stop there. In kindergarten, my teacher asked us to learn our birth story for homework. The next day, my teacher randomly picked me to share.

"Roni, tell the class about your birthday."

Proudly, I weaved to the front. I faced my peers.

"My mom found me on the side of road under a rock. I was a turtle. She took me home and loved on me until I became a baby girl."

The room fell silent. My heart sank. From their expressions, I knew Sheri had struck again. But this time, I felt anger. I felt like her joke. I hated being her entertainment. But regardless of my wishes and my feelings, she took pleasure in my pain.

She laughed when I walked into glass doors, bounced off, and fell behind her at the toy store checkout counter. She burst into an obnoxious cackle, bent over laughing. She failed to help. Instead, a store employee lent me a hand. I brushed off my embarrassment. Deep feelings of abandonment simmered.

For the first time, I started to feel apart from my mom. I started to feel alone in the world. She continued to use me as her punchline. It didn't matter if I was hurt or humiliated. It didn't matter if it was in private or public. No matter what, she laughed at me.

One night during Bible study, I repeatedly pushed my purse further and further under my chair. I fell headfirst onto the floor. My legs stuck straight up. My panties were exposed. My feet were flailing. She roared. She slapped her knee as I struggled to right myself. The elder on stage stopped the meeting to ask over the microphone, "Can someone please help Sheri?" An older lady rescued me and comforted me. My mother did not.

When her cackle wasn't directed at me, I enjoyed my mother's warped and wicked sense of humor. I often imitated her style. We went to great lengths to make each other laugh. Humor became our coping skill and favorite pastime.

At home, we plotted and planned to startle and scare each other, graduating to more creative, sadistic pranks over time. As one of us turned a corner or entered a dark room, the other jumped out and screamed, "Gotcha!" As one of us bathed, the other threw ice-cold water over the shower curtain. As one of us stepped outside, the other locked the door. We lived for the element of surprise, but we also lived cautiously. We were always suspicious. We were always on guard.

No place or activity was safe from a prank. No one could make us laugh like each other. Together, we were two giggling idiots who required constant intervention to behave. We often lost our composure during quiet, sad, serious moments. I have countless memories of our uncontrollable laughter disrupting events.

To a child, she was a fantastic comic who, unlike other adults, welcomed laughter during the most inappropriate times. She modeled and encouraged ill-timed silliness. Another Bible study evening, I was bored, tired, and drawing cartoons while the adults analyzed Scripture. My mom glanced at my drawing: a cowboy worm roller-skating up a tree. She busted out. Lost it. Neither of us could regain control. The rest of the Bible class glared.

"Sheri, do you two need to step outside?" the elder called out abruptly.

Embarrassed, we ceased laughing and turned into statues. We

couldn't look at anyone, least of all each other. My mom discreetly tucked the drawing into her purse. She kept it for years and showed it to everyone.

As a child, I failed to understand that my mom was an adolescent girl in an adult's body. She never fully developed. She was never loved. Never secure. I sensed her raw vulnerability, but I was unaware of the depth of her fears. Unaware of the depth of her sorrows. Unaware of the root cause of her suffering. Unaware how her brownness was birthed. Without this knowledge, I vacillated between feeling safe with her, wanting to protect her, and, after I turned five, fearing her.

Even though she stood strong and held her own amid husbands, enemies, and authority, she inevitably crumbled into a defenseless, scared child around her family. In their presence, her stance shifted from easygoing to alert. She was never fully committed to the scene. She was always ready to bolt if given the chance or fight if she was pushed.

Squashed among four sisters and one brother, my mom was born fourth in her family. The sibling order was Pat, Lottie, Jerry, Sheri (Mom), Winona, and Roy. Each of them could scare the shit out of me. Their unpredictability coupled with their failure to regulate their emotions, handle their alcohol, maintain relationships, or problem solve without aggression proved unsettling.

Each responded with either fight or flight to most situations. On family reunions, holidays, and weekend visits, I prayed for more flighting and less fighting. However, when three or more were together, violence ensued. Events inevitably ended in hurt feelings and deep, lasting wounds. I can't recall a period when all my mother's siblings were on speaking terms.

Because of this, my mom kept her distance and raised me several hours from her nearest sibling. It was obvious all my mother's siblings suffered greatly. Depressed and dejected, life had wronged each one of them. Life had whipped them. Repeatedly. For years. The fallout from their childhood warped their adulthood, rippling to the next generation and beyond. However, they each possessed such personality. If life had smiled on them, they would have been extraordinary, though none of them ever considered this possibility. Their trauma did not allow for such beliefs, let alone normalcy, stability, or dreams.

Though all my mother's siblings shared a traumatic childhood, each wore their trauma differently. According to my mother, her oldest sister, Pat, was the most disturbed. She was a virtual stranger to me. Fearful, my mother purposely, deliberately, avoided her. As a child, I enjoyed Pat stories like I enjoyed horror films. I was all eyes and ears for every gory detail of her severely beating her children. Frightened, but not shocked—my mother and all her siblings had tempers. I felt a chill, however, at the stories of Pat's "demon possession" allowing her to move objects with only her mind. As far as I could tell, I was related to the bogeyman.

Lottie, the second in line, was my favorite. She picked my middle name, Layla, based on Eric Clapton's hit by the same name. Even though she exhibited a wide range of emotions around her siblings, on her own, she felt comparatively stable. Married twice with three children, her second marriage was to my dad's best friend. I adored their family. In their presence, I felt safe and connected. We spent many weekends together between their house in Abilene and ours in Fort Worth; the end of our time together often brought me to tears.

Jerry, the third, was broken and sensitive. Instead of growing callused, she developed a soft shell. She had a great laugh and a sweet demeanor. I didn't see her often, but when I did, I wanted to hug her, protect her, and wrap her in Bubble Wrap. Severely bullied as a child, Jerry latched on to a boy just as scrawny and poverty-stricken as she—a kindred spirit and kind soul who grew to be her loyal husband.

Together, they provided the best attempt at a stable, loving home for their children.

My mother and Winona, born after her, were both striking, little, mentally ill, and mean as hell. It was difficult to tell them apart as they both had long, black hair with petite figures. Even their personalities were similar—both free, strong, and wild. Winona raised, trained, and sold Dobermans. She kept one as a pet, named Satan. Though bigger than Winona, he was somehow her canine incarnate. Winona married, had a son, and divorced.

Jerry raised Roy, the baby and only boy, until he was old enough for the army to finish raising him. He married and had two children, but even as an adult, whenever my mom spoke of him, she spoke of a young, immature, incapable boy. He perpetually looked lost and in need of guidance, or maybe in need of a mom. As the youngest, Roy suffered both the most and the least.

Deep in her bones, my mom craved family and unconditional love. She craved her tribe. Over the years, through trial and error, her grandfather "Pa" proved to be the sole person with whom my mom felt secure. When we saw him, she melted in his arms and fawned over his words.

In turn, I warmed to Pa and eagerly anticipated trips to Oklahoma, looking forward to his antics. During family reunions, Pa positioned himself in the center of the action. For kicks, as one of us ran by, he deviously placed his cane on the ground and snapped our feet from under us, chuckling as we tripped and tumbled.

With his towering stature and crooked wooden cane, I don't remember Pa any age but old. He lived in Antlers, Oklahoma, before traffic lights existed. Once they were installed, Pa refused to stop at a red, still driving straight through intersections. Knowing his stubbornness and temperament, everyone, including the police, gave him a pass. Known as Boss Crain, he was equally respected and feared by all.

A full-blooded Irishman, Pa came to Oklahoma in 1918 on a covered wagon. On his path, he came upon the Choctaw tribe. As an elderly man approached, Pa pointed out the woman he wanted. However, the man suggested a different girl.

"Younger, prettier," the man said.

Pa declined.

"I want her. The strong and sturdy one," he said, pointing again to my great-grandmother. Pa and Ma had five boys and a girl—my grandmother Lena Mae.

Even though my mother and her siblings had two parents to claim, neither their mother nor father was a parent. Her father was the town drunk. She never spoke of him. I never even knew his name. I knew more about Lena Mae. Ahead of her time, she owned a beauty salon, took pilot lessons, and fancied alcohol and partying. Unfortunately, as Lena Mae gallivanted around town, her children attended school dirty and hungry. This alone set them apart from their peers, prompted bullying, and caused fights. Pa and Ma often intervened, searching for Lena Mae, scolding her for leaving the kids. Urging her to go home.

Throughout my mom's childhood, she and her siblings literally fought for survival—food, water, clothing, and shelter. And they had to fight one another when their resources dried up. They tried to forget these gruesome facts. They tried to stuff them down. They tried to erase them. If I ever complained, my mom responded, "You have no clue. As a little girl, I went to sleep hungry every night. I pushed my pillow against my stomach, so it didn't feel empty, and I could sleep."

And with that, I stopped complaining.

Over the years, their group conversations often landed on those foodless times. These conversations triggered the most trauma. The darkest emotions. The deepest hurts. The saddest stories. During one visit after a few drinks, Aunt Lottie stared in space and got quiet.

Eventually, she called me to her side. I hesitated. My gut warned me. She motioned for me again. Reluctantly, I complied.

"You know, I saved your mom's life when she was a little girl. If it weren't for me, you wouldn't be here," she said.

My body stilled. Hypervigilant.

"Since we never had enough food to feed all of us, we became quite desperate. Shit, we were kids."

My body shook.

"One morning, I heard Pat planning to kill your mom," she continued.

I wanted the story to be over. I wanted her to stop. But by her look, I knew she wanted to see my reaction. She wanted to scare me. See me squirm. She smirked as she placed the weight of the memory in my lap. I caught my breath. She continued.

"I think Pat was jealous of your mom. You know, she's the prettiest. Maybe Pat was just hungry. Hell, if I know. But when I heard those sounds from the other room, I knew what was happening."

She paused. I braced myself.

"I ran toward the bed. Pulled Pat off your mom. She was suffocating her."

I sat in disbelief. I tried to block out the images. It all felt too wrong for this world. But apparently, it was not too wrong for my world. Not too wrong for this family. For these siblings.

"Your mom knows I'll always protect her," Lottie finished after a few quiet moments.

The air felt thick. I couldn't move. I couldn't talk. I realized then my mom's pain was rooted in this incident. Rooted in the fear of death. The fear of family. The fear of a cruel, motherless world.

Whenever my mother was drunk, sad, or particularly brown, she recounted the horrific, grim story of her mom's death.

"Last time I saw Mama, she brought us groceries home. While we unloaded them, she sat in the car. She didn't say nothin'. She might've been drunk. I don't know. She waited in the driveway. As soon as she saw a diesel truck, she put the car in reverse and hit the gas. The truck decapitated her. I was only fifteen," she shared. Flat.

The story always ended there. No more details. No more discussion. None of her other siblings ever spoke of their mom's death. But whenever my mom spoke of it, it was with a cold, emotionless matter-of-factness to which I eventually became accustomed.

When Lena Mae died, the older siblings were already married with children. The younger ones, like my mom, were extracted from hell and split into separate foster homes. I knew this, but my mom never discussed it. She never uttered a word. She never dealt with it. None of them did. And I knew not to ask.

In the late 1960s, still in high school, my mom moved to California with relatives who graciously opened their home to her. Those were her happy, fun years. She was in love. Throughout my childhood, various songs prompted her beautiful smile at the memory of her high school sweetheart and their love. I lived for these stories. Her tone would soften. Her eyes would flicker with happiness. Her brown would glow golden, and I was so grateful she had moments when she felt wanted and loved. If only those years could have lasted, we all may be different now. Softer now. More secure.

After she dropped out of school, my mom reluctantly traveled to Texas and left her love behind. On her first night home, Aunt Lottie begged her to go out. Tired and disheveled from traveling, my mom sat alone in a bar booth. She nursed a beer. After a while, she noticed a tall, handsome blonde doing the "Funky Duck" to Santana. Nine months later, at the age of nineteen, she gave birth to me—a life born out of chaos into chaos.

2

Fathered

A fatherless girl thinks all things are possible and nothing is safe.

—MARY GORDON, *THE COMPANY OF WOMEN*

I have never been small in being or personality. Never small in vision or dreams. Nor small in voice or tongue. These are all qualities I credit to my dad and my initial attachment to him. He was my first encounter with love and safety. From the moment I entered this world, I was loved, and I loved. Even though I can't recall, I am quite certain the all-consuming, deep affection implanted in me at inception and solidified in our initial encounter was love at first sight.

My love for him was more than an infant seeing her father. It was like I was a part of his body. I looked like him. Both blondes. I was named after him. Both named Ron. I acted like him. Both clowns. I was of him. Inseparable. Attached. We were one. Whatever he taught me, I trusted. Whatever he did, I copied. Whatever he felt, I sensed. I was daddy's girl. Completely devoted. Completely his. From birth to five, he was my world. My sunrise. My sunset. My green. My everything. I was proud he was mine. All mine.

On August 9, 1972, I was born in a small hospital in Jackson, California. However, by the time I could walk, we were back in Texas.

Almost as far back as I can remember, every time we passed the Fort Worth City Jail, my mom would announce, "Your dad saw you take your first steps through his jail cell window. Look! That window, right there." After all she put our little family through, I'd barely turn my head at her lies. I never asked for details. Never wanted them. Never appreciated her stories of my dad. I know she loved him. I know she loved me. She just had a demented way of showing affection and attention. Her stories, whether true or false, were hurtful.

With his tall, all-encompassing stature and Robert Redford looks, I felt smart and special by his side. Felt important and significant. He spoke to me as his equal and hung with me as his mate. We had less than nothing, but we also had an entire world to explore together. Therefore, we had it all. My awe and wonder were born from him. Developed by him. He expanded my worldview beyond our house. Beyond our yard. Beyond our little family. He taught me to reach out and grab life, play with it, touch it, turn it over in my hands, and set it back in its rightful place. Unharmed. Intact. Give it love and set it free. He believed all living creatures are equal and in need of love and consideration. He taught me nature would reveal itself and unfold before my eyes as long as I treated everything with kindness and respect.

Like two astronauts on a new planet, we inspected the earth and discovered its beautiful secrets. Trees, land, animals, insects, and clouds were all subject to our analysis. In them we found our entertainment. With his gentle ways and hands-on teaching, I stayed engaged. With my enthusiasm and zest, he soaked up the experience through my eyes. In those moments, his inner little boy came out to play. His heart swelled with tenderness. His greenish-blue eyes sparkled with sweetness. He, too, was in love.

It's possible his love for me was unmatched. I was the first thing that was truly his. The first person to unconditionally love him. To experience his gentleness. To see a hopeful future within him. To believe in his potential and possibility. His parents saw no such thing—they birthed him and his older sister and then literally left them. Neglected them. Abandoned them. Locked them outside from morning to evening. Demanded to be left alone. An unfeeling mother and a traveling father, they provided zero compassion or empathy. Provided no education or guidance. Provided no real social or adaptive skills. Then mocked him whenever he failed or proved incapable. Bad-mouthed him for not returning home, for not maintaining a relationship with them.

My father and his older sister became independent and resilient out of necessity. They were unmothered. Unfathered. And at his first opportunity, my dad left home. Left them all.

"I was born to the two most selfish people on the planet," he would say, and it showed. Because of his shaky foundation, my dad trusted no one and loved few. He loved animals more than humans. He navigated the world with nothing more than his God-given talents, street smarts, good looks, and great comedic timing. He hitchhiked around the country, lived in various states, shared homes with friends, and worked odd jobs.

This trial-and-error life proved harsh in the beginning. He had no one to depend on. No one to call on during hard times. No one to give a damn about him. Fortunately, and unfortunately, his past, his upbringing, and his decisions collectively led him directly to my mom. They were both broken and beautiful. Both orphans, lost and free.

As if it was fate, my parents unconsciously collided at a local bar the night my mother moved to town. They were also fated to fail. Their whirlwind relationship played out between two states. Commenced in Texas. Culminated in California. Crashed back in Texas. Looking back, they seemed destined to implode, though no one could have convinced them of this undeniable fact. They had no family. No money.

Ron, Sheri, and Layla

No high school diplomas. After their fateful meeting, they hitchhiked back to California and walked the streets, two in-love hippies. They slept where they could and built a home wherever God led them.

I still remember the happy times—the three of us filled with love and laughter. Maybe it was my imagination, maybe it was religion, or maybe I remember the better part before the end part. Or maybe, just maybe, I was too young to decipher. Too young to understand love, life, and loss. Maybe I just wanted my parents together. Wanted them happy. Wanted them to love each other. Wanted them to love me.

I know my parents were in love. I felt it. I saw it. I remember the love in my dad's eyes as he stared at my mom from across the room. I noticed how he admired her beauty. I could see he was thankful she was his. I recall my mom's satisfied smile as my dad entertained their friends. I remember how she looked up at him from her petite vantage point with delight in her eyes, gazing with love and pride.

I remember our happy. I thought it was here to stay. Thought they were mine to claim. Maybe I just wanted what every child wanted. For a while, I convinced myself I had it. A beautiful mom. A cool, loving dad. Two parents at home. Clothes. Food. Friends. Health. We looked like other families. I thought we lived like them, too. I felt firmly planted in the world and attached to our family of three.

Aunt Rebecca, my dad's sister, found God in the Jehovah's Witnesses. As the beliefs and principles captured her mind, she preached to those closest to her. She converted my parents and their dear friends Lloyd and Karen Melendy—a sweet, loving family who lived across the street from her. They had a son one year older than me and one on the way. Aunt Rebecca was also pregnant with her first at the time.

All three couples studied and explored the Bible together. They wanted to please God. Wanted a better future for their children. They acclimated to the people and culture. Attended the meetings. Attempted self-discipline. For some time, religion held us together and breathed life into our family. Transformed our world. Stopped the fighting. Offered my parents a purpose.

The more they learned, and the more God permeated their hearts, the more they stopped their worldly ways. My dad shaved his beard and cut his hair. He went from hippie to conservative. They ceased smoking. Watched their drinking. Stifled their tempers. In a particularly sad change for me, we stopped celebrating holidays and birthdays.

Before their conversion, I enjoyed spending holidays with my dad's parents. I appreciated the opportunity to know and have a relationship with them, regardless of my dad's feelings and experiences. I loved Pappa Dave and Mema. They gave me my favorite thing: Roni Rabbit.

My best friend. But my dad and Aunt Rebecca wanted to break the cycle. They envisioned a different life for themselves. For their children. They revered the Scriptures and abided by God's proclamations. Therefore, holidays had to go.

When my parents learned of God's original intent for man and woman—marriage—they ceased "living in sin." So, on April 3, 1975, my dad's birthday, they got hitched in a quaint wedding ceremony hosted by the Witnesses with me, their two-year-old, in tow.

In their wedding photos, my parents' expressions were captured along a continuum. At times they look hopeful and happy. At others, they look scared as hell. In all photos, they are young and poor. In my eyes, the marriage made us more bonded. In God's eyes, we were complete. In the law's eyes, we were official. We all went with it.

For a brief, blissful time, we lived with Mrs. Reeves, a random, elderly lady who needed help. She lived in her big house. We stayed in the guesthouse. Her property spanned several green, manicured acres where we roamed alongside the animals and my parents worked. Mom cleaned and nursed. Dad mowed and tended.

When my dad worked away from home, I waited impatiently for him to return. Uninterested in others, I looked out the window and watched the door. Waited for his green. When his car appeared, I shrieked and ran to him, beaming at the sound of his voice. If my dad was between jobs, which was often, and had finished all the chores, I didn't leave his side. I loved waking to him in the morning. I loved seeing his face first.

On my days home with dad, I followed his every step. Nipped at his heels. Our time together was easy. Effortless. Free. Fun. With his unique wit, he dealt with our day. Dealt with my mom. Dealt with the present. Dealt. He spoke of neither the past nor the future.

Like my mother, he used comedy to cope and contend, but his sense of humor was distinct. Different. Clean. Appropriate. Child-friendly. He often hurled dad jokes in a silly voice to make me laugh. To keep me on my toes. To ease our situation. Between his gentle nature and comedic ways, I never felt anxious with him. Never worried. Never wanted more.

My dad and I spent many days together as "two scallywags" tramping around the property, both shirtless, he in pants and me in a diaper. With our naturally laid-back attitudes, people joked that our hearts barely beat. Inside, we explored the world of entertainment—music, movies, shows—followed by naps. When we woke, we went back to watching TV. We ate peanut butter and banana sandwiches. Snacked on sardines with saltines. Learned about artists and songs. Listened to Greg Allman and Pink Floyd.

Once we sufficiently investigated inside, we moved outside. Hours passed as we roamed the green pasture and nearby streets. I played naked in the water hose. We swam in the pool. I pushed the kitties in my buggy. Waved to the birds. Talked to squirrels. We were lost in our curiosity. Lost in green. Lost in search of life. Lost in search of tarantulas.

Once the spiders were in our possession, I was afraid, but my dad sparked compassion and interest within me. He wanted to calm my fears. Wanted to watch my brain work. As the tarantula crawled up my arm, I marveled at each velvety leg. Each fang. We petted the creature, counted its legs, and discussed its colors.

When we were satisfied with our spider inspection, we released them and visited the horses. These massive creatures fascinated me, but my mom didn't want me near them. Didn't want me riding them. She voiced her opinion loudly and boldly, but we ignored her and did as we pleased. I squirmed with happiness as my dad carried me toward them. After I watched intently as his hands ran across the horse's body, I copied his movement. Slow. Gentle. Methodical. My tiny hands looked almost insignificant next to my dad's strong and substantial ones. He held me in one hand and managed the horse with the other. My mom may have been scared, but I wasn't. Not with my dad navigating. Not with him holding me.

Once as my dad carefully placed me on the horse's back, the horse kicked and bucked. I flew high into the sky. Held my breath. No time to cry. I am sure a million emotions filled my dad's heart, and even more thoughts cluttered his mind. However, he still positioned himself perfectly and caught me. As soon as I felt his arms, I scrambled to his neck. Clung tightly. Safe. Secure. Saved by my Super Dad. I never doubted him.

Eventually, though, our bliss was interrupted as religion's inspirational influence waned. Old wounds and old cracks festered and broke open. Whatever my parents attempted to bury resurfaced. Whatever God mended ripped apart. We made a slow, tumultuous descent into three individual pieces. Their path echoed their song, "Wild World" by Cat Stevens. Theirs was a delicate dance between two magnets. At times inseparable. At times repellent. Constantly prepared for the other to bolt.

My mom started bad-mouthing my dad in his absence to whoever would listen. Sometimes she exaggerated her stories. Sometimes she spun completely false tales. I will repeat none of them. It was like she forgot I lived in the house. Forgot I had his eyes and ears. Forgot I loved him more than life. Forgot I was of him.

I knew her words were twisted. Fabricated to turn my dad into a monster. But others didn't. They were in the dark. Engulfed in her brown. They liked gossip. They inhaled her stories. Believed her. Felt sorry for her. They were engrossed in each elaborate detail. Engrossed with each plot twist and turn.

One summer day, her audience was so engrossed and focused they forgot about me. Forgot I was in the pool. Forgot the dangers. Forgot I couldn't swim. I floated around the pool in a donut. This cheap 1970s floatation device encircled my waist and buoyed me atop the water when it was right-side up. However, if it accidentally flipped upside down, it could hold me under the water.

This particular day, I kicked and played for a bit, but got unlucky. I flipped over. My head submerged. My legs thrashed in the air. I couldn't right my inner tube. I kicked. I flailed. I panicked. I almost drowned.

My open, desperate eyes burned from the chlorine. From my underwater vantage point, I could see my mom still sitting. Still talking. She had no idea her daughter was fighting for life. From across the pool, a stranger jumped in. Saved me.

The stranger placed me on the side of the pool. I gasped and spat. Tried to breathe. Tried to calm my body. I burst into tears. My mom failed to notice. Missed the commotion. She was still busy disparaging my dad when the stranger approached her. Clued her in. Pointed her in my direction. Finally, my mom rushed toward me.

For the first time, I didn't feel safe with her. For the second time, I felt separate from her. Angered. Disappointed. Embarrassed. Her apology meant nothing. She felt incompetent to me. Dark. Reckless. Incapable of keeping a living thing alive. I wanted my dad. I wanted her to shut up about him. On the way home, she begged me not to tell him. I stewed and bubbled. Focused on a few key offenses. Mulled them over in my mind. If my dad had been present, I would have been safe. His eyes would have been on me. In fact, he would have been in the pool with me. Empowered and fueled by my anger, I told him as soon as I could.

Our bliss also started to crack with their arguments. Without forewarning, it became a thing. Became a consideration. Became a worry. Became my mom's favorite pastime. She was never content. Never grateful. She was unconcerned if I was present or not for their fights. Unconcerned by what I heard or witnessed. She hurled insults like confetti. Ranted and raged. Conversely, my dad wanted me to be a kid. He tried to refrain from exposing me to adult problems. He watched his behavior in my presence. He never cussed. Never yelled. He sat calmly while she purged and prodded.

I often crawled into his lap and waited for her gas to empty. After she quieted or exited, my dad would sit in silence. Deep in thought. I sat silent with him. After a few moments, he snapped out of it, so I snapped back as well. Then we got back to living and exploring. Eating and laughing. I wasn't sure if he knew or cared why she was mad. I knew I didn't. As long as my dad was with me, her tantrums were a blip on my radar.

Perhaps I should have been concerned as our home environment began to spill over everywhere. The arguing became our fourth family member. At any second, in any place, an argument could walk through the door. It took on a pulse. Breathed our oxygen. Suffocated us all.

When arguments failed to evoke fireworks, my mom became the aggressor and deliberately caused altercations. She leapt toward my dad. Without warning. Without just cause. With fists locked and loaded. With the intent to incite. With the intent to fight. She soared. She struck. She wanted a story. Wanted the drama. She couldn't live without it. She provoked my dad until his green flickered and dimmed. His ugly side emerged. He would have to hold her back. Stop her. Then she would play the victim to everyone around her. Little did they know, she was never the victim at home or anywhere else.

While visiting Aunt Rebecca one evening, cozy in my footed pajamas, my mom imploded. She yelled, jumped toward my dad. He snatched me up. Tried to get away. She advanced. He turned the furniture into barricades between us. She lunged. He dodged. From the couch to the chair and back again, he protected us. Kept us safe. I jostled in his arms as they played cat and mouse but was perfectly content.

I didn't want to go with her. She looked crazy. Acted scary. Once she tired herself, she fled across the street to the Melendys with new stories in tow. My dad and I watched TV then went to sleep. Those were always the best sleeps. Brown gone. Blanketed in green. Just him and me. Safe. Calm.

At four, I didn't equate fighting to anything, especially not to an ending. I believed fighting was the norm. I didn't know about divorce. I'd never heard the word. I didn't know any divorced adults. I knew my mom was unpredictable, moody, and half-cocked. I knew at times she was angry with my dad. But that was her. I knew my dad was exasperated with my mom. And I knew often he retaliated against her. But that was him. I loved them both. Sometimes I was fearful of my mom and their fights. But that was me. This was us. This was how we lived.

But she couldn't leave well enough alone. She wanted to burn our entire family to the ground, unsatisfied until our ashes smoldered. Until everyone hated my dad. Until we were all asphyxiated in her brown. She didn't care what she was doing to our family. What she was doing to me. To him. To his reputation. She didn't care that her stories implicated the love of my life. Didn't care her actions separated us and pushed him away.

Doesn't she understand how much I love him? How much I need him? How much we need each other? Doesn't she care about our feelings or understand what a dad means to a daughter? Apparently, she didn't. Such things were lost on her. We remained at the mercy of her wishes and whims. At the mercy of her tantrums and tales.

After being raised by his detached mother, my dad had the unbelievable bad luck to fall in love with my mom. Captured by her beauty. Imprisoned by her madness. With one look in her deep, black eyes, he let his guard down. Got sucked up in her brown. He miscalculated, and he paid the price. In her wake, my dad suffered years of grief and heartache, and so did I.

I never thought he would leave me. Never thought I would be without him. Without my green. Without my heart. Without my best friend. With everything that I am, I never thought he would ever, ever go.

3

Ignored

I hate my stepdad.

—ME, IN RED CRAYON IN MY
FIRST-GRADE JOURNAL

Muffled sounds. Muffled movements. Air hanging hot and heavy. My white, wispy hair laid damp on my cheeks as they panted and petted in the front seat. Hot and bothered at the drive-in, my mom and George were aroused by the 1976 rape revenge movie *House by the Lake*. This was no film for a four-year-old. No scene for a child. But I huddled in the back seat, so small and tangled up in my emotions. I was not allowed to watch the movie. Not allowed to watch them. Told to keep my eyes closed.

"Go to sleep!" George said. But the sounds alone piqued my interest. Stoked my curiosity. Waved sleep away. A curious child, I peeked at the deeds on and off the screen. At carefully chosen, stolen moments, I gathered as much intel as a few seconds afforded me. Through the fogged windows, I made out a hand angrily rubbing a breast on the screen. *Slap!* As the woman screeched through the speaker, the windows rattled, and the seats vibrated.

My mom jolted and gyrated. Her brownness pulsated. With each rip and tear of the actress's clothing, my mom moaned. I squeezed my eyes shut. Curled into a confused ball. Wanted my bed. Wanted my dad. Wanted anyone but them. Frightened by their sounds and secrecy. Shamed by my mom's behavior.

At some point, I believed my mom was hurt. I jumped up. Lunged toward her.

"Lay down!" he yelled.

My mom attempted to smooth the situation. My tears fell. I couldn't be consoled. In his frustration, neither could he. The damage was done. The image seared in my brain. Played over and over. His pants unzipped. His underwear open. His hand between my mom's legs. They continued undeterred. Sounds of cackling and fighting on screen became our evening's soundtrack. I rubbed my foot back and forth on the seat as I cried. The repetition soothed, calmed, and lulled me to sleep.

My first memories of George are flashes of hair and jeans in the shadows. He hid. He dashed. He peered. He whispered wildly through our apartment windows. His white man 1970s afro bopped from window to window in search of my mom. In search of his future. In search of my dad's family. Sometimes my mom smiled at the sight of him. She grew giddy. Other times she appeared frightened. Shooed him away. Every time her eyes darted to me, seemingly unsure of what her four-year-old daughter witnessed. What she could convey.

He was inconsequential to me then. Barely a thought. Forgettable. Short. Bad teeth. Perverted eyeglasses. Too-tight jeans. George wasn't a handsome man by anyone's measure. I wasn't sure what my mom saw in him, since my dapper dad stood six foot four and was blonde with model looks. George was younger than my mom. He filled the room with energy and testosterone. Perhaps through her lens, he filled her future with hope and possibilities. Through my lens, however, he felt chaotic, selfish, and immature.

Regardless, my mom fell captive. Slowly and with intention, she moved toward him. Moved methodically away from my dad and me. Most felt it was too soon. Most called it an affair. I was four. I called it nothing. I couldn't fully grasp the situation. I just wanted my dad home and George gone.

I had no idea what occurred between my parents. No idea how to paint green back in the picture. No idea how to bring my dad home. My four-year-old brain failed to understand all the changes.

Where's Dad? Who's that guy? I wondered.

One moment we were all together attending Kingdom Halls in our Sunday best. The next we were separated by address and circumstance. All their decisions were made behind closed doors. All the details remained hidden. They spoke in hushed tones with Witness elders. With dark hues. With family friends. Without me. Nothing felt comfortable or settled.

All their beginnings felt wrong. Wrongness in George's presence. Wrongness in my mom's actions. Wrongness in the air.

To my disbelief, against my wishes and without my dad's consent, my mom and George returned from somewhere. They were married. I wasn't invited. In the photos, she wore a brown dress. George wore a suit.

Adults arrived and mingled for their marriage celebration. Hovered happily. Ruffled my hair. Tried to hold me. As people picked me up, I grabbed two fists full of my white hair and shook crazily. On cue, like a reflex, they planted me back from where they plucked me. Sometimes I strutted away. On this day, I ran and hid. Some of them tried to be silly and coax me out of the shadows. Evoke laughter and dance. Stubbornly, I remained in hiding. Refused to be persuaded. Refused my new life.

Some people thought their union was a good idea. A hopeful endeavor. I wasn't part of that "some." I hated that our family friends even attended the celebration. Smiled. Modeled acceptance. *What traitors!*

I was Team Dad. Team Green. I was consumed with sadness. I felt sorry for him. Sorry for me. I felt life pulling me against my wishes. Nothing felt right.

George never felt right. He didn't want me. He didn't like me. He feigned affection for me in the presence of others. He pretended to be interested. Pretended to be stepdad material. Without onlookers, though, his pretense became annoyance, and he ignored me. He wanted my mom, so he tolerated me. I refused his fake love.

As he attempted to show the partygoers his new daughter, his new relationship, I aggressively fought him and ran. I put on a show for all to see. A show that proved my alliance to my dad. A show that painted George as the villain—another dark figure in the picture. Thankfully, my mom let me be. Didn't require me to return George's regard. Didn't require my participation in the party. Instead, we all pretended I didn't exist, and the party resumed.

Tucked away in a safe hiding place, I saw George's mom kneel on the floor in front of me. She gabbed and giggled by me, but not with me. I stayed stoic. She rambled on and on. Eventually, she revealed the candies in her hand. I perked up. After the sweets, she left. She didn't attempt to move me. Didn't attempt to include me. Didn't require anything of me. From that moment, I adored my new grandmother.

Betty understood my situation. She understood the irony. She understood my sadness. She knew her son. She was clear on the way things were. Thankfully, she became my cheerleader. My fan. When the other adults clubbed and partied, she often babysat me. When my adults forgot their responsibilities. When my adults forgot my dad's child.

Betty adored my dad like I did. Their longtime friendship was, in fact, the reason Sheri and George met in the first place. Betty was a classy, good-looking, sociable lady. She also worshipped as a Jehovah's Witness. For years, she and my dad playfully flirted at social gatherings. My dad respected her. He eventually introduced Betty to his dear friend Bob, one of his colleagues at Borden's. Quickly following introductions, Betty and Bob married; they cherished one another for years until they passed.

Betty and Bob became my grandparents. They felt safe, loving, and inclusive. So inclusive that I slept between them when I stayed over. They had hens and baby chicks I could love and talk to. For every sleepover, their kitchen was stocked with our favorite bedtime snack: peanut butter and saltine crackers. Each night we stuffed our bellies and snickered until we sat full and sleepy. Most important to me, though, she spoke highly of my dad when most spoke unkindly. Most pretended George was a good, viable replacement for him. Betty and I pretended no such thing.

A little too rapidly, "till death do us part" turned into "fight to the death." Sheri and George's three-year marriage, marked by three different trailer park lots, became a destructive, explosive mess beginning with the words "I do." As we moved from lot to lot, their behavior escalated from partying to bickering to fighting to violence. Their relationship descended into brown. Into darkness. Into complete chaos.

The first trailer park lot was set off from the main highway in Mansfield, Texas, and consisted of one street full of trailers. One street full of hooligans. It was a pitiful, dirty place to start a family. A pitiful place to learn your place in society. A pitiful place to learn that you, too, were a degenerate.

George and my mom enjoyed the first few months together. They wrestled. Laughed. Partied. They appeared to be in love. They pretended to be normal. They tried to make a nice home. My mom decorated my new room and bathroom in various shades of patterned pink from floor to ceiling. I walked on pink carpet. Slept in pink bedding. I closed out the world with the pink curtains surrounding my bed. I appreciated her gesture. Appreciated her attempt to ease my sadness.

While my days and nights were filled with pink, their days were filled with work, hangovers, and arguing. Their nights were filled with friends, discos, and alcohol. I felt separate from their life and routine. We never felt like a cohesive family of three. We existed along separate paths. They swerved along an ignorant path to nowhere, while I constantly searched for any path to my dad, oblivious to my mom and George's whereabouts. I only knew they existed with the ebb and flow of yelling in the background.

When their erratic episodes exploded, I ran to my room. Closed my curtains. Hid in the covers. Longed for safety. As their voices rose and doors slammed, I cried. As their fight escalated, I prayed. I begged God for more visits with my dad. For summers with Pappa Dave. For weekends with the Melendy kids. For respite from their insanity. For hope. All consumed with my wants and needs, I failed to realize my mom was in trouble.

Like most partiers in the 1970s, George and my mom drank alcohol and drove along the Texas roads. Windows down. Fleetwood Mac on the 8-track. No seat belts. No concerns. As I jostled about the car, my mom waved at the cops with a beer in hand. This was the era before Mothers Against Drunk Driving (MADD). Before DUIs. Before common sense. If common sense did exist in the 1970s, it wasn't George and my mom's thing. They drank in all life had to offer. They drank and dressed for the club. They dropped me with Betty. Fled to fun.

After a few more days at Betty's than I was used to, I grew curious. Unsure. Insecure. *Where's my mom? Why hasn't she picked me up?* I noticed hushed whispers when I entered rooms. I waited. I worried. I slept. One day George emerged out of thin air. In silence and with no explanation, he took me home.

Still and sober, my mom sat on the couch with a scarf on her head. No personality, or at least, not my mom's personality. She tucked me into pink, kissed me, and exited my room. No explanation. No clarification. In the morning, I rose for breakfast. As I entered the kitchen, my mom cleaned. Organized cabinets. Straightened drawers with a frantic, robotic movement. Throughout the week, she didn't dress. Didn't do her makeup. Instead, she bathed, wrapped her head in a scarf, and got busy cleaning. I saw her brown deepen to black.

George lived with impatience. He snapped when my mom failed to recall conversations or details. Snapped at her strangeness. Snapped at his new life. Every so often, I gathered the courage to ask my mom if she was okay. With a Stepford Wife glare and tone, she replied, "Of course!" I returned to my room. Became invisible. She returned to weirdness. Became lost. For weeks, I inquired. Observed. Worried.

Unaccustomed to trailer park culture, naively I briefly socialized with a few of the other children. I followed a foul, unkempt girl and boy into the boy's trailer. We tiptoed into his parent's room. Quietly opened the bottom dresser drawer. Gently withdrew several issues of *Hustler*. With creepy grins, they flipped through pages of breasts and vaginas. I bolted in horror and ran like a crazed cat to my trailer. I burst through the door, wild-eyed and panting. Motionless and expressionless, my mom sat with her wrapped head. She was ignorant of my fear. Oblivious to life around her.

Two days later and one room away, my mom rested in a deep, dark stupor. The same nasty boy visited my trailer. He started a strange conversation with me. Described how he and the girl fondled each other daily. I didn't understand his words, but I grasped his actions. His motives. His heavy breathing. As he rehashed their sordid deeds, he rubbed his hand up my leg to the threads of my cutoff shorts. He gave one a tug. Without warning, I hurdled him and jumped off the bed. Sprinted to my mom. Squeezed beside her. Almost underneath her. He bolted. Slammed the door. Shaken to my core, I calmed next to her motionless body.

The phone rang. Startled us into movement. In minutes, we were in George's car at a salvage yard. I marveled at such a place. Car after car waited for salvation. Waited to be rescued or made anew. As my curious eyes studied each mangled, disfigured form, our car stopped. George and my mom exited the car and walked toward a heap of metal. I moved to the front seat. All eyes. All ears. Slowly I realized the heap was our missing car.

"Mom, what happened? What are you doing?" I yelled out the window.

They returned with random belongings and papers. I climbed into the back seat. I rapid-fired question after question. George grew annoyed, but my mom finally opened up.

"Remember when I was gone for a few days?" I nodded eagerly. Glued to her eyes. Glued to her story. "We had a bad wreck. A truck plowed into us while George tried to turn into the trailer park."

With each detail, tears filled my eyes.

"Because I was asleep in the back, my head was trapped. They used the Jaws of Life to save me." Luckily, she survived. Luckily, I wasn't left with George.

I blamed George for the crash and my mom's injuries with gusto. Blamed him for the trailer kids and for trailer living. Blamed him for my sadness and my dad's absence. Blame and depression twisted inside me. My feelings became poor behavior and spilled over everywhere. I'd experienced too many changes in too short a time. Too many wrongs in my little life. I hated George. I hated reality. But I especially hated mornings. I couldn't cope with being jolted back to a life with a step-dad. Back to a life of divorce and remarriage. Back to a life of sadness.

On school days, no one wanted to wake me or deal with me. My mom dressed me while I slept. I often woke to school staff dragging me from the car. In my grogginess, I wrestled the teachers. When I finally freed myself from their grasp, I bolted and screamed after my mom's car, frantic. Desperate and breathless, I ran down the carpool lane. She never stopped. Never turned around. Never even slowed.

I began calendar time each morning with snotty sniffles. During class, I became aggressive toward my peers. Called another little girl a "bitch." Pushed her to the ground. Mad she stole my seat after the Pledge of Allegiance. My temper swelled. Became its own entity. Became a concern. I had zero tolerance. Zero coping skills. Zero respect for kids or adults.

I walked the kindergarten halls, pissed and tired. I had no interest in schoolwork. No interest in stupid kid games. My depression took my energy. Took my time. Took everything I had. Though awake, I craved sleep. I needed the escape. Needed the recurring dreams of my dad and me frolicking in green and living like two outlaws. Living with no mom. No George. No other humans.

"Is it naptime yet? Can I get my mat?" I asked my teachers after an hour of schoolwork. Though I suspect they grew annoyed, they allowed me to retrieve my mat early. I was always the first to lie down. The first to sleep. The first to leave the teachers alone. And I was always the last one to wake.

The very sight of George when I arrived home each afternoon triggered more sadness and sent me into darkness. Sadness consumed every cell in my body. Once I started crying, I could not stop. No one could calm me but my dad, who was only around for visitation. More often, he was gone. Away from my mom. Away from me. My mom and Karen Melendy searched for him. Searched the phone book. Searched everyone and everywhere. Called until my dad surfaced. Called until I calmed.

After weeks of residing in a deep hole, my mom convinced George to buy me a puppy. The puppy would lift my spirits. Get my mind off my dad. After much debate and a few arguments, they brought home a blonde Labrador. I leapt. Squeezed him. Thanked my mom. Ignored George. I could not muster a kind emotion for him.

I promptly, deliberately named my dog Pepe after our neighbor's dog, Pepe. George always flirted with the other Pepe's owner. Now, every time George left the neighbor's house and called for Pepe, both Pepes barreled toward him. George had to scramble to get our Pepe in the house and the neighbor's Pepe back home. Pissed and bothered, George cussed at them. Yelled. Often bored, I would purposely let my Pepe loose just to watch the George Show. I took great pleasure at George's expense. As if he knew, George gave Pepe to our friends. A calculated revenge move in our game of chess. I missed my dog, but not as much as I missed my entertainment. Regardless, my mind remained on my dad.

When I was in first grade, we moved to the second trailer park. This one was in Evermen, Texas, and placed us closer to Aunt Rebecca, my cousin Terr, and the Melendys—all my favorite humans. With the move and time, my mom's personality returned. Her head injury subsided, and she was feisty once again. Aggressive. Fun. Punkish. Unpredictable. George could no longer pop off without consequence.

Reluctantly, he returned his balls and the family pants to her. But the transition proved rocky. Their arguing morphed into fighting. It was the same pattern. Her pattern. When they fought, regardless of where they were, my mom inevitably left. Grabbed her purse and bailed. At a store, she left. At the house, she left. In the car, she screamed, "Pull over this fucking car!" She left on foot. I was thankful she removed herself, but I did not like being left with George. However, as soon as her feet touched the pavement, I sucked up to him.

Though we despised each other, I needed a few things from him in those moments. I needed to return home before my mom destroyed the trailer. Destroyed everything in her path. Though embarrassing, I kissed up to him. I had to protect my record player, my red apple penny bank, and Roni Rabbit.

"Don't you think we should go home? I don't want her to be madder at you," I'd say in a sweet, concerned voice. George rolled his eyes.

"Oh, you like me now. You need me, huh?" he said, never missing an opportunity to barb me.

"I want to go home," I would reply.

Calm and tipsy, my mom sauntered over to George when she returned. They retired to their room and reconciled. The needle moved back to one. It started all over again.

I lived for my intermittent time with my dad. I moped around the house between visits and perking up as they approached. I packed days before I left and talked about my dad incessantly. I said goodbyes like a farewell tour, irritating everyone in my orbit. Two days before one visit, George, my mom, and I drove home from dinner. I sat in the back but hung over the front bench seat between them. Caught up in green, I sang every word to every song on the radio.

"Make her stop singing. It's all I can hear!" George yelled, caught up in his ego.

I sang louder. "My dad lets me sing," I said.

"Sheri, I'm serious! I can't think," George growled.

My mom tried not to laugh but intervened.

"Scoot closer to me and sing softly in my ear," she said.

For the rest of the ride, I sang to my mom but stared directly at George, as if my gaze could penetrate the side of his skull. After the tense ride, my mom tucked me into bed. Placed Roni Rabbit on my chest. Closed my curtains. Within minutes, they were arguing. I jumped up. Pressed my ear to the door. George fumed. Roared. My mom yelled. Thundered. They tossed my dad's name around the trailer.

A dagger. Unsure of the cause, I continued to listen. George dialed the phone. Yelled something. Cussed.

"Ron, meet me now!" he yelled.

The phone crashed. George's boots rattled the trailer. The front door slammed. My mom's footsteps neared my room. I hopped in bed. Pretended to sleep. Praying and apologizing in the silence. *God, please protect my dad. I'm sorry I sang too loud. I promise to be nicer to George.* George returned after an hour or so. I was mid-prayer and mid-groveling. He forcefully flung our trash compactor open and closed. I held my breath. Tears fell.

He must have cut my dad into little green pieces and discarded his remains in the trash. I prayed. The thought refused to leave my tiny mind. I cried all night. Wiped my tears with Roni Rabbit's ears. I worried. I ached. I wanted to check the trash, but I could not bear to see my dad dead. The next day, I called my dad. He answered. He was alive. In one piece. I was still going to see him.

As my green drove me home after our visits, he broke the sad silence with comedy.

"Get ready! I'm going to slow down to twenty. When we get in front of your trailer, you open the door and roll out of the car," he'd say.

I giggled. He didn't want to deal with my life situation as much as me.

When I returned from my dad's, I vowed to be kinder to George. Decided to engage with him. Make an effort. Typically, I hibernated in my room when George came home. But because of the deal I made with God, I stayed in the living room and continued watching *The Bugaloos*, a program about a teenage fairy and her furry friends. George and his work buddies plopped on the couch with their beers and snacks.

As I watched, I tuned into George and his gross friends. They gawked at the fairy. Took turns commenting on her skimpy outfit. Verbally and mentally undressed the teenage girl.

"Look at those perfect boobs and nice ass."

They salivated. They high-fived.

"I would tear her up!"

I slipped into my room. Primal and perverted, they continued after I left. I no longer viewed George as a stepdad. He was creepy. Sexual. I no longer let him tickle me or touch me. And I no longer wanted to be alone with him. My vow of renewed kindness lasted a week. I was sure God would understand.

A few weeks into second grade, I burst through our front door and announced a name change. "Don't call me Roni anymore! From now on, I am only answering to 'Layla.' That's final!"

My mom laughed. I was not joking. No girl at my school had a boy's name. No girl at my school had a bowl haircut. Since I was lazy and refused to comb my hair, I welcomed the short cut because I thought it would be easier. However, after the fifth stranger said, "What a cute little boy," my mom pierced my ears.

I believed the problem was solved, but I miscalculated my situation. Miscalculated my cruel peers. Miscalculated popular culture. Ronnie Milsap, a country singer, kept turning out hits on the radio and TV. Kids started calling me Ronnie Milsap. The clever ones sung his songs to me. I boiled. My patience depleted.

School was my respite from George. I could not be tortured there, too. I could not handle any more stress. I figured God gave me two names for a reason, so I decided to go by my middle name. After that day, I no longer answered to "Roni." I ignored the teasing. Ignored everyone. Eventually, everyone learned to call me "Layla" or "Susie" if they wanted a response. It felt good to have control over something. Felt good to be empowered.

For the third and final move of my mother and George's marriage, we relocated to back left side of the same trailer park. No longer in front, right off the main road, it felt like a new beginning. A hopeful lot. So I unpacked. Straightened my trinkets. Danced and swayed to Smokey Robinson's "Being with You." Each time the needle slid to the end of the 45, I replayed the tune.

Around the fifteenth rotation, I heard a deep, guttural sound emanating from my mom in the other room. I left Smokey and went to Sheri. Bent over and crying, she pulled me close. Through joyful tears, she whispered, "You have a brother. He's coming home."

She sent me back to pack a weekend bag. After a few steps, I turned. "What's his name?" I asked.

"Judah," she responded through her beautiful smile.

Confused, I delicately gathered information on the ride to Abilene. "How do I have a brother? Where has he been? Is my dad his dad?"

"He is your real brother. He was kidnapped as a baby, and we are bringing him home," she answered, blissful and brown. "Now, close your eyes. If you go to sleep, we will get there faster."

Questions bubbled in my throat, but I knew to stop asking. George drove in silence. Unsure how to navigate this situation. I woke upon our arrival. Our first court-ordered visitation with Judah was at the Taco Bell in Abilene. Nothing made sense. The brother. The setting. The explanation. None of it. As Judah walked closer with the case manager, I realized my features were not uniquely my own. He looked like me. Same green eyes. Same button nose. Same smile. We were a year apart, but as close in appearance as twins.

After an awkward hug, we chased each other round and round the fountain as fast our feet could fly. With each lap came a new emotion and a novel thought. I became dizzy, almost drunk on happenstance. Drunk on the gravity. Drunk on the absurdity. Drunk on the luck of my newfound brother.

Sheri, Judah, and Layla

Lunch was ready just in time for my legs to collapse from exhaustion. Sweaty and weird, we sat next to each other. We both ordered tacos. Both dumped all contents out of the shell. Both just ate the insides.

When lunch ended, the visit ended. Judah was back to being gone. On the long ride home, I daydreamed of my brother while my mom wept. Replayed the visit. Wondered if my dad knew. Tried to envision Judah's life. Struggled to place him in mine. Grateful for him. Thankful he had a home. I wanted to protect him from my life. I worried my life, my mom, or George may hurt him. *Please, God, keep Judah safe. Keep him far, far away from our family. Please forgive me.*

For months, my mom remained preoccupied with court orders and obligations. She was consumed with all things Judah. Met with attorneys. Filled out paperwork. Scheduled visits. Met deadlines. Contacted friends and family to testify. Decorated Judah's room in cars and blue. She was her best self. A bright, glowing brown. A role-model parent. A perfect citizen.

George and I sat on the sidelines. Pushed together by incident. On occasion, my mom sent me with George to clean pools. Both of us balked at the idea, but we complied. She brushed me out of her hair to assist George. At least, I thought my job was to assist George. I planned to wear official gloves. Use the pool net. Save insects from drowning.

Instead, I found myself inside the client's home. No pool. No net. No gloves. George and the woman pushed me toward her daughter's room. With disinterest and disdain, I sat with the four-year-old and watched her play with Strawberry Shortcake dolls. Moments passed, and I decided to venture out for a drink. Spy on George.

I tiptoed to the kitchen. No adults in sight. No one by the pool. No one in the main rooms. I returned to the child and dolls. I stewed. I cussed in my head. I was angry he left me. Wanted my mom. Hated the kid. Despised the dolls. After an hour or so, George opened the door. "Ya ready?"

I seethed with rage in the car. The air was thick with defiance. Thick with guilt. Thick with silence. When we arrived home, I planned to tell. Planned to spill my guts. But I was not sure what George did. What could I say? In my confusion, I paused. My mom floated in the room on sheer hope. Her hair and dress tousled prettily as she glowed with the anticipation of her son. She looked at George.

"How'd y'all do?"

George met my gaze. With each breath, with each sentence, he concocted one lie after another. I withdrew to pink. Smashed my snow globe. Bloodied my finger. Retreated behind my bed curtains.

As the court case approached, the caseworker conducted a few home visits. Stress became my mom. She insisted we clean every inch of the trailer before each visit. We cleaned under beds and atop cabinets. We cleaned door handles, closets, and both the front and back yards. George helped sometimes. He was absent other times.

My mom acted strange and submissive in the caseworker's presence. She needed constant reassurance, but the caseworker stuck to standard speak. "It looks good. Your attorney will get my report."

Nothing more, nothing less. My mom trembled as she dressed for court. Conservative, motherly clothing draped her. I was not allowed in the courtroom. I stayed with my grandparents, the Melendys, or George's family. I rotated through a whirlwind of babysitters. I never knew where I would be. Never knew where I was going. No one told me anything about the court case, not even my dad, so I snooped to find the details. Whether with my dad or mom's side of the family, I sat silently around adults, hoping they would forget my presence and gossip.

Based on my investigation, my mom's story of Judah's kidnapping was not everyone's story. Some believed my mom left Judah as an infant with her best friend and never returned. Some thought she left Judah for a short time with her best friend, and once she returned, they were gone. Nowhere to be found. I remained confused. *Why would my mom leave her baby? Who was her best friend? Why wasn't she searching for him every day? Why did she keep me? What does my dad think?*

Answers were never provided, apparently lost in brown and green. In the evenings, my mom returned red-faced and puffy-eyed, beaten and bruised from the day's events. She withdrew to her room. Slept in her clothes. Vacillated between brown and black.

I attended the final day of court, but sat with my aunt in the hallway, directly across from the courtroom's tightly closed doors. We wanted to be the first to congratulate my mom. The first to hug Judah. The first to take him home. We waited. We paced. We played games. My heart pounded. My mind raced. I daydreamed of life with a brother. Going to school together. Showing him off to my friends. Laughing until our cheeks hurt. Eating ice cream until our stomachs ached. I was not ready before, but I was now.

I decided to cancel my previous prayers. *God, please bring Judah home to us. I know I asked you to keep him far away, but now I want a brother. And my mom needs him.* After an eternity, a strong hurricane wind seemed to blow the courtroom doors open and interrupted my prayers. People rode the wave through the doors. I could hear my mom. But I couldn't see her. Too many people. Too chaotic. My mom's screams and cries filled the halls.

"No! He's my son! You bastards!"

Two or three people were holding my mom an inch above the ground, carrying her out of the courtroom exit. She kicked, spat, cussed, and screamed. Defeated, she melted down to a puddle of brown. An adult grabbed my arm and rushed me to the car. As the wave receded, Judah was gone for good. No one ever mentioned his name again. His room remained blue with cars, hollow and forbidden. Darkness blanketed our home. Guilt consumed me.

To help my mom, she and I visited Lottie and Winona in Abilene on random weekends. George remained behind doing whatever George did. My mom and her sisters drifted between sober and drunk for days. With each drink and song, my mom stuffed Judah back in his place. She tried to resume life, but the gravity of loss and her past decisions inevitably changed her. Altered her. Destroyed her.

She morphed into a fragile, unpredictable, distant, moody, and often aggressive human. My spankings increased in frequency and intensity. Our home became entrenched in rage. Engulfed in a thick, dark-brown cloud. Everyone and everything pissed her off. But at the same time, she might also mourn roadkill. Her unpredictability and violent undertones scared me.

For the first time, her meanness was directed at something other than her husbands. Her cruelty and viciousness spewed randomly into our days and nights. Anyone could be subject to her wrath: a waiter, a bank teller, a friend, a teacher, another driver, a passenger, or her child. Upon returning home from a weekend trip, my mom noticed the house was spotless.

"Why is the house clean? You did this?" she poked and prodded George. Her tone hovered between sarcastic and hostile. Her brownness spewed as she moved to her room. George continued to watch TV. Nervous. Guilty. He was caught not despite, but because of his attempt to cover his deceit. His broken vow. I stood frozen, shifting my eyes from George to my mom. Waiting. Prepared to leave. Prepared to call for help.

She noticed the bed tightly made with fresh sheets. Like a rabid spider monkey, she pounced. I fled. Ran down the street. Within seconds, I heard a chorus of violence. My mom screamed. I turned around. Sprinted for her.

As I opened the door, I saw George pin my mom down. He kicked her repeatedly in the face with his steel-toed boots. I dashed outside. Stopped in the middle of the street. With all my energy, all my might, with clenched fists and a tense body, I screamed as loud as possible until someone, anyone helped. The neighbor flung his door open. He ran to my side.

"He is beating my mom! Help!" I pointed and squealed.

Alarmed, the neighbor ran in our trailer. He pulled George off my mom. Hurled him out of the trailer. George tumbled down the steps. I called the police. Before they arrived, George peeled out of the trailer park. Stayed away for days. My mom, determined to end their charade, plotted and followed his every move. Led her to a hotel room. She hid in the shadows. She caught George with his mistress, entwined in sin.

My mom filed for divorce while repeatedly listening to "I Will Survive." I was euphoric. Vindicated. Free. George crawled back to his previous life.

Then my mom attempted her first suicide.

4

Adored

To truly laugh, you must be able to take your pain and play with it!
—ATTRIBUTED TO CHARLIE CHAPLIN

As my thoughts transformed into stories and my experiences morphed into memories, a deep distrust of my family formed. Those who orbited me were broken. Absent. Immature. Unfit. Scary. Lackluster bloodlines wrapped in pure ignorance paved the path for my fucked future.

My only hope—my only remotely dependable family member—was Pappa Dave, or PD. He showed up when he said he would. He helped me when I needed it. He loved me unconditionally. He was my kind, hilarious grandfather. My lifeline. My touchstone.

My being the first grandchild from his oldest child and only son solidified our special bond. Everyone knew he adored me. I believed he lived for me. He was a proud grandfather. Proud of me. And I was proud of him. I beamed in his presence. Smiled from ear to ear at the mention of his name or the sight of his face.

I enjoyed all things PD. His smell. His dapper style. His pristine Chrysler New Yorker. His comedic bent. His gift for music and story-telling. And he acted as though he loved all things me. PD convinced my mom to let me stay with him in the summers. He allowed me to bring one cousin, drove hours to retrieve me, and returned me before school started. At Christmas, he passed out trinkets and dollars to his other grandchildren. But then he would present me with a new red tricycle, nice clothing, or money.

No one was jealous of the way he doted on me; they knew my reality was mired in madness. Tension existed between PD and his own children, but I dismissed it. Even so, my father and Aunt Rebecca never told us negative stories about him. I wouldn't have entertained them if they did. I adored him. His relationship with his grandchildren proved healthier than with his own children. Different from his own. Better than his own. Age and his second wife, Shirley, our Mema, stabilized him. Molded him. Grounded him. And I came after Mema. After all his poor decisions.

PD grew up in Pennsylvania, the baby of his family. A mama's boy by all accounts with the nickname "Babe," he was loved and spoiled by his mom to the core. Unexpectedly, at the age of fifty, she died of a heart attack while cooking. The event devastated PD. Hardened him. Shaped him. Life-changing events and near-death experiences seemed to follow him after this. Most were due to bad luck. Others were due to bad decisions.

He almost lost his life during the Korean War, not at the hands of the enemy, but a true predator. While in the jungle stalking the enemy, a fifty-foot anaconda fell from a tree onto PD. The monster squeezed, attempting to suffocate him. With quick reflexes and a pocketknife, PD slayed the anaconda. Grateful for his life and grateful the war ended, he returned to the United States, promptly married his first wife, conceived two children, and then divorced. He drove diesel trucks and picked his guitar across the country. After the divorce, he left my father and aunt to protect themselves from their abusive, neglectful mother. PD knew the situation but continued to drink, drive, and terrorize each city for the hell of it.

At one point, he jackknifed his diesel truck and ended up in a body cast. He lived the life of a spoiled brat, which perpetuated and validated the stories his children knew of him. Mema, the only grandmother I ever knew, saved PD, and we were so grateful. She brought him home. Settled him.

At their first encounter, PD charmed her through the cell bars while Mema bailed her brother out of jail. Armed only with wit and comedic stories, PD entertained her for freedom. He needed Mema's help. Her sympathy. Her bail money. Since my grandparents met at a jail, a low point by most standards, I suppose there were only highs to be had after that.

Once freed, they dated, married, and birthed a daughter of their own. Mema loved and welcomed all parts of PD. Attracted to his rambling, gambling ways, she accompanied him several times a year to Vegas. By all accounts, PD lucked out since he and his needed love. Mema couldn't help but love. She was made of love stuff. She loved everything in her path. Animals. Friends. Elders. Children. With Mema and their daughter by his side, his outlaw ways curbed. By the time I arrived, she had loved on PD until he changed and matured. Morphed and molded. Compromised and conceded. I only knew him as a trustworthy family man. A reliable businessman. An amazing grandfather.

Time and time again, PD voiced his concerns regarding my living situation and my mom's poor parenting. From the time I was young, he often attempted to remove me from my mom's grasp. Her influence. Her abuse. My mom repeatedly told a story about PD and Mema "kidnapping" me as a young toddler. With no memory of the incident or accounts from other family members, my mom's details became my understanding. She painted them as villains. She, however, was simultaneously the victim and hero. Whenever my grandparents defied her, this story, this incident, justified my mom's consequences. Her revenge. Her hate. The tale would spill from her lips.

"After one of your visits with them, they never returned you to me. I tried to get you back, but I couldn't reach anybody. Finally, I got Shirley on the phone. While Dave was working, I set up a time to visit you. Shirley was so nervous when I arrived that her cigarette shook in her hand. I called out to you, but you wouldn't come to me. You didn't know me. Slowly, I moved closer to the porch. Then I grabbed you and ran to the car. You were screaming, reaching out to your Mema," she spun.

Horrified and unsettled, I never filed the story away as my mom desired. Under kidnapping. Under victim. Under hero. I failed to understand why I was *left so long* that I did not recognize my mother. *You didn't know me.*

To me, this story meant that my mom got around to bringing me home at some point after partying. After living childless. After running free. Disgust often bubbled in my gut when she retold this story. Instead of arguing my point, correcting her, or amending history, I sat and stewed. *God, why didn't you leave me with Pappa Dave? Seriously? Are you listening? Do you see what is happening here with this lady?* I prayed while she rambled about her quick getaway. Quick thinking. Quick skills. As she saw her cape blowing in the wind, I ignored her and filed the event under "B" for "Bad Mom."

On occasion over the years, perhaps because of jealousy, perhaps because of control, my mom forbade my visits with PD. However, the ban never lasted long. Inevitably, and possibly because she needed a sitter, she allowed my summer stays. I was unaware of how the adults reconciled. Unaware of the man hours needed to resolve matters. I was just grateful for the truce. Grateful for the visits. Grateful for our borrowed time.

My first recollections of my grandparents were summers spent on PD's farm. It was heaven on earth. A grandchild's dream. A place I never wanted to leave. A place with all my favorite things. Land. Animals. Grandparents. My cousin. And my sanity.

Each morning, with sleep in my eyes, my senses were overwhelmed with the sounds and smells of my sacred summers. The creaking floorboards under PD's alligator boots. The aroma of breakfast intertwined with PD's hairspray and aftershave. Mema's newspaper rustling as she lit a cigarette. The geese and roosters calling out to me. Begging for me. Barky, PD's beloved dog, impatiently waited for me to awake so he could be my first encounter. He licked me to consciousness. Herded me into the kitchen. Wanted to eat. Wanted us all together. Throughout the day, Barky babysat us at PD's request—a role he took seriously.

In my toddler years, Barky positioned himself in doorways so I couldn't leave or enter restricted jurisdictions. In my stubbornness, I attempted to crawl under him, but when I plopped on the floor, Barky sat down. When I clumsily stood, he stood. He fiercely protected us, tracked our daily journeys, and followed our every step.

When Barky and I entered the kitchen in the mornings, I basked in my grandparents' blissful smiles at my presence.

"Well, there's Layla Pots! She's awake!" Mema said. I listened to their banter as I anticipated the day's events.

I ate my usual—scrambled eggs mixed with jam. Terr, my favorite cousin, joined me for my summer visits and added to mealtime fun with his hatred of food. All food. He packed each bite on the inside of his cheek until it was the size of a golf ball. He never swallowed. But he also never complained. In fact, he grinned constantly though he only consisted of bones and white hair. We both laughed as I quietly, deceptively ate his food. I was ready to play. Ready to be free. I could not wait for him any longer.

Layla, Pappa Dave (PD), and Terr

Our days were filled with animals, guns, and frolicking. The geese alone provided hours of sheer entertainment as they terrorized Terr. The faster and harder his skinny little body fled, the more aggressively our feathery friends chased him.

"Terr-A-Torries!" Mema yelled as she attempted to save him. His arms flailed when their beaks grabbed his diaper and violently pulled him to the ground. Terr's cries and screams were music to my ears. I was of no help. I laughed. I snorted. I rolled until my belly hurt and Terr was rescued.

Babies of any kind being born were my favorite moments on the farm. Intrigued by the process, I watch every birth that occurred during my visits. Each experience solidified my innate love of animals and developed my empathy for God's creatures. We learned life's intricate, delicate way of creating. We learned how babies, whether a litter or a clutch, whether fur or feather, are born in protective sacs or hard shells. How all newborns immediately summon their mothers. How the weak ones are eaten or abandoned for the sake of the family's survival. How all creatures crave love and acceptance. And how all living organisms have an important role in life.

Once the newborns were safe, PD taught us how to shoot BB guns—a rite of passage for every Texas child. Although beer cans were the only prey we hunted, our chests puffed with pride at our outlaw ways. On those summer days, I wanted for nothing. I was never alone. Never bothered. Never more loved. My heart still drooped sometimes as I longed for my dad and wished he and PD got along. I wished my dad could traipse around the farm with me so we could discover life together again.

In the evenings after dinner, PD spun tales of his life's adventures. Tales of his childhood, of the anaconda, and life on tour with Merle Haggard and George Jones. Ever the storyteller and compelled to captivate, he wanted our undivided attention as he recounted each story with great detail. He wanted to make us laugh. Wanted to shock us. But most importantly, he wanted us to believe. And we did. Always.

Once we demonstrated the emotion he was seeking, he fell quiet and reveled in his storyteller's splendor. After the stories waned, he set the mood with his country songs. Terr and I beamed at the sight of the guitar. From PD to Hank Williams to George Jones to Merle Haggard, we crooned and swayed until bedtime. Giddy at the first note of my favorite jam, "Coca-Cola Cowboy" by Mel Tillis, I belted out the chorus with PD at the top of my lungs.

"Last song!" PD forewarned us multiple times. We ignored him and kept twirling. Once the curtain closed, we reluctantly dressed for sleep, drained. As if on cue, Terr or I complained of something hurting—anything to delay sleep. Anything to hold on to the fun.

Cranky, fussy, teething, or sick, PD's solution to all childhood ailments was alcohol. For teething, he rubbed Jack Daniels on our gums. For all other illnesses, he provided us a nip of beer in our baby bottles.

His medicine cured the symptoms. Mema's love tucked us into bed. We woke again to the sounds of farm life. Our summer days played on repeat. And we all pretended the summer was here to stay.

By the time I was in elementary school, PD had sold the farm and moved into town closer to his used car dealership, Skaggs and Reese Motors, which he owned with M. A. Skaggs. Devastated by the news of their move, I cried. I obsessed. I worried about the animals. Dreamed about them.

"Where did they go? Are they okay? Do they miss me? Are they lonely?" I asked.

My mom refused to converse about such things.

"Shut up about the animals. I don't have any answers for you. Ask Pappa Dave," she replied. I intended to do so. Once the school year wrapped up in June, I packed for Abilene, ready to leave behind George and my mom. Ready to be loved by my grandparents. Like clockwork, PD pulled up to Aunt Rebecca's in Fort Worth to retrieve me in his pristine New Yorker. Always a different model. Always shiny and inviting.

My early elementary school years were my Terr-less summers, as he was visiting his father in California. Consequently, my grandparents focused on keeping me entertained. I spent some days with Mema visiting her "old people," as she called them. One was M.A.'s wife, Matty Skaggs, who had Alzheimer's. Mema started checking on Matty after she left the stove on and set the kitchen ablaze. Kindness and sweets pulled me through Matty's door, though her two poodles with painted nails hated me. They yipped and nipped. I sat stiff and uncomfortable, not daring to cause a ruckus. I didn't dare make a peep.

Mema's other old person was Reecey. She scared me. Her cloudy eyes confused me. I wasn't sure if they stared at me or tried to possess me. I refused to meet her murky gaze. I wanted to get out of her house the minute we arrived. She smelled like her insides were rotting. Though I adored my days with Mema, I did not adore her old people.

A few times during the week, I accompanied PD to work. These were my favorite days. He was ever the comedian. Ever the clown. He devised a skit of sorts for us to mess with his customers, props and all. The skit entertained only the two of us, and mostly him. After he outlined the plan, the script, and our roles, we rehearsed until customers showed.

My role was as a child mannequin wearing Groucho Marx glasses. A brilliant idea. A home run. I was down. I understood my role. I was born to be a Groucho Marx mannequin. PD's primary role was to sell cars at all costs, his secondary role was to pretend I was a mannequin and not a real child. Not his granddaughter.

"Be very still and quiet," PD said repeatedly. "Even if the customer talks to you, stay frozen."

We rehearsed with me sitting somewhere in his office—on top of the desk, in a chair, on the filing cabinet, or even on the floor. Then we rehearsed my mannequin skills. After rehearsals, PD worked while I was on the lookout for customers in the doorway waiting for someone, anyone to drive in. I took my post seriously. I didn't play. I didn't talk. I didn't dare leave or venture from the door.

Once an unsuspecting victim pulled in, I ran to PD's office and yelled, "They're here!" I put on the glasses. PD positioned me on a perch. He ventured outside to make a sale. Inevitably, his charm lured them into his office. There I sat. Motionless. Mute. White hair. Big green eyes framed by Groucho Marx glasses, complete with bushy eyebrows and a bushy mustache. Neither of us ever broke character.

As the customers tried to focus on PD's sales pitch, they subtly, but not so subtly, cut their eyes at me. Some walked closer to me, others drifted away with confused expressions. PD continued with his pitch and never acknowledged my presence. I never adjusted my pose. The customers never asked, but by all accounts, they were sufficiently creeped out.

As they swiftly, fearfully exited the dealership, we laughed and congratulated each other. I returned to my post, anticipating the next victim. PD never made a sale during our skits, but we didn't care.

One evening we were nestled in, cozy, and the phone rang. PD and Mema were startled. I looked up and then continued playing with my Barbies. For a few seconds, we shared confusion. The phone never rang during our nightly viewing of the ultimate country comedy show, *Hee Haw*. On the second ring, PD closed his recliner, rose to his feet, and moved toward the phone. On the fourth ring, he answered. Listened. Nodded. Reluctantly, he agreed to a request from the other end. Without saying goodbye, he placed the receiver on the base, returned to his chair, reclined, and sat, stoic.

I continued to dress my Barbie. Blue velvet coat. White high heels. Pink plastic purse. PD and Mema shared a strange stare, but Mema asked nothing and continued stroking the dogs, smashing fleas between her fingers.

Within minutes, the doorbell rang. PD told me to answer it. I flung the door open to see my dad and a small, attractive woman smiling nervously. I soared into my dad's arms. My heart filled with happiness. Almost exploded. Time and miles between us collapsed. My dad introduced his friend. "This is Priscilla."

I said nothing. My grandparents acknowledged her but barely noticed my dad. After a few awkward seconds, my dad hurried Priscilla and me to the back room and closed the door.

"Priscilla and I are getting married," he eked out in a serious, hopeful tone.

I flipped on the bed. Backward. Forward. Sideways. I refused to look at either of them. Flip. Flip. Flip.

"Layla, are you listening to me? Stop for a second."

I stopped flipping and began jumping.

"Layla?"

I flopped to a seated position. Looked at the carpet. Dangled my feet.

"Priscilla and I are getting married. I wanted you to know. Wanted y'all to meet."

Words failed me. Emotions overwhelmed me. I didn't know how to respond. I was beyond thrilled to see him. I wasn't thrilled with the circumstances. I was unsure how to feel. Unsure how to act.

"I will remain living in Abilene. We aren't moving," my dad continued.

I kept searching for a response. My stomach ached. I wasn't sure if I was hungry or about to be sick. Before I could form a sentence, before I could find a syllable, my dad asked for a hug and left. He came and went like a mirage. It all came and went so quickly, I wasn't sure it occurred at all.

PD attempted to talk to me. I remained silent. Fought back tears. Mema tucked me in. Kissed my forehead. As soon as she turned off the light, I cried silently. Replayed the moment. Wanted a second chance. Wanted my dad to return. In my sorrow, I never found the right response. Never spoke to my dad about his wedding. About his new wife. About his new life.

The day before the ceremony, my dad took me to a department store.

"Do you see a ring or necklace you like?"

He purchased a pearl heart ring for my ring finger. A kind gesture in exchange for my understanding. A kind gesture in exchange for my absence at his wedding.

By the end of elementary school, my grandparents moved to Lake Abilene, another dream location for grandchildren and another amazing escape for me. As soon as I arrived at the lake each June, my dad scooped me up, and I stayed with him and Priscilla the first week of every summer vacation. PD half-heartedly agreed to this arrangement, but only because he knew I hadn't seen my dad all year and I lived for this week. He knew I adored my stepmom and craved my dad.

Each summer, PD collected me from Aunt Rebecca's house in Fort Worth. Then my dad retrieved me from the lake. After a week, he returned me to PD. I appreciated their truce to work together for my benefit. I soaked up all things dad in those few days. His jokes. His mannerisms. His smell. I pretended I lived with him. I imagined my life as their daughter in their house.

I especially loved the visits after my little sister was born. Sweet and soft. Warm and fuzzy. Perfect and mine. I watched her sleep. Held her when she woke. I wanted her to know me. Wanted to be her sister. Wanted to teach her about life. As soon as Priscilla drove away, even if my sister was napping, I deliberately woke her. My visits were not long enough for naps. I needed as much time as I could steal. So we got to cuddling, tickling, and giggling. Repeatedly, I whispered in her ear, "I'm your sister." And repeatedly, Priscilla returned to a wide-awake baby.

By the time I returned to the lake from my dad's visit, Terr resumed his role as my summer accomplice. He never stayed for as long as I did, but I took full advantage of our time together. Since we only had a week or two, I immediately created a schedule for us. Allocated time for hygiene, meals, Yahtzee, fishing, checking the mail, and so on. Every hour was planned and every activity detailed. We got busy getting busy. I got busy bossing Terr.

In retrospect, I am eternally thankful but completely shocked that Terr never bucked my schedule or questioned my tyrannical system. He never complained. His compliance reinforced my dictator ways. I started pushing the boundaries and tested the Terr waters. Tested his loyalty. Tested his resolve.

As the days progressed, I went from fun activities all day to needing a scheduled break, but only for me, not Terr. During my hour break, I scheduled time for Terr to iron his underwear. While he ironed each piece, I got a snack, walked the grounds, checked the fishing line, or watched soaps with Mema. Periodically, though, I checked on him. Checked the iron. Checked his work. To my delight, each piece was crisp and smooth. He proved to be a loyal, loving cousin, up for any challenge.

Often, I granted him time off for good ironing. At some point, the power went straight from my head and spilled onto Terr. He quickly graduated from soldier to general. We discreetly chose which neighborhood kids played with us. Who was allowed in our presence? Who was worthy? Once we decided but before fun commenced, we required the chosen to bathe with actual soap and water before playing with us.

To ensure the baths obediently occurred, we provided our bathroom. Towels. Water. Soap. As they bathed, we watched TV. Once sufficiently clean, we dictated the neighborhood games until supper. Strangely, and to our surprise, PD and Mama never stopped this ritual. The baths provided them with a lifetime of laughs and jokes.

My favorite evenings were our dinners at Luby's. On random days after work, PD rounded us up and drove us into town for a Luann Platter and Jell-O. For the long car ride, Terr and I played silly, impromptu car games with intricate rules and guidelines. Deep in our imaginations, excitement, and hunger, a horrid, rancid smell pulled us back to reality. In seconds, we went from happiness to suffocation, coughing, and gagging. We fought for our lives, for oxygen.

PD grinned and giggled in the rearview mirror. Mema was tickled, too. PD tricked us every single time. And every single time, we fell for it. Classic PD—he did anything for a laugh. Instead of driving the fastest route to Luby's from the lake, he chose the longest route that wove past the dump and singed his grandchildren's nose hairs.

By the time we arrived at the buffet—the feast, the extraordinary display of treats—our memory of the smell was long gone, and PD was forgiven. He knew we couldn't stay mad at him.

One night at Luby's, however, proved unforgettable. Instead of the usual PD tales, he told us a story for the first time—the story of his time as an actual prison inmate. In a serious, solemn tone, PD articulated the details of his prison experience to Terr and me. With each word, we sat stunned with mixed emotions. It was kind of cool to have a family member who went to prison, but it was kind of scary as well.

All the typical, important details like his age, the prison location, or his offense were absent from the story. Instead, his account focused on one particular event. One particular night. As he slowly told his version, he paused in between each sentence as if the retelling was hard.

"You know, kids."

Pause.

"I was in prison once."

Longer pause.

"After a while in there, I decided to break out."

Even longer pause.

"But once I was on the outside . . ."

Longest pause yet.

"I was so bored."

Pause we thought may never end.

"I broke back in."

The table fell quiet. Confused, we waited for more of an explanation. When none came, we resumed eating. Over the years, the prison story became a staple. No more and no less details provided. Same account. Same reaction.

As September stole my summer, we prepared for the unavoidable. The harsh reality. I must return to my trailer. Return to my mom. A melancholy mood encased us all. The thought that I wouldn't see my grandparents until Christmas was more than I could bear. Goodbyes were never good to me. They never felt like anything other than abandonment. I was never sure if this goodbye was the last goodbye. Never sure if my mom would allow future visits. Never sure. Never secure.

In the several days leading up to my departure, I hugged a little more. Laughed a little harder. Loved on all things lake and family. As our final ritual before leaving Abilene, we purchased school clothes. Then, with the coveted Gloria Vanderbilt jeans packed nicely in my suitcase, we trekked back to Fort Worth. Those hours he drove me home were the only times PD fell quiet. No stories. No shenanigans.

Without forewarning, without knowing, without understanding, one of our summers was our last.

5

Displaced

You must learn to live on fault lines.

—SULEIKA JAOUAD, *BETWEEN TWO KINGDOMS*

A fresh start. A stepdad-free life. All wrapped up in grandparent love, I returned home from my summer visit giddy with anticipation. Giddy about our future. I imagined all the new activities my mom and I could do. Daydreamed of my parents reuniting. Rested happy. Woke content. Lived lighter. Felt freer.

Of course, my mom had to work harder. Of course, she needed help. We were single now. We each had a new role. Each had to do her part. Life would adjust. Routines would change. It would take time. But I felt certain we would find our way and establish our groove.

I never considered the alternative. My mom was strong. She was resilient. I knew any day she would wake. Leave her room. Play with me. Get to rebuilding. Get to living. So I waited. Waited for days while she slept. Made lists of fun places we would visit. Watched TV. Explored alone. Cleaned the house. I wanted everything perfect when she woke. But instead, the next day was the same as the last.

Eventually, Karen Melendy showed up at our trailer. She sat with my mom for a bit. Packed my bag. Placed me in the car. Drove me to her house.

"Your mom needs to rest," she explained in the car.

I agreed. My mom seemed groggy when I kissed her goodbye. She was barely able to lift her head. Initially, I worried about her. I briefly spoke with her each day, but I enjoyed the Melendys' home. It was easy to get lost in the fun and play. Lost in the love and care. After a week or so, with my belly full and feeling secure, my mom appeared out of nowhere.

"Susie, let's go!" she yelled, dark and wild.

I reluctantly moved toward my mom while looking at Karen. I didn't want to leave. Not this way. Not with my mom in a rage. But she didn't care. Didn't ask me. Wasn't in the mood to negotiate. Karen pleaded, but my mom ignored her.

She squeezed my hand a little too tightly and jerked my arm a little too hard as we walked briskly out the door. We sped home. Her music drowned out the ability to communicate. Drowned out my ability to cope.

Without Karen to babysit me, I accompanied my mom to work. With a few weeks of summer left, she had no choice but to bring me along. She could have swallowed her pride. She could have apologized to Karen. But in my mom's mind, those weren't options. She was right. They were wrong. No gray in the equation.

I never knew the details of her fights. I never understood why she argued with everyone. I simply witnessed people around, then people not around. Then, after a certain amount of time, some people were around again. I mourned their absence and appreciated their presence.

Time with others became precious and delicate. I cried often when leaving loved ones, afraid I would never see them again. But with Karen, I knew she would return. The Melendys were never gone for long. We couldn't live without one another. I just had to wait it out. Let my mom's pride deflate.

So, before the third grade, while my mom was in a fight with Karen, I went to work with my mom. I helped her dust and empty trash cans. I chilled on the couch and watched TV when I got tired. I took pleasure in seeing my mom transform a dirty house into an immaculate home.

I'm sure her clients were grateful, though I wouldn't know. My mom required an empty house on cleaning days. It was mandatory. She was incapable of working with or around others, and we needed the money. Therefore, she worked alone.

I enjoyed having the houses to ourselves. Sometimes we snuck food from their fridges when we got too hungry—a slice of cheese rolled into lunch meat or a few cookies held us over. We didn't use plates or silverware. We chewed and swallowed quickly, cleaned up immediately, and didn't leave any evidence.

After an hour or two, the home was spotless. At this pace, we cleaned two or three houses in a day. I loved the feeling of leaving the last home as the last door locked. With checks in hand, we promptly went to the bank. My mom taught me to fill out deposit slips. With "less cash" in her wallet, our first stop was Taco Bueno. Our second stop was for gas. Then home. The next day came. Repeat. Our summer routine felt right. Our partnership worked. I liked spending my days as my mom's helper. I liked feeling needed. Liked making her day easier.

"I found a sitter for you in the trailer park. She's sixteen, and her younger sister is your age. Her mom will be there but stay out of her way. I will be back after work," my mom blurted out one random morning.

I wasn't happy. I didn't want to stay with strangers. I wanted the Melendys.

"Why can't I go play with Robby and Jamye?"

She pretended I said nothing.

"Go get whatever you want for the day."

I pretended to comply. Went in my room. Destroyed whatever I could find. Something breakable. Something mine. I pouted. Then I placed random, insignificant items in my bag. Nothing of any importance except Roni Rabbit. As my mom knocked on their trailer, my heart pounded. Heavy footsteps ran to the door. An ugly blonde teen answered.

"Hi, Sheri. Are you Layla?"

I nodded and looked at my mom. My eyes begged.

"You'll be fine. This is Melissa. Mind her. Okay?" My mom rushed on. "Is your sister here?"

As the words left her mouth, a beautiful, ratty-haired girl poked her head around the door.

"Hi," she said.

Melissa introduced us.

"This is Katelin. Y'all are in the same grade."

I smiled as if being in the same grade fixed the situation. My mom forced her goodbyes. I started to cry.

"You'll be fine. I'll be back before you know it," she said, trying to reassure me.

As my mom nudged me into their mangled trailer, I took a few steps and the door closed. The smell of must, cigarettes, and cheap perfume filled my nostrils, attached itself to my clothes, and stained my brain. Melissa walked away. Katelin stared at me.

"Who's here?" a gruff voice barked from the back.

"The kid I'm sittin' for," Melissa replied.

Their mother crawled out of a dark cave. A short, stocky figure hobbled straight for me. I, still frozen by the front door, contemplated running home, but my legs wouldn't bend. She moved unevenly toward me. Closer and closer.

"What's your name, little girl?"

I failed to find my tongue. I couldn't make anything work. Her appearance frightened me. Everything about her was rough and scary. I searched for any feature that resembled a female. Resembled a mom.

"Her name is Layla," Katelin said, saving me.

"Now, listen to me. I sleep during the day and work at night. I better not hear a thing outta ya. Don't make me come out here. Hear me?"

"I know, Mom," Katelin bounced around and answered.

I remained a statue.

"You? Do you understand?"

Her eyes met mine. I tried to become wallpaper. Melissa put her hand on my head and shook it up and down.

"She heard ya."

Their mother stared at me a bit longer and then returned to hobbling. The trailer rocked. I scrutinized her bizarre movement. Was one leg longer than the other? Was one leg twisted to the right? I was fixated. I studied her gait. Examined her silhouette. Melissa bent down and positioned her face in front of mine.

"Hey, you're okay. That's my mom. You can call her Ms. Trina. Well, when you start talking," Melissa said, laughing. Katelin ran from one room to the next. She smiled as she passed.

I was stunned. Freaked out. Wanted to walk home. I asked God for my parents or Karen. Tears swelled. I continued to stand as a frightened mute in the living room. Refused to sit on their nasty furniture. Clutched my bag. Watched the clock. Declined to play. Picked apart the trailer. Noticed everything wrong. The interior resembled an indoor garage sale. Nothing matched. Everything was old and broken-down. Nothing was worth more than ten dollars. Melissa tried to include me.

"Katelin is watching TV. You can go in there."

I stood still. Moved my eyes only. My mouth wouldn't work. Eventually, my legs tired and shook. I gave in and sat on the filthy carpet right where I stood. When I got bored, I ventured into my bag of random crap and wished I would have packed better. I pulled out Roni Rabbit. Pulled out comfort.

"You ever gonna move from there? Let's do sumpthin'," Katelin said.

With each comment, each question, my anger boiled. I stuffed down the urge to slap her. Melissa entered the kitchen to make lunch.

"Katelin, come help. Leave her alone."

They stirred in tandem from the fridge to the stove to the table and back. I watched. When they looked at me, I looked away. Focused on Roni Rabbit. Katelin whispered to Melissa. Both laughed. I grew angrier. Melissa made me a plate.

"Come eat. You can't eat on that floor."

I refused. Didn't move.

"Starve then."

Katelin laughed at her sister. I stewed. Felt tears but refused them. They ate. Cleaned up. Left the room. In the middle of the floor, I fell asleep. I woke to my mom shaking me while laughing.

"She's stubborn. Same time tomorrow?"

In shock, I glared at my mom until my words pushed out of me.

"You're leaving me there again?"

She pulled into our driveway. Slammed on the brakes. Raised her voice. Grabbed my arm.

"Listen. Melissa is your sitter. I have to work."

She paused.

"Yes, you're going tomorrow and every day until school starts."

My blood turned hot. I wanted to scream, but I didn't want a spanking. Instead, I grabbed my bag. Withdrew to pink. Smashed my jewelry box.

The next few days were a carbon copy of the first day. Mad. Statue. Mute. I moved my protest to their couch. There was no need to be angry, dirty, and on the floor.

I was determined to teach my mom a lesson. I wanted her to feel sorry for me. To apologize. To take me back to Karen's. But she never even acknowledged it. Never said anything. After Melissa informed her of my daily actions, she shot me a dirty look. Returned to the car. Drove home.

On Friday, she dropped me off in the morning, and I immediately fell asleep on the couch. I fully expected to wake up to my mom. When I woke, the sun hung low. The living room was dark. Shadows danced on the walls. My body was humid and damp. I left the couch in search of humans. I heard Ms. Trina stirring and walked quickly in the opposite direction toward the girls.

"Where is my mom? She should be here by now."

Both girls were astonished to see me awake. Moving. And talking.

"She's not comin'," Katelin joyfully blurted out.

"Your mom needs you to stay here for the weekend. She'll get you on Sunday," Melissa said.

I dropped to the ground. Tears fell out of me. Ms. Trina entered. I stopped.

"There's food for dinner. Make y'all somethin'. And Layla, dry it up. It's enough! See y'all in the morning."

When she left the trailer, I called my mom. No answer. Roni Rabbit and I cried ourselves to sleep. In the morning, the smell of donuts woke me. The girls were cooking. I sniffed them out.

"Take some dough. Roll it into a ball. Put it in the oil pan for three minutes. Then move it to the paper towel. Wait a few seconds. Then put it in some sugar or cinnamon. Then eat," Melissa instructed.

Amazed by the process and excited to eat donuts, I completely forgot my situation. I focused on cooking and eating a bazillion holes. No one told me to stop. I ate until the ingredients disappeared. Ms. Trina shuffled in. Tired. Annoyed.

"Girls, get dressed. It's time to clean the bar. Melissa, when did you put my clothes in the dryer? Shit, everything is wet."

She touched the clothing. Slammed the dryer door. Hobbled back to her cave. I escaped into the bathroom. Locked the door. Changed my day-old clothes. Pulled my hair into a ponytail. Brushed my teeth. Repacked my bag. I wanted to be ready in case my mom came early. Katelin banged on the bathroom door.

"Are you done?"

I jumped. Exited. Called my mom. She didn't answer. The three of them got ready one by one, and then we packed into their messy, filthy car. Food, gum, bottles, and tissues decorated the floor and seats. I stared out the window. I wondered what my mom was doing. If she missed me. I realized wherever she was, there must not have been a phone.

We arrived at the bar. Piled out of the car. Ms. Trina cussed and barked as she fought the lock. Pitch-black and cold, Ms. Trina turned on the lights as fast as her legs could hobble. Melissa retrieved the cleaning products. Katelin and I helped some but mostly played video games and roamed the grounds, which I enjoyed. I explored every inch. Crawled in the nooks and crannies. Danced on the stage. Rolled up in the curtains. At times, I even spoke to Katelin and included her in my imagination. In my elaborate games and scenarios.

When Ms. Trina called, we ran to her side. I didn't dare cross her. Whatever she asked, I did. Then resumed playing. After a day's work, we returned to their home. Ms. Trina went to sleep. I watched *The Incredible Shrinking Woman* with the girls and dozed off. I woke to Katelin rummaging through my bag.

"That's mine. Give it back! I'm tellin'!" I yelled.

She laughed and teased. I recovered most, but she refused to hand over Roni Rabbit. As she twirled around me, she taunted me. Held

Roni Rabbit close to my face and then pulled him back as I grabbed for him. Over and over, she teased.

"Stop it, bitch!" I screamed.

Melissa turned the corner. Snatched the rabbit. Pulled Katelin's arm.

"Shut up! You want my mom to hurt you? Don't wake her up!" Melissa hissed.

I ran to the phone. Called my mom. No answer. I retreated to my home base, the couch. Sad and mad, I lay with Roni Rabbit on my chest. Questions consumed me. *Where is my mom? Why won't she answer? Why hasn't she called me? Does she wonder if I'm okay? Why did she leave me here? Who are these people? How does she know them?* Eventually, I fell asleep with no answers.

Around 11:00 p.m., my eyes fluttered opened. Laughter and chaos bellowed from the girls' room. They jumped when I silently appeared in their doorway.

"Shit, you scared us!" they said.

Both girls held beer cans. Acted silly. Ms. Trina was at work. Katelin bounced toward me. "Wanna sip?"

I rolled my eyes and fled to the bathroom. When I returned, they whispered and snickered at me. Melissa dialed the phone.

"Peanut? I'm sending this girl to your house. Meet her outside."

When she hung up, I knew by their expressions that "this girl" was me.

"Are you cool? If you are, you will run an errand for us."

I stared through her as she talked.

"Walk to the end of the street. A guy named Peanut will be there to meet you with a pack of cigarettes. Then come right back here. Got it?"

"She's chicken. It's too dark. She's not gonna do it," Katelin said, drunk and stupid.

I opened the door. Looked at Melissa.

"This way?" I asked.

Terrified, cold, and pissed at my mom, I ventured out. Quickly, I walked down the dark trailer park road toward a stranger named Peanut. I wanted to turn around. Wanted to run to my trailer. Wanted to cry. But I kept taking steps. In the distant light of the streetlamp, a tiny guy stood smoking a cigarette.

"Peanut?" I yelled.

He waved. Once I reached him, I grabbed the pack and sprinted back to the trailer. Melissa stood in the doorway. Both girls were dizzy with excitement.

"Have you ever smoked before?"

I shook my head.

"Well, tonight you will."

Melissa pulled out three cigarettes.

"Copy me. Hold it like this. Put it up to your mouth. Light it. Inhale. Blow."

Melissa enjoyed her first cigarette of the weekend as she taught me.

"Watch me," Katelin interjected.

I observed.

"My mom says I'm allergic to smoke," I declined.

But the girls were not satisfied.

"You have to. We don't want you tellin'."

I refused. Katelin inched closer to my face. Held her cigarette up.

"I'll burn you if you don't."

I grabbed the lighter. Lit the cigarette. Barely inhaled. Hated the smell. Hated the taste. Coughed as they laughed. I pretended.

"Do you like Peanut? He liked you. Wanna go back over there?" Katelin questioned, humping the couch arm while laughing. Their drunken unpredictability frightened me. I ignored them. Fake puffed. Threw the cigarette out.

"Is there dinner?" I was curious and starving. I hadn't eaten since the donut holes.

"We're just drinkin' tonight, girls," Melissa chuckled.

I withdrew to the couch and fell asleep to cigarette smoke, obnoxious cackling, and hunger pains.

"Layla, pick up the phone!" A loud growl filled the living room the next morning.

My eyes jolted open. I jumped from the couch to the phone.

"Get ready. I'm on my way." My mom's voice trembled. Elated, I dressed and waited. Positioned myself by the door. Looked out the window. No one in the house stirred. In minutes, my mom flew into the driveway and honked. I ran out the door. And like that, they vanished. Hell was over.

My mom appeared disheveled. Worn out. Depleted. I noticed, but I selfishly focused on getting home. Because of her state, I didn't bother to tattle. I kept quiet. Behaved perfectly. Didn't want to cause any problems. Didn't want to be sent back. I hid in my room for hours. Grateful for my things. It felt good to bathe. Eat. Be near my mom.

As I crawled into her bed, she turned on *All in the Family* and then *Johnny Carson*. We cuddled until she rolled over for the night. Once on her side, she made her final nightly request, "Gimme your leg." I automatically flipped my leg over her waist.

In the morning, I woke up happy. Ready. Rested. My mom didn't. I made breakfast. On a bed tray, I delivered her food and a sweet note.

"Mom? Wake up. Breakfast," I whispered loudly.

She rolled over. Smiled. Sat up. Ate. As I took the dishes to the kitchen, she cried out. To me. To herself. To God.

"I can't do this anymore. I don't want to be here. Let me die. I want to die."

I paced. Unsure of how to help or what to do, I waited until she calmed down.

"Mom, are we going to work?"

It was a workday, but she remained in bed. No signs of movement.

"Give me minute, okay?" she said.

I returned to my room. She talked on the phone. Hung up. Went back to sleep. For days. I played alone or with my imaginary friends. When hungry, I ate whatever I could make. Whatever we had available. When tired, I curled up next to my mom. I lay still. *Why does she want to die? Is she sick? Why does she want to leave me? Why doesn't she like our life? Our home? What's wrong with my mom?* Twisted in thought, I fell asleep.

When she randomly woke in the night, I woke. Excitement consumed me, but I tried not to overwhelm her. I moved slowly. Talked softly. However, her awakened state was fleeting—over before it began. Her body drifted from the bed to the bathroom. Then back to sleep. She floated from the bed to the kitchen. Then back to sleep.

Though her body bustled about, her mind lay dormant. Her eyes looked at me but didn't see me. Her ears heard me, but her mouth remained silent. Things went in, but nothing came out. The sad shell of a mom.

After a week of living with a zombie, my new friend, Jane Garcia, invited me to her house. I reluctantly accepted. I worried about leaving my mom, but I needed a break. Needed to be a kid. Needed to see people. If I couldn't go to the Melendys, then I would go to the Garcias.

I didn't know Jane well, and our relationship was built in proximity to our moms' friendship. The Garcias were new to our lives—basically strangers. I wasn't even sure how we knew them. They were fringe Jehovah's Witnesses, but they weren't friends with my dad, stepdad, or the Melendys.

Even though they lived next to our trailer park, they didn't attend our Kingdom Hall; nor had I seen Jane at school. One moment they weren't in our lives, and the next they were all in our business.

Regardless of all this, I prepared for a sleepover. I grabbed Roni Rabbit, kissed my mom, and left with Jane and her mom, Irma.

About three minutes later, we pulled into the driveway of a small tract house that looked exactly like all their neighbors' homes. Upon arrival, Jane led me to her room. Twin beds and a chest of drawers greeted us. A few clothes hung in the closet. Nothing on the walls. Nothing on the floors. Nothing out of place. Nothing to be out of place. An overwhelming craving for my mom rushed over me. I wanted out.

"You want a snack or drink?"

I declined, but I followed her to the kitchen. Noticed the sparse decorating throughout the house. One couch. One TV. One dining table. It was as if they had been robbed and left with nothing. I soaked it all in. Jane ate. By the looks of her, she frequented the fridge. While she complained of a rash from her thighs rubbing together, her oldest sister appeared.

"Hi, I'm Maria."

Unlike Irma or Jane, Maria was exotic—dark hair, brown skin, effortlessly curvy. She exuded a worldly, friendly personality. After introductions, however, she retreated as fast as she entered. After Jane polished off her food, we explored the outside world. We walked the street. Observed the creek. Talked about everything and nothing.

Irma called us in for dinner in the evening. A large Mexican man, who I learned was named John, impatiently waited at the table for his family and food. I sat. He yelled for the others, and his deep, annoyed voice startled me. Like scared minions, girls came running from all directions. Irma snapped to attention and waited on John. They all cowered in his presence. The girls feared their father. Treated him like a dreaded king. They took turns feigning affection and normalcy. Laughed a little too hard at his jokes. Hung on to his every word. Craved his attention but were scared when he gave it to them.

While they feigned and faked, I ate with my head down. If they feared him, then I did, too. I was certain they had a good reason. I sat confused. My emotions distorted. I didn't want him to notice me but felt weird that he hadn't acknowledged me.

Sophia, the sister between Maria and Jane, started a conversation about her dance routine. John and I were both bored. While she talked, I inspected her. She appeared to be adopted. Didn't resemble either sibling. Seemed innocent and fragile. Her body was skinny, underdeveloped. But she proved to be the most attractive. She rattled on and on. In mid-sentence, John retreated to the garage. I felt spared. Sophia looked jilted.

The following day, the house swarmed with secrecy. The girls oozed pity and mystery. All in the know but me. However, Jane seemed oblivious while fastidiously cleaning her eyeglasses. Whispers ceased and smiles appeared when I entered rooms. Irma asked us to play outside, which seemed reasonable. We had planned to anyway.

Several neighborhood kids swarmed the street. Played games. We joined. Entertained ourselves for hours. One by one, I met the crew. Most were immature and quite ordinary, but I immediately liked Joey. He lived directly across from Jane. He was a tall, blue-eyed thing. Cutest kid on the block.

Once we met, we were inseparable. We had a lot in common. We were both third graders with single moms. Both blondes. Both liked to joke around. We could have passed for siblings. By the end of the day, we ruled the pack. Just as we established our power, dinner was ready. Same routine. Same scene. After dinner, I showered.

In the bathroom, I heard the word "hospital" and other words I didn't understand through the door. I pressed my ear to the door. Someone was in the hospital. But I was unable to determine anything else. Then it dawned on me. I was staying another night. I hadn't spoken to my mom.

Fear metastasized from my head to my toes. Grew and pulsated. I flung the door open and ran to Jane's room. In her own world, she rubbed Vaseline on her thighs. She looked at me, puzzled. I decided to call my mom. Walked to the kitchen phone with determination. Maria and Irma stopped talking. Stared at me. I dialed and waited while the phone rang. Listened to our answering machine message. The sound of my mom's voice drew tears. Everything went dark.

The hospital felt cold and chaotic. It smelled of sickness and desperation. As I meandered through the white halls, my insides battled. Anxiety. Bravery. For days, I had longed for my mom. Longed for her brown skin and brown eyes. But now I feared what she looked like. On the outside, I appeared stoic. Calm. Dissociated.

The nurse held the door for me. Slowly, methodically, I moved to my mother's bedside. Several machines were attached to her body by cords as she clung to life. I took a deep breath.

"Mom?"

She didn't wake. Didn't orient to my voice. Didn't know her daughter was present.

"What are these black lines and smudges?" I asked the nurse, pointing to my mother's face. Choosing her words wisely, the nurse gently described the process of pumping a stomach. Apparently, charcoal is used. I must have appeared confused. The nurse made a second attempt to explain.

"We pump the stomach to remove any harmful or foreign objects."

I nodded like I understood, but I didn't. *Objects? Why would my mom swallow objects? What objects? My mom ate objects?* My brain tried to compute the information. I thought of LEGOs. I felt alone. I had no one to confide in. No one to process with. No one to comfort me.

I held my mom's petite hand until it was time to leave. I always loved her hands and long nails. I inspected them a little longer. Rubbed my fingers over her chewed fingertips. She often chewed away her fingerprints in stress. I couldn't look at her face. She appeared lifeless. She never opened her eyes. Never saw me.

The plan was to start my third-grade year living with the Garcias to allow time for my mom to recover and stand on her own two feet. Reenter life. Then I could return home. I complied, but I hated this plan. I wanted my mom well, but I detested living with the Garcias. My life had been interrupted. I was displaced. Arrested.

Each morning, when I woke in Jane's bedroom, I drowned in the sensation of being lost. Homeless. Parentless. Lifeless. I was an item being shuffled about. A thing. A porcelain doll. As if while God played with dolls, I was moved from one dollhouse to the next. Moved from the floor to the table to the bed. My clothes might change. I might sit with strange dolls. God rearranged my life on a whim. Uprooted. Unfamiliar. Uncomfortable. Hard.

As I trudged through each day, the weeks turned into months. The sun rose and set. Shined on cue. Kept its daily routine. Nothing was disrupted but me. On school days, I played the role of a girl with a typical life and normal family. I refrained from telling teachers or peers about my mom. I avoided any conversations on the topic. On weekends, I focused on the neighborhood kids. Ran the streets. Stayed outside.

I carried on as if with zero care. The imaginations of us poor, latch-key children dictated the day's events. Took us on unknown journeys. I gladly surrendered and escaped. With the sun high, we played hide-and-seek and freeze tag. When the rain poured, we floated on our backs down the creek. As the sun descended, Joey and I told scary stories. Recited them as truth. As the moon rose to its rightful place, our crew retreated home.

I retreated inward. My least favorite moment of the day was

returning to the Garcias' blank walls. Blank world. Blank faces. By my choice, whether inside or outside, Jane and I lived in a constant state of play. The pretend world became my only world.

After a month or so, I noticed the Garcias' lives rarely collided. Behind the tract house façade, they lived as separate entities. Each orchestrated their own parallel existence. Kept up pretense. Ignored cracks. Dismissed reality. And for good reasons. Out of fear. Out of distress. Out of survival.

The older sisters were stuck between adolescence and adulthood. Consumed with activities and hormones, they kept to themselves. Lived as scared little girls. Irma busied herself with the role of mom and wife, almost consciously ignorant to the problems in her home. John occupied himself with his career and his mistress. Openly entangled in all things female. Openly arrogant and heartless. Purposely cruel. He used aggression and terror to manipulate and control his females. His objects. His property.

The beatings were infrequent but effective. I observed two in nine months. I never noticed anything brewing before the beatings. To me, the aggression exploded from nowhere. Occurred behind closed doors. Lasted longer than any child should withstand. As I walked through the kitchen, John violently pulled Maria into her room. Slammed the door. Wailed on her body over and over. Sophia hid. Irma said nothing. Did nothing. Nervously roamed the house. Jane waved me into her room. Noises rose and fell. Groans and whimpers continued. The house turned nervous and anxious. Everyone diligently worked on nothing.

I was shocked that there were no screams, pleas, or cries. But John apparently didn't allow it. Wouldn't have it. After a long period, he emerged. Maria didn't. Never left her room. In the morning light, she looked deflated. Destroyed. Impaired. After that beating, automatically and unconsciously, my behavior changed. With my sense of security warped, I moved about like a scared cat. Cautiously. Quietly. Guarded. Alert.

A few months later, John exploded on Sophia. Same pattern. Dragged her into her room. Beat her continuously. Muffled sounds carried between the walls. Tired and satisfied, he materialized. Sophia didn't. She needed time to absorb the beating. After this incident, I trembled at the sight of his cold, empty eyes. Fell asleep praying to God for my parents, the Melendys, or my grandparents. I was terrified. I had to leave. I feared for myself. Feared for Jane. Who would be next?

With terror and time, John transformed the girls into ghosts. Shells of humans with silent cries. Hollow entities that lived in the shadows with no voices. No opinions. No ability to feel pain. No light behind their eyes. They floated in and out of reality. With terror by his side, he did as he pleased. Acted how he wanted. He carried on an affair openly and brazenly. He took Jane and me to "work" with his mistress. *Who would tell? Who would ask? Who would care?* As they flirted and tinkered, we dreamt up games. Pretended we weren't there. Pretended she didn't exist. We never spoke of her. Irma never asked. They taught me the useful power of pretending. I used it as I pleased. Like they did.

"Layla, your mom is here," Irma yelled to me one evening between dinner and bedtime.

Surprised but thrilled, I grabbed my bag and frantically gathered my belongings. Thanked God for answering my prayers. I said my goodbyes in my pajamas and without shoes, one frozen foot already out the door. I ran to the car. Threw my bag in the back.

"Hi, Susie! I've missed you!" she said with a smile.

I shared the sentiment but wanted her to drive. Move on down the road. Head home. Instead, we sat with the radio on, and the heater blowing.

"I'm sorry, but I'm not taking you home. Not yet. Okay? I just wanted to show you my new car."

Her words pierced my heart. Oxygen left my lungs. I couldn't talk. Slowly, I noticed her new silver Honda. The word "my" instead of "our" rattled around my brain. The words "not taking you home" numbed my senses. Manically, she talked and talked about her car. About the John Lennon song playing. About how she needed more time. But she never said where she'd been. Never said why she hadn't called. Never asked how I'd been. Never asked about my living situation or about school. Never asked me anything.

When her "favorite song" ended, she placed my bag on my lap. Kissed my forehead.

"Susie, it won't be much longer."

I shook my head. Opened the door. As I shivered, tears streamed down my chin. She skidded away with the music blaring. The walk back to the house was mired in shame and abandonment. I was embarrassed to see any of them. Embarrassed my mom didn't want me. Embarrassed no one wanted me.

The next day, I physically couldn't get out of bed. An invisible weight pressed on my body. Jane asked me to get dressed. A friend of hers was joining us for the day. But I couldn't move. I couldn't hear her. I couldn't focus on her needs. My willpower to deal with the Garcias was gone. My brain was full. Like clouds, scenes of my mom, her new car, the song repeatedly came and went. If I focused too long on one scene, it dissipated. But another one immediately formed. Jane, angered that I hadn't obeyed her, lashed out.

"If you don't get up soon, we aren't playing with you."

Her words meant nothing. However, I wanted her to shut up and leave me alone. So I dressed and fell back in bed. Jane's friend surfaced. No name. No face. I didn't care. They played in front of me. Jane attempted to entice me. But quickly, my inaction enraged her.

"Whenever she wants to play with us, don't talk to her. Don't even look at her."

I was familiar with her antics. Our pattern consisted of playing nicely, then fighting horribly. I decided to find Joey. As soon as I sat up, Jane and her friend laughed and pointed at me.

"Look at her dirty ears! Were you playing in the dirt? Do you bathe?"

I ran to the bathroom mirror. Noticed the dirt packed in my ears. Started to cry. I realized no one was on my team. I had no mom or dad to watch over me. To care if I was dressed appropriately. To care if I bathed, brushed my teeth, or cleaned my ears. To care for me. To ask about me.

With this realization, I screamed. Ran to the phone. Picked up the receiver and dialed the Melendys. Pressed the phone to my ear.

"Hang up the damn phone!" John yelled on the other end. I dropped it. Ran and hid in a closet. Heard his footsteps down the hall. Terrified he would beat me. Jane poked her head in.

"What's wrong? I'm sorry!" Jane pleaded.

Fear, humiliation, and confusion.

"Get me a knife. I can't do this anymore!" I cried out.

Jane sat stunned.

"Get me a knife. Now!" I screamed desperately.

A few days later, on my mom's schedule, she and her friend Barbara took me to lunch. I was certain the Garcias involved my mom out of concern. They needed her to process the incident with her daughter. Find answers. Help.

However, Barbara conducted the meeting. Apparently, she was my mom's mouthpiece. As she talked, my mom remained quiet. Stared at me. Ate her food.

"Susie, what were you going to do with the knife?" Barbara asked.

I became angry instantly. I didn't appreciate her calling me Susie. That name was for family only. Wrapped up in rage, I didn't answer. Glared at her. Refused to eat.

"It's very important you tell us why you asked for a knife."

If my mom can try to kill herself, then so can I! I wanted to scream. But I remained committed to my silent protest. If my mom was silent, I rationalized, then I would be silent. Barbara continued with her best interrogation tactics. Tried to crack me. But I never answered her questions. Never spoke to her. Barely looked her way.

"When am I going home?" I asked my mom.

She started to answer, but Barbara interjected.

"She isn't ready yet."

"Then take me back to the Garcias now!" I said, full of piss and vinegar. *What is the point in prolonging lunch? What is the point of this lunch? What is the point of this entire year? What is the point of it all?*

As third grade came to a close, I sought out riskier activities. Joey and I discovered a way to walk in the street drains. We weaved our way through dangerous underground tunnels daily. We peeked at people through the street gutters. I secretly hoped and prayed to God we'd drown or get trapped.

In the evenings, Jane and I played a strange game. I would breathe deeply three times while crouched down and then stand quickly and hold my breath. Jane anxiously waited for me to transform into a crazy, unpredictable girl. At the right time, on my exhale, I growled. Hissed. And creepily moved toward her. This character let out all my aggression. All my fears. All my pain. Once sufficiently terrified, Jane tried to hit the spot on my back we'd decided would jolt me back to reality. Back to Susie. Back to nothing.

I often made it difficult for her to press the right spot. I liked pretend-land. Liked being crazy. Liked expressing my insides. On my final night in Jane's room, mid-game, mid-character, almost per-manently transformed into a crazy, bitter girl, my mom brought me home.

But only for a time.

6

Loved

At some point in your childhood, you and your friends went
outside to play together for the last time, and nobody knew it.

—ANONYMOUS

Theirs was a place of God. A place of compassion. Consideration.
Children. All living organisms inhabiting the ten acres grew
from all good intentions given to man. Lloyd and Karen Melendy possessed the kindest hearts and the souls of angels. They lived for their
children, opened their home, and took in strays. They exuded love.
They sacrificed. They gave. They surrendered all to God.

I was one of their strays—a special stray, but a stray nonetheless.
However, that fact meant nothing. I could breathe with them. I could
forget. I could be me. Be a child. Be free.

Karen and Lloyd encouraged us kids to claim our stake in the
family and the world without force, criticism, or malice. They culti-
vated an environment where each child could grow and claim his or
her rightful destined place. They created a perfect world for the five
of us kids, and it was all ours. In order, we were Robby, me, Jamye,
Keisha, and Micah. Staggered in age, some of us were blonde, some
brunette, and each was better looking than next. None forgotten.

None more important than others. Each of us lived wild and free. Each of us was innocent. Except me.

We were a tight, small army. A brood. An assorted crew. Young, immature, and full of boundless energy, we were each endowed with a double dose of imagination.

We found limitless games to play on the property—a plot of land adorned with a creek, a pond, chicken and rabbit coops, a dirt race-track, a jungle gym, an above-ground pool, and a trampoline. We had no off buttons, sense of time, or concept of structure. From eyes open to eyes closed, we discovered. We crafted. We grew.

We played to our hearts' desires and caught fireflies until Karen called us in at dark. A call we hated and resisted. But the fun didn't stop inside or with a parent's cry. Our brains conjured up new games with new rules and new characters for the new setting. We played until we fell soundly asleep on the floor in our regular clothes and shoes. Dead to the world. Dead to all we adored. Secure.

The little house built with Karen and Lloyd's hands on Road 600 was home to me. I spent much of my childhood there. And when I was whisked away, I was always trying to get back. I wanted to stay there and never leave. The decision, however, was never mine, and honestly, it was never the Melendys'. They were keen to raise me and keep me as their own.

Sheri embodied two people in one petite body. When she dropped me off with the Melendys, she shone. All smiles. All charm. She needed a sitter. Needed their help. Needed me away. She told cute stories of life since their last encounter. Some stories of me. Some of her. All fluff and fun. Then she bolted. Once she left, we got busy being us. Got busy forgetting her.

After weeks of being a Melendy, Karen would make the call. The hard call. She'd ask my mom to let me stay with them. For good.

Forever. I often wonder who I would have been, who I would have become, if I had been a Melendy. *Would I have been as kind as them? As forgiving? As secure? As honest and good? Would I have been free from stomach pains, anxiety, and nightmares? Would I have been free to be me? Free to belly laugh? Free to love and be loved?*

The answers were lost in Sheri's reality. Lost in her patterns. Lost in her tantrums. She wouldn't allow my happiness to settle. Wouldn't have it. In fact, she fought against it. Like a bad, recurring dream, Karen's call triggered my mom. Triggered her presence. Triggered chaos.

At pickup, Sheri seethed. Bubbled with ego and pride. Stormed through the front door, hot and hostile. Sometimes, she was so mad that the only thing she could yell was my name. Other times, she spewed a few choice words at Karen before she dragged me away. Pissed she had a child. Pissed the Melendys were gracious. Pissed they called her bluff.

While she peeled out down the driveway, her noise and obscenities filled the car. I cowered. I felt like an inconvenience. An afterthought. A nuisance. As I sat as a passenger of Sheri's, part of me remained with the Melendys. Part of me withered in shame. Part of me shook to my core.

After years of this cycle, time away from the Melendys became a constant. An inconvenient fact. A reality I tried to forget. Comings and goings plagued my youth. Robbed my time. Disrupted my favorite distraction. As soon as I left the Melendys, I scrapped and scrambled. Begged and pleaded to return home. Return to them. Return to my family. No matter how long the absence, no matter what prompted the return, when I laid eyes on the picturesque scene of their home, I exhaled. I calmed.

My time away felt miniscule, as if no time had passed at all. In my young, egocentric brain, I needed to believe that no events transpired without me. The scene—my home—was reminiscent of a postcard I

Robby, Jamye, Keisha, and Layla

tucked safely in a box. No movement occurred without my acknowl-
edgment or touch. My retrieval and recognition. My permission and
inspection. Life on Road 600 needed me to exist. To stir. It needed
me to hold it in the light and manipulate it this way and that for time
to pass.

Once I wafted color onto to the page and jostled oxygen through
their lungs, each family member resumed their roles and activities.
Each got to living. Each got to loving me. With a flip of the postcard,
all the kids barreled out of hiding and belted out a million ideas for fun,
as if the ideas accumulated while they awaited my homecoming.

When I did return, we immediately resumed the seriousness of our
play. We organized and delegated. Collected and positioned. Sweated
and panted with play. Any object, any room, or any closet could be
transformed into an elaborate game in seconds. Tennis rackets became
our guitars. Hairbrushes were mics. After rocking out for hours to the
Happy Days soundtrack, we draped sheets over furniture to build our

tent. Our haven. Our home base. A quaint, private area filled with essentials and snacks.

When we were bored of the tent, the nooks and crannies of every-thing became tests of courage and trust. We took turns locked in an antique chest for the fun and for the terror. Stuffed under piles of thick blankets, void of light and oxygen, questions swarmed my mind as the lid closed. *How many knocks or screams before I'm freed? Will I suffocate? Will adults intervene?*

Other days, the above-ground pool became our private ocean with currents and waves. Round and round we went. All of us swam in sync. Once the pool swirled with force in one direction, we let go. Floated on our backs. Let the water carry us away.

Waterlogged, we jumped and slid on the trampoline in our bikinis, taunting the boy next door and horrifying his poor mother. At night, we converted it into our bed under the stars, blankets and pillows stacked high.

To my delight, I constantly had real babies to mother. With five children of her own, Karen provided us older kids with live babies to feed, dress, and love. And when the babies proved tedious or exhaust-ing, we visited the rabbits and chickens with attention and care. We named them all. Although we may or may not have eaten Snowball, Keisha's pet rabbit.

Once we disrupted every inch of land, we plopped in front of the TV and played a VHS. We watched *Parent Trap* a bazillion times. Disney movies played on repeat. How lucky were we? Anything and everything was for our entertainment. Karen and Lloyd didn't really possess things of their own. New furniture? We immediately ruined it. New dress? We tried it on. New makeup? We ruined it in a day. We left nothing undisturbed. Nothing unturned. Nothing well enough alone.

I rested at the Melendys in a way I never rested anywhere else. A deep, calm, secure, safe rest, which I never experienced between my stays there. A rest in which I didn't need Roni Rabbit. A rest so deep, I often refused to wake without body shaking, cover removal, and at times, a splash of water. I couldn't wake up like the others. My body needed more time. More sleep. More coaxing.

Whether church or Six Flags awaited, I was a sloth, although I was slower on church mornings than Six Flags mornings. The Melendy kids understood about church. They struggled to wake and dress as well. Their understanding and tolerance was nonexistent on Six Flags mornings, however. My laziness infuriated them. All the kids woke up ready for the adventure. All woke except me. As they kicked and shoved me to consciousness, I begged, "Just leave me. I don't want to go." And at some point, the kids agreed.

Sunday mornings, however, came once a week, a fact I fought with gusto. The Jehovah's Witness faith consumed the Melendys' life, decisions, and schedule. Three to four times a week, we either attended a meeting, participated in a Bible study, or preached door-to-door. I cared for none of it. I was a kid. I wanted to play, sleep, and explore. So, on Sunday mornings, I slept hard. Deep. Drooled. Dreamed.

In my unconscious state, I heard rustling in the distance—chaotic movements as the kids dressed in their Sunday's best. Micah played and laughed. He ran from room to room until Karen scooped him up for grooming. Jamye searched for a matching outfit in slow silence. One matching sock. One matching shoe. He rubbed his eyes and mumbled in frustration. He seemed to search for years without a clue. Robby, the oldest by one year, had an established social life. He dressed first. Spiffed and shiny, he waited at the table for others to eat.

"Hurry up; you're going to make us late," Karen would say.

She mommed everyone, prodding her brood into various stages of ready and dressing when she could. Lloyd smiled at the cute mess of his disorganized crew. He hurled one-liners with his thick country accent while preparing biscuits and gravy.

All the while, I hid under covers until someone confiscated them. Since Keisha and I shared a room (and a soul), she had the unwanted task of waking me. In between dressing herself and avoiding her task, she pleaded with me. She wanted me up. Wanted me with her. Wanted me to fix her hair. Wanted our day to begin.

Keisha and I were inseparable. We dressed alike. Acted alike. Talked alike. We vacillated between being sisters and best friends. But in the mornings, we annoyed each other. Eventually, I emerged. Though clean, my hygiene may have been a bit compromised and my attitude a bit surly. I could have been described as groggy and irritated, even. Either way, I emerged.

Almost late and all bothered, we piled in the station wagon (or Suburban, depending on the year) and headed to the Kingdom Hall. Once in the car and down the road a piece, Lloyd made an abrupt U-turn back to the house. A turn that could only mean we left Jamye again. As we drove down the driveway, Jamye stood outside the front door. An all-too-familiar sight, Jamye lived perpetually detached from everyday events. When we finally arrived at Sunday meeting, Lloyd placed his briefcase and Bibles strategically to save us all seats. We took up an entire row—an unorganized, loud, chaotic row.

Once the meeting commenced with the first talk, I got to ignoring by engaging in anything but listening or learning. I sat. I stared. I drew pictures. I picked scabs. I brainstormed ideas for play later. My favorite pastime was simply observing us and all that we entailed. We were a constant source of entertainment and energy. I'm not sure how Karen or Lloyd heard the talks or learned a thing.

For any behavior besides peace and quiet, Karen shushed us loudly. She often handed us a Bible and pointed our attention to Scripture. But

I didn't understand the Bible. Adults all over the world debated each word, line, and character. *What can I add? How can I be expected to understand?* But as I attempted to focus, Jamye inevitably sneezed and blew ugliness all down his face. Keisha and I roared, rolled, and ribbed. Micah snored. Robby ignored. Karen searched her purse for a Kleenex. Our row was a living, breathing daycare.

With five children in every meeting, at least one of us was mad each minute. One needed the restroom. One acted up. One was too loud. One was asleep. I envied the sleeping babies, who usually were laid out on the floor or across two chairs. They twitched. Sweated. Dreamed. *How is that fair? Why can the young ones sleep? I'm just as tired.*

On the road home after church, Keisha and I piled in the back to entertain Micah and, honestly, ourselves. We adored his squishy, juicy smile, his blonde locks, and his delightful ways. He returned our love by complying with our requests and repeating whatever we asked. He mimicked hip phrases like, "No doy!" and "Gag me with a spoon" in his cute little voice. Delighted, we continued until Karen called for us to stop. Jamye may or may not have made it into the car.

About halfway home, all of us deep in planning for the day, our stiff clothes became unbearable. Uncomfortable. One by one, we shucked an accessory. Shoes off. Ties undone. Hose torn. Belts unbuckled. Before the wheels stopped, the doors were already opened.

We toppled to the ground and barreled through the front door. First on the agenda? Star Wars. Keisha portrayed Princess Leia while Jamye vacillated between Han Solo, Luke Skywalker, and Chewbacca. I, of course, played "Princess Layla." Our minds explored George Lucas's fictional universe. We used our powers for good and trekked across foreign lands, barefoot and brave, with lightsabers in hand. We met intergalactic species and solved their woes in a "galaxy far, far away" until we were jolted back to earth and reality.

Pain. A sticker weed. For most humans, a sticker is an inconsequential fact of life in the country. However, I am not most humans. Pain never suited me, and drama consumed me. I cried. Screamed. Gyrated. Hopped. Following our well-established routine, Keisha ran for Karen. Jamye stood confused, caught between earth and another galaxy, as if wondering how a Jedi fell prey to a sticker. Inconsolable, I wailed that I might never walk again.

"Just leave it alone! Don't touch it! I'll live with it!" I begged as Karen approached.

"Be still. You're being silly. Let me help you," Karen said, attempting to grab the sticker. But I continued to plead with desperation. Eventually, with lightning speed, she removed it and saved my life. Keisha stood by until my tears turned to laughter. Jamye rolled his eyes. Robby sped away on his motorcycle. And Micah ran by naked.

None of us were strangers to painful accidents on Road 600. Huguley Hospital, the local ER, knew Karen and Lloyd by name. While nothing but love flowed between us kids and no one intended to hurt the other, it happened all the same. Any and every activity posed a hidden danger, and we quickly uncovered it. We had too many accidents to count, but the shock and pain of what seemed benign made a few stand out. We learned something can turn wrong in seconds.

One day we were fishing in the pond and waiting for a bite. I stood still, calm, and apparently too close to Robby. His next cast sent his hook deep into my leg. Our serenity turned to horror. Our silence turned to screams. Lloyd eventually cut the hook free.

Another time, we were building a tent and securing the sheets under large rocks. I stood up, disturbing the structure, which somehow dropped a rock directly on Robby's head. Another accident. Another concussion.

A year later, while the older kids babysat, Micah dug in a "dirt pile." Through the window, his contentment was obvious. He was busy with his methodical, intentional digging. We turned away, and within minutes, black fire ants covered his entire body. Another accident. Another ER visit.

Years later, Keisha and I fell off the jungle gym and landed on Micah. Broke his arm. Broke his spirit. Another accident. Another cast.

Oddly, Jamye caused his own problems. Once he pushed candy deep into his ear, leading to the doctor's and a vacuum. Then he did it again. Another accident. Two more ER visits.

The worst accidents involved motorized vehicles. Our entertainment did not need speed. Our imaginations did not need gas. Motorcycles wrecked. Go-karts crashed. We collectively plowed over a boy with a large tractor, pushing him into the depths of the dirt. Another accident. Another heart attack. Thank God we all survived, unscathed and intact.

Depending on the incident, I either yelled, "I'm tellin!" or whispered, "*Shhhh*, don't say anything!" Both pleas were accompanied by bribes or punishments. If the young ones disobeyed, Jamye and I mouthed our conversations until they believed they were deaf, caved, and complied—or until they ran scared.

If we could solve our problems without involving the adults, we would. If we couldn't solve something, Karen or Lloyd proved understanding. They were never scary or punishing. I enjoyed their parenting. They processed with us and gave us guidance. It was a stark but comforting contrast to Sheri's vindictive, aggressive parenting style. Karen's talent was momming everything around her—a talent I soaked up. At worst, we got a gentle yet firm lecture. As Karen left the room, I often whispered to myself, "Mom." It was my one-word prayer. I had an innate need to bond us by name. I needed to be hers. I needed her to be mine.

On weekends, we often day-tripped to visit Lloyd's huge, kind, loving family in Waco, which wasn't far from the house on Road 600. One weekend on the way there, Karen told us *The Wizard of Oz* was playing the next night. As a result, we were extra giddy and full of anticipation all day to the point of exhaustion, and we all fell asleep on the way home. When we arrived, Lloyd carried each of us from the car to our beds. Half awake, his gesture felt like love. Like belonging. Like I was one of his.

The next day we ran around like crazy, searching for anything to occupy our minds and keep us busy until Dorothy. We walked the creek bed, played in the car, and checked the clock. We roamed the property and checked the clock. An hour from showtime, we prepared and checked the clock. We gathered blankets and pillows, picked our spots, made popcorn, served ice cream, and checked the clock. We sat. We waited. We anticipated. Then we sat and waited some more.

Finally, the MGM lion roared, and the show commenced. We giggled at first, but then we focused. We were glued to the TV. Glued to the moment. Glued to one another. We were the stillest and most engaged we'd ever been. We laughed at the munchkins, feared the witch, and winced at the flying monkeys. Micah was asleep on the floor by the time Dorothy met the wizard, and Keisha wasn't far behind. Robby, Jamye, and I barely saw Dorothy click her heels. Karen turned off the TV and Lloyd turned off the lights as my eyelids grew heavy and closed.

Just as I fell into a comfortable slumber, just as I settled into my life, just as I let my guard down—Sheri returned. Like a tiny ball of brown chaos, the Wicked Witch appeared and dumped on everyone in her way. Groggy and confused, I tried to wake up. Tried to understand. Everything became tangled and dismantled. Emotions and good sense got lost in the fray. Karen followed us to the car as we left the warmth for the cold night air. My bare feet froze to the ground.

In a soft voice, Karen tried to reason with Sheri. Tried to reason with her best friend. I wanted to cry. Wanted to jump in her arms. Wanted to plead my case. *Don't let her take me! I am happy here! I will be yelled at. Ignored. Forgotten. I haven't said goodbye. Keisha will won-der where I am.* But I couldn't speak. Fear held my tongue. As the tires spun out of control, I wished for Dorothy's shoes. I wished to click my heels. To return home. Instead, I trembled and watched Karen retire to our house. Tears fell. I simply mouthed, "Mom."

"You have plenty of food. Don't call anybody. I'll be back," Sheri yelled. These were her parting words before the first time she left me alone for days. The sun had not yet cast shadows on our trailer since last night, and the events were not yet a blur. With a heavy heart, I tucked the postcard of my home and my family back in its box.

7

Visited

Nothing can replace the influence of
unconditional love in the life of a child.

—ATTRIBUTED TO MR. ROGERS

I woke to a quiet, deserted house. Unaware of the time. Unaware
of the cause. Unaware. Step-by-step, I cautiously moved through
the Melendys' dark home. Not one of them was in sight. No Karen
or Lloyd. No kids. No pets. My head swiveled as my body felt drawn
toward something outside of myself. Something beyond my control.
My body gently pulled me through the front door. By a lifeline. By an
umbilical cord.

Outside, an extraordinary pink sky glowed, blanketing the ceiling
as the sun and moon stepped aside. The scene was desolate and bare, and
I wondered if this was the Armageddon adults debated. Anticipated.
Feared. *Have I been left behind? Have I been bad? Has God removed
everyone from me? Am I truly alone now?* I wanted to cry for my dad, but
I fell slave to the moment. To the experience. To the visual.

I tried to absorb the familiar landscape. The ten acres of lush play-
ground that defined my childhood looked dry. Burned. Forgotten. A
light breeze disturbed my ponytail. Chilled my skin. Blew the leaves

and dirt about. In the distance at the front of the property, a white tent came into focus. Untouched. Uninterrupted. Peaceful, but out of place.

I turned back to look at the house, still in search of the Melendys. Still in search of familiarity. Still trying to understand. But the home, my home, appeared to be abandoned and dejected. No signs of love and laughter. No signs of family or God. No toys. No color. No windows. All was black and gloom, from the foundation to shingle, as if all humans had left years before. I looked away in sorrow.

But before grief consumed me, the tent was upon me. I drifted through the opening. To my delight, several children of all ages and genders were gathered on the ground. They smiled and welcomed me. I returned their love. As I continued to scan the space, I saw an older man with gray hair and a long, wispy beard approaching from the back corner, his arms spread wide.

"Sit, my child," he said. I obeyed.

He joined the circle. As he spoke, an innate sense of well-being consumed me—a feeling I had only felt with my dad. I listened, my attention, senses, and emotions heightened.

"Do not be afraid. For you are with me. You are of me. I will protect you," he said. His softness filled the tent; love penetrated all my cells. Washed over me. Settled me. For a time, we sat with satisfied hearts and bellies. No longing. No craving. No grieving.

I awoke calm and safe. I believed I belonged. Believed I was protected. Believed.

8

Diagnosed

The truth will set you free. But not until it is finished with you.

—DAVID FOSTER WALLACE, *INFINITE JEST*

Cold. Sterile. Inhumane. Underfunded. Understaffed. Crowded with mental illness. Crowded with people in need. Crowded with despair.

As Sheri signed in, the receptionist acted annoyed. Impatient. I ignored their situation. I stared, inspecting each patient in the waiting room. Each caregiver. Each movement. All the faces looked dejected. Vulnerable. Miserable. Misunderstood. Flat.

Down deep, I knew we were them and they were us. But if one behaved or looked stranger, I put them in a different category than us. I created distance between us with justifications and labels. Rationalized. I set us apart based on appearance alone.

Sheri didn't look crazy. She wasn't babbling or rocking or undressing. She was strikingly brown and moved across the waiting room with ease. She had dressed effortlessly in her favorite blue jeans. Her hair was curled. Her makeup perfect. Sheri's eyelashes fluttered while she smiled at the others.

As we found our seats, she cracked a few jokes to calm my nerves. To cheer me up. To help me forget our morning. She felt bad about our earlier fight. Felt bad about yanking, pushing, and hitting me. Felt bad about screaming and cussing. She offered to play Hangman and I Spy. I agreed. I softened. We occupied our jitters for an hour.

"Sheri Finch?"

She rose and returned to the receptionist. She raised her voice when her inquiries were ignored. The receptionist cut their conversation short and dismissed her. This wasn't unusual. For any stressful situation, Sheri yelled going in and cried going out. Yelling was Sheri's preferred stress response including, apparently, when at MHMRA (Department of Mental Health and Mental Retardation), a state-funded clinic. I understood her responses. I wanted to scream and cry as well.

The waiting room had the ability to make people feel forgotten. Exiled from life. Set apart from humanity. Contagious.

Sheri sashayed down the hallway—hopefully toward answers. I waited. Swung my feet. Stared. Didn't dare move from my seat. Tried not to touch anything. Played with my fingers, then my zipper. Talked to myself. Bored. Tired. I wished I had a book, activity, or Roni Rabbit with me.

An elderly woman seated across from me dug in her purse. The sound annoyed me and continued for too long, but I couldn't look away. I wanted to see what prize she had. After a few seconds, she met my stare and pulled a peppermint from her purse. She asked with her eyes and a smile if I wanted one. With caution, I moved toward her. Just as I took the candy and smiled a thank-you, a familiar, loud cry billowed up from the hallway.

I rushed back to my seat. I watched the scene unfold. Inconsolable, dark, and dramatic, Sheri walked with a lady. Nodded her head in agreement. Cried. Wiped her nose. I walked toward them. The lady attempted to describe Sheri's diagnosis. She tackled the medications.

I listened intently. Wanted to help if I could. But I understood nothing. I'd never heard the words "manic depressive" or "lithium" or "cycling."

I tried to make sense of it, but it sounded like a foreign language. The lady repeated herself to penetrate Sheri's hysteria. Not sure if it worked. Not sure what Sheri absorbed. After three repetitions, the lady said goodbye. We paid our fee. With prescriptions in hand and black makeup dripping down Sheri's face, we left crazier than we entered.

Still confused, I eavesdropped. Listened to Sheri's discussions with Karen and others. Pieced together tidbits. Sewed a seam of one-sided conversations.

Apparently, "manic depressive" caused her sleepiness. Her absences. Her suicide attempt. Her darkness. All of Sheri was wrapped in this diagnosis. "Lithium" was the cure. If she took the medication, she would be fine. Hope overwhelmed me. Each day, I deliberately watched her take the pill. Smiled as she swallowed. Skipped away unburdened. Thanked God for the help.

After some days, Sheri acted happy. Light. Calm. Her happiness felt like the good old days. The days before Judah. Before George. Before mental illness found her. She seemed coherent and clear. The pill made her interested in our life. Interested in me. She morphed into a mother. Started cooking, sewing, and reading to me. She ceased all spankings. Ceased tantrums. Ceased profanity.

During the week, Sheri cleaned houses by day and waited tables by night. I stayed home the nights she worked, but this time she called every hour, on the hour, to check in. To check on me. To stick to a routine. I hated the late nights alone, but at least I could reach her when I got scared.

Plus, I enjoyed the perks. Each night, she placed all the loose change from her tips into a big jar. My allowance. Mine. I frequently counted my dough. Sorted my coins. Organized my loot. I loved the quarters and dimes.

On Tuesday and Thursday evenings, we drove to Burleson and attended the Jehovah's Witness meetings with the Melendys. On weekends, we wrestled and laughed. Pranked each other. Played outside. Unexpectedly, Sheri made plans and kept them. She showed up when she said she would. Followed through. Completed tasks. She even planned and executed our move from Kennedale to a new trailer park in Fort Worth. We had a new yard with a levy. I went to a new school. We had a new start.

Sheri's health was infectious. Attracted others. Triggered optimism. Our family and friends were filled with gratitude and hope. We had visitors stop by to witness the transformation and see the new neighborhood. Old and new friends alike invited us to dinner. To events. To share in life. We were on display, and I was proud to show off my new mom.

As fourth grade lurked in the summer shadows, Sheri announced two morsels of good news.

"There is a girl in your grade I want you to meet. I wait tables with her mom at Rollies BBQ. This way, you will have a friend on your first day of school. Whatcha think?"

"Okay," I half-heartedly agreed. "What's the other news?"

Sheri moved closer.

"Roy is coming to stay with us for a bit!"

I smiled. Mimicked her elation. I was thrilled to have him, though I did not know him. As with all encounters with Sheri's family, I was two parts anxious and one part excited. On his first night with us, we chatted nonstop. We listened to his army tales, told war stories of our own, and stayed up too late. The next morning, I woke to a panicked mom.

"Roy, wake up! Hurry!"

I scurried to the living room and sat on the couch. Wiped my eyes. Waited for the adults. As they entered, Sheri led Roy to the front door. My intense gaze followed them. I gasped.

"Roy, if you did this as a joke, just tell me. I won't be mad! Did you do this?"

Roy scanned the door, silent and shocked. Three crosses had been drawn in a red substance. One large and two small. While in some religions the cross is a holy symbol, for Jehovah's Witnesses, a cross is satanic. Demonic. Sacrilegious. Roy couldn't speak. Shook his head.

"Roy, it's okay if you thought it was funny. Be honest. Did you do this?"

"No! I swear. I went to sleep with y'all. I promise," Roy replied, holding his hands in the air.

"Have you seen Pat?" she immediately asked, sensing he wasn't responsible.

Roy nodded.

"I stayed with her for a few days before coming here."

I shuddered. I wasn't sure why, but I knew his answer was the wrong answer. Anything with Pat was wrong and scary. Sheri freaked. However, this freak out wasn't typical. It was measured and minimal—appropriate for the situation. The lithium calmed her cells.

"Did she give you anything? Do you have any of her things here?" Sheri pressed.

Roy walked to his room. Dejected. Guilty. Frightened. He returned with a quilt.

"She gave me this."

Sheri grabbed it. Left the house. Threw it in the dumpster. They spent the morning scrubbing the crosses from the door. After this, Roy felt weird and insecure. Sheri moved about anxiously.

True to form, Sheri never directly spoke of the incident to me. Never offered assurances. Never processed or parented. To me, she pretended it never happened.

I wanted some explanation. I didn't understand. The red substance washed off, but an imprint of the crosses remained. Unable to afford a new door, we lived with three faint, freaky crosses. They confused me. Terrified me. Gave me nightmares. Whenever I passed them, I ran, scurried, or skipped. But the crosses followed me. Peered at me. And each night, I prayed for God to protect me.

Sheri and Roy's conversations returned again and again to Pat and the crosses, though not in front of me. After an awkward week, Roy left early and returned to wherever he had come from. We slowly returned to our lives.

Sheri scheduled a meet-and-greet for me and Debra, her friend's daughter. I reluctantly complied. I never enjoyed meeting new people; however, I needed a friend at my new school. Butterflies filled my stomach as we walked to the door, but quickly dissipated. As I met everyone, it was impossible to be anything but comfortable around them. Carole, funny and easy, was the mom of three beautiful girls. She loved her family. Loved life. Loved laughing. I understood why my mom gravitated to her.

Debra was the youngest, sweetest, and most laid-back of her siblings. However, I also liked her older sisters. They both were wickedly honest with a great sense of humor, but also as different as night and day. Debra's father stood taller and larger than anyone I knew. His presence filled the room. He didn't say much, but he didn't need to—the females in his life never stopped talking.

After introductions, Sheri and Carole gabbed about work. Debra and I moved to her room and listened to "We Got the Beat" by the Go-Go's. We were instant friends. Instant sisters.

On the first day of school, Debra walked me around the campus and introduced me to her circle. She showed me off. Guys and girls in all grades respected and liked Debra. She was popular, but unfazed by her status. Unfazed by her natural beauty. She was tall. Skinny. Dark skin. Dark hair. Brown eyes. Beautiful smile. Easy laugh. Cool. I felt special around her. Lucky. Protected. Safe.

As soon as class started, I physically couldn't stay awake. Consciousness was not an option. Even though school began at 7:30 a.m. and ended at noon, heat penetrated every pore of my body. Every cell of my brain. Every inch of our school building. Castleberry Independent School District was mostly housed in old, dilapidated structures with no air-conditioning. During hot months, the district adjusted the school schedule to accommodate cooler temperatures.

For weeks, I was confused. I didn't realize one could opt out of AC in Texas. Even though I was dirt poor, cool air blew freely in our trailer. I quickly learned that without temperature control, my body wanted to melt into a puddle or burst into flames. And when neither occurred, I passed out. As soon as I arrived in school and took my seat, the heat lulled me to sleep. My teacher, Mrs. Hill, allowed this behavior for a week or so, until she snapped.

"Layla? Layla? Wake her up!"

The boy sitting next to me pushed my arm off my desk. I woke. Hair dripped with sweat. Belly and butt wet. Drool puddled on my desk. As I scanned the room, kids chuckled at my confusion.

"Layla, it is time to join the class. We are working on times tables. We are on sixes. Do you know your times tables through the number six?"

"I know them up to twelve."

Mrs. Hill balked.

"Well, then, come show us. Recite your times tables starting with the number six," she replied after a few seconds.

Groggy, wet, and annoyed, I moved to the front like a sloth, faced my new peers and began reciting. Mrs. Hill grew giddy with each new number sequence. When I finished with the number twelve, she could barely contain herself and pulled me in for a hug.

"Well, class, that's how it's done! Layla, you may resume sleeping."

Those words were music to my ears. Kids sighed. Mrs. Hill allowed me to slowly acclimate to the heat. As winter blanketed us in white, I was still ahead academically and now participated in all activities. After school, I crossed the street to Jack in the Box and played Pac-Man for an hour until Sheri arrived. Once we got home, Sheri changed, made dinner, and left for work. I watched TV, finished my homework, and talked to Debra on the phone. Fourth grade sailed by.

For the first summer ever, I drove away with PD feeling confident. I wasn't worried about leaving Sheri. I wasn't fleeing a bad situation. Sheri and I were a year in without incident. Without drama. Without a Sheri meltdown. Apparently, lithium allowed us to lead normal, functional lives. This summer, I drove away secure and waved good-bye to my beautiful brown light.

My summer was filled with love. With wonder. With all things grandparents. At first, Sheri called frequently. We rambled about our day's activities. About songs. About nothing. I enjoyed our calls and felt her positivity. More than that, I enjoyed knowing where she was. How she was. How to reach her. Her brownness glowed through the phone.

Gradually, though, the calls decreased to once a week. Then to only when I called. Though when we spoke her voice sounded the same, she acted the same, she laughed, joked, and griped about work, a little worry lingered in my mind. Seeped through the cracks.

Pushing off my misgivings, I immersed myself in PD's world. I listened to all his tales. We danced to our favorite tunes. I loved on Mema, played with Barky, and visited my dad. As the summer concluded, PD loaded the car for Fort Worth, and we drove to Aunt Rebecca's. Sheri showed up on cue. She looked a bit loopy. Smiley. Goofy. Deep brown punched my stomach.

"Mom, are you okay?"

"Yes! I'm just so happy to see you!" she said with her big, beautiful smile.

She immediately drove to Taco Bell, my favorite place. Over tacos, I talked her ear off and told her all my PD tales. She laughed. Asked questions. Always enjoyed his antics. His stories. I left out all things Dad, of course. I didn't want to trigger anger. Didn't want her inquiries about his address or phone number. Didn't want conversations about child support.

Sheri also talked and talked. Quickly. Wildly. Out of sequence. Out of context. She told tales of her summer. Of work. Of being lonely. Of missing me. She left out all things chaotic, of course. All things true.

The following days, I watched her behavior. I knew she was off. Way off. My insides twisted into knots. My brain told me to investigate. I tried to listen to her conversations. Tried to determine if she had stopped taking her meds. Tried to figure out what the fuck was going on.

She overcompensated. Lied. Dodged. Danced. Dreamed up fun ideas for the day. For the night. I followed her lead. Pushed anxieties deep into my toes. She used comedy and terror to transport us out of our reality. Out of boredom. Out of drama. Out of poverty.

When we watched TV or movies, we couldn't communicate. I couldn't ask questions. She couldn't lie. I couldn't side-eye her every movement. We sat in silence with eyes wide. Her brown throbbed. If we weren't watching *Saturday Night Live* or *Benny Hill*, we were watching *Scream of a Winter Night*, *Night of the Living Dead*, and *Invasion of the Body Snatchers*. Sheri craved fright. She didn't care that I was too young for blood and guts; she wanted a thrill, so she lugged me to the drive-in.

I never understood why she watched scary movies. They absolutely terrified her. On some level, though, they pleased her. The sheer anticipation energized her. She was giddy on our way to the drive-in. Excited for the previews. She shrieked and grinned when the actors appeared. Her brown eyes glistened in the cinema light. I marveled at her beauty. At the first thump or bump, we covered our eyes, only peering through the gaps in our fingers.

I trembled and squirmed. Quaked and struggled. Just as our hearts leapt from our chests, she kicked the speaker out the window, delightedly frantic with fear. We watched in silence, glued to the screen until we physically couldn't take another scare. At home, tucked safely in our sheets, we wrestled with nightmares. We were unable to sleep. She was unable to wake up for work. Unable to function. Unable to focus on life. I was unable to determine what the hell was wrong with Sheri. She was definitely turning darker.

As fall dripped shades of orange, life within our flimsy walls proved interesting. Sheri continued to descend with a slow detangling of certainty. An inability to maintain reality. Her lies became convoluted. Unorganized. Rushed. What she told one person was not what she told another. What she told me one day was different from the next. Her perceptions unraveled.

If I questioned her, she barked, cussed, and pushed me toward my room. I vacillated between two lands: a land of fear and a land of rationalization. With each bizarre behavior, fear emerged. Then, I rationalized. I wanted to make sense of it all. Of her. Of her diagnosis. Of her treatment.

With each passing week, my rationalizations piled up and eventually needed their own rationalizations. My head pounded. My stomach stirred. I felt responsible for her when I was at school. I felt as if she needed me to hold her cells in place. As if while I was away, she would flicker to black and implode.

I decided I needed help. The Melendys needed to know. I couldn't just call and tell them, though; I needed them around her. Maybe they would notice and help. Maybe they would calm my fears. Provide an explanation. Provide sanity.

I practically begged Sheri to attend a meeting in Burleson. She agreed. Suspicious. I never wanted to attend meetings, and recently I had enjoyed not attending any. She emerged from her room. Smiled wide. Dressed in a turquoise terry cloth strapless dress with heels. The color illuminated her tan skin.

On the way to the meeting, she made an abrupt stop at a liquor store.

"Wait here. I'll be right back."

She returned with a six-pack. Downed one beer in the parking lot. Pulled out another. Placed the remaining four in the trunk. She smiled at me.

"Let's go, Susie!"

She peeled out with Fleetwood Mac shrieking. I stared at her. She met my eye.

"What? Lighten up! We are going to the meeting. Smile."

Sheri hauled ass down the highway, late for the meeting. Late for reality. Late again. A police siren in the distance caught our attention over our blaring music. Sheri pulled over. Before exiting the car, she shoved her cold beer at me.

"Here, put this up your dress," she said with her wicked grin and sadistic black eyes.

In shock, I obeyed. She strutted over to the cop. Batted her eyelashes. Cracked a joke. Cast her spell. He chuckled. When the bottle touched my stomach, I giggled. The police officer poked his head through the window. I immediately stopped.

"What's so funny in here?"

I grinned. Said hi. He nodded. Stared awhile. Issued my mom a warning and left. Beer in hand, Sheri sped away in a cloud of glee. Sang all the way to the Kingdom Hall. Walked in like she owned the place.

Like she was attending a cocktail party. Smiled. Waved. With an odd intention, we both listened to the entire service. No shenanigans. No movement. Once the meeting concluded, she hugged the Melendys. Engaged in small talk. Charmed. Lied. Left.

She drove us home, a beer in hand and a grin on her face.

"How'd I do?" she asked. "Is that what you wanted?"

Christmas caught me by surprise. On a wink and a prayer, I left Sheri to spend the holidays with my dad's family, but not my dad. It was a long-standing tradition and a much-needed break. Sheri didn't celebrate Christmas, but she allowed me to partake.

The Reese holidays were filled with jokes, alcohol, food, presents, love, laughter, and PD's stories. As I dressed in my footed pajamas, I heard PD's guitar and ran to the living room. PD sang. We danced. After Christmas on their way home to Abilene, my grandparents dropped me off at home.

I heard loud music through the door as I inserted my key in the lock. I waved goodbye to PD and Mema. Acted normal. As I entered, Sheri was cleaning the house. In high heels. In a Led Zeppelin world. In a drunken haze. A statue, I stood at the front door. Took it all in. The absurdities. Her heels. She noticed my stares.

"What? I'm working on my calf muscles."

Muscle tone was not a concern she had ever expressed. I slowly turned the music down.

"Turn that shit back up!"

I retreated to my room. Sat stunned. There were no rationalizations for this one. Sheri was black.

"Get dressed. We are meeting my friends for a drink," she walked in and said.

I said nothing. Within minutes, we walked into a bar. Dark. Seedy. Barflies only. Once again, I became a statue.

My thoughts swarmed. *Where are we? Why am I here? Why would she bring a ten-year-old to a bar? Who is this friend? Who are these people? How does she know them? What is wrong with her?*

Sheri yanked my arm. Pulled me toward her friends. Pulled me back to the bar.

"This is Susie."

She rambled. I heard nothing else. She handed me quarters. Pointed me in the direction of the arcade games. As I inserted each quarter, Sheri downed another beer. Her volume escalated. Her flirtation amplified. I stuck to the Centipede Game. Too ashamed to join them. Too embarrassed to look at her. Randomly and annoyingly, one of her guy friends came over to watch my game. Attempted to engage me. Bribed me with quarters. Breathed down my neck with his beer breath. I ignored him.

I wanted to go home. Wanted her to shut up. Wanted to run away. After three hours of nonsense, as the sun peeked over the horizon, she drunkenly drove us home. I escorted her to her room. She fell on the bed. I asked if she wanted food.

"Close the fucking door! Go to bed!"

That meant no. She passed out in her clothes. I made dinner. Bathed. Fell asleep counting down the weeks until summer with PD.

As fifth grade ended, I found myself spending more time at Debra's, and not at Sheri's request. She didn't care. I felt helpless. Felt alone. I wanted companionship. I didn't stay away long, though—a weekend at most. I struggled to leave Sheri, even though when I returned, she was often gone—at work, with friends, or who knows where. Sometimes she was gone physically, sometimes mentally. Either way, she was lost to me in the inky abyss.

When she did appear, her mood and behavior were unpredictable. I never knew if a question or request would invoke anger, aggression, compassion, laughter, or a viable answer. I grew afraid to ask anything, whether about homework or a difficult task. I never made frivolous requests. I wore fear like a backpack I couldn't remove. It weighed on me. Suffocated me. Slowed me down.

However, it was almost the end of the school year, and I needed her help. For weeks, I saved up for a Barbie doll swimming pool. I stopped playing Pac-Man at Jack in the Box and instead walked home after school. I saved. I saved my quarters. I saved Sheri the hassle of picking me up. And I counted. I dreamed of my Barbies in the water. Tan. Fit. Splashing around with Ken. Once I saved enough money, I wouldn't stop talking about the plastic pool. Unfortunately, to buy it, I needed Sheri to drive me to the mall.

"Ask your dad. What has he done for you lately, if *ever*?" was her drunken response.

"Shut up about the fucking pool! Go to your room!" was her angry response.

"Can we talk about this later?" was her sleepy response.

"I'll do it this week!" was her happy response.

Finally, "this week" came. Sheri promised to buy the pool after work. I paced as I watched the clock. Once again, she was late. One hour went by. Two hours went by. Karen came to the house and waited with me. Three hours went by.

Without warning, Sheri burst through the door like a wild tornado. Sweating. Panting. Telling a tale of a car chase. A guy chasing her through a neighborhood. A crazed person who cut her off. Blocked her in a driveway. Pulled out a machete. Attempted to kill her. Sheri's eyes and aura were black. Chaotic. Crazy. She talked in circles. Talked fast. Arms and hands flailed. Body roamed.

The more she talked, the angrier I became. I looked back and forth from Sheri to Karen. I couldn't believe what I was hearing. Couldn't believe Karen was buying it.

She is off her meds. She's drunk. She's lying to you! I wanted to scream. But I stood frozen. I didn't want to be slapped or beaten when Karen left. I was frozen in disbelief. In fear. In anger. In realization that my mom was off her meds. Way off her meds.

It had taken me almost a year and a machete story to admit it to myself. *Why couldn't Karen see it? Why wasn't anyone helping us? Helping me? I should've tried harder. I should've made her take the meds. Why did I leave her alone? Why didn't I tell someone? Why won't my mouth move? And now, my mom is gone.* While I was deep in thought, Karen tried to calm her, but Sheri was crazed. On another planet. Black. She went on and on. Once she finally fell silent, Karen rubbed her back.

"Where's my Barbie pool?" I asked.

9

Disturbed

The worst part about having a mental illness
is people expect you to behave as if you don't.

—ARTHUR FLECK, *JOKER*

Sheri let herself in. Waved at the boy. Motioned me toward the couch. Walked to a back room. No explanation. No introductions. No concern. For the third time in two weeks, I waited in this living room. Waited in a stranger's home. Waited for an hour or so. Stared at the TV. Stared at the older boy in a recliner. Stared at the wall. I listened to the adults laughing. Talking. Socializing behind closed doors. The boy ignored me. Drank Big Red. Flipped through the channels.

I waited. I took in everything around me with all my senses. I smelled an unusual scent I had only ever experienced there. On the third visit and after an hour, the boy in the recliner spoke.

"Do ya know what they're doin'?" he asked, defiant.

I shrugged my shoulders. Tried to be cool. Tried to be in the know.

"Whatever. In case you want to know, they're smoking pot," he said.

I nodded slowly. Pretended to be fine. On the inside, I boiled. Anger bubbled. Shame simmered. *No wonder she acted weird when we left. No wonder I couldn't go into the room. No wonder she's an idiot.* The longer I waited, the madder I became.

Sheri finally emerged with a dumb, wide grin. I immediately left for the car. Sat in silence. Refused to engage. Refused to look at her. She searched for a song. Cracked jokes. Appeared unbothered by my silence. She headed for an unknown destination. I didn't ask for details. The sun was low on the horizon when we pulled up to a house.

"Let's go! We won't be long. Fucking smile, would ya?"

A furry man opened the door. He beamed at the sight of Sheri from beneath his long hair and beard. He did not seem happy at the sight of me. Sheri noticed his unpleased look.

"Do you have a guest room? She can go in there."

Once again, I was an afterthought. Something to be placed somewhere. Away from her. Away. They pulled each other close. Sheri flirted. They held hands as we walked down the hallway. He motioned toward the room.

"She can lay in here."

Sheri took his lead. Turned on the lamp.

"Layla, lie here for a little while. Try to go to sleep," she said in a soft, sweet voice.

I sat on the bed. They exited and closed the door. The sounds of giggles and kisses faded. I scanned the room. No pictures. No TV. No clock. No phone. No warmth. A strange room with a bed, side table, and lamp. I fell back on the bed. Feet dangling. *Who is he? Where are we? What is she doing? Why can't she be normal? I've got to get out of here. I have school tomorrow. I have homework.*

I tried to plan my escape, but my plans involved a phone, which I didn't have. I thought about crawling out the window, but I didn't know where we were. I wasn't even sure where the smoke house was. *Why didn't I pay more attention?* I was mad at myself. Mad at Sheri. Ridiculous situations occurred constantly. They kept escalating. Always absurd. My mental tantrum was disrupted by noises. It sounded like Sheri was in pain.

"Mom?" I yelled, afraid she was in danger.

I waited. Heard more noises. Sat up. Waited.

"Mom!" I yelled.

Within minutes, black appeared. Annoyed. Pissed. Aggressive. She yanked back the covers. Flung my legs on the bed. Covered me. Dug her fingernails in my arm.

"Stop, that hurts!" I whimpered.

She dug deeper. Positioned her lips close to my face.

"Don't say a fucking word. I mean it! Go to sleep! If I come back in here, you'll be sorry!" she whispered through gritted teeth. Then my loving mother turned off the lamp and left.

I cried. My arm bled. Hours passed. I never slept. Thoughts circled. *No, she'll be the sorry one. I'm telling Karen. I'm telling PD and my dad. I'm even telling my teachers. She'll be sorry when I fail out. When she has no friends. When she goes to jail.*

We arrived home at 3:00 a.m. At 6:30 a.m., I dressed for school. When I got home at 4:00 p.m., Sheri was sleeping. I never saw the furry man again.

During the sixth grade, Sheri and I orbited the same city and lived in the same trailer. At times, we even shared the same space. But we were broken. I preferred Debra's house. Her family. Our friends. I preferred anywhere but my home. Anywhere Sheri wasn't. I immersed myself in my social life.

When I did return home, I returned to an empty trailer where only traces of Sheri existed. While I was away, she showered. Changed. Cleaned. Ate. Left before I arrived. She called me periodically from Rollies BBQ where, if she wasn't working, she was partying. I knew she was mostly calling to make sure I hadn't called Karen. Hadn't ratted her out. Hadn't burned down the trailer.

When she returned, she returned late and with a man. Waited until

I was asleep. Snuck him in through the back door. For months, I didn't see his face. Only heard his voice. Smelled his BBQ scent. Thankfully, it was the same man. And thankfully, he left before I woke.

Sheri acted casual in the mornings after. Pretended the man didn't exist. I pretended the same. Nothing was gained by confronting Sheri. Nothing but lies and a beating. She always hung herself. Always inadvertently tied her own noose. She tied it tightly with a long rope made of deception. I just needed to sit back. Be quiet. Collect information. And wait. Her slip-ups often happened late at night or early in the morning. Alcohol and bipolar didn't mix.

One night, deep in sleep, I woke to screaming. Moaning. Panting. Slapping. Struggling. I leapt from my bed. Flew to her room. The sounds intensified. I tried to open her door. Tried to rescue Sheri. But pillows, blankets, and stuff pushed back. With all my weight and force, I pushed through. Fell on a mound of stuff. Fell at the foot of the bed. Fell at their feet. All three of us froze. I noticed their naked bodies. I realized the situation. I ran.

After an hour or so, Sheri slithered into my room. Sat on my bed. Put her hand on my leg. I recoiled. Said nothing.

"Layla, I've been dating Mark for a while now. This isn't someone I just met. He's the owner of Rollies," she crooned. She attempted to process. Attempted to parent. Attempted to explain. Her words meant nothing.

We moved about in silence, both of us too ashamed to look at each other. Too ashamed to talk. I couldn't erase what I saw. What I heard. What I experienced.

In an attempt to connect and change our scenery, we headed to Abilene to visit her sisters. In a moment of drunken honesty, I overheard Sheri talking about her meds.

"No, not anymore. I stopped taking lithium a while back. I didn't like how it made me feel."

I wanted to burst into the room and yell, *Normal? Because it made you feel normal! You were finally normal! I knew you stopped your meds! I can't believe you stopped!*

"I feel great now," she continued, "Everything is good. Mark and I are in a good place. Susie's doing great in school."

My jaw dropped. I couldn't breathe. I watched my cousins as they danced. Blank. As they sang. Stunned. As they played pool. Pissed. Sad. Paralyzed. The sisters joined us. As soon as Sheri uttered a syllable, I stood up.

"I want to see my dad!" I yelled.

And with that, I exited the room. Sheri followed. Tried to console me. Promised to make summer plans with my dad. Begged me to dry my eyes. But I couldn't stop crying. I wanted my dad. I wanted hope. I wanted a normal mom. Sheri left. Made some phone calls. Within a few hours, Aunt Winona appeared. All smiles. All fun. I softened.

"I have a surprise for you," she said, walking toward me. Surprises from Aunt Winona weren't unusual. She often bought me clothes and toys, but she had nothing in her hands. Instead, she told me to sit. Sheri beamed.

"I was at a client's house when I saw her son abusing a cat. He had it hanging upside down and he'd cut off the end of its tail. I pulled the cat down. Screamed at the boy. And told his mom to either give me the cat or I'd call the police. The cat has been at the vet for two weeks now. She is pretty and sweet and ready to come home. And she's yours," Winona said, smiling.

In gleeful shock, I leapt into Aunt Winona's arms. A gray-and-white cat named Snuggles became my best friend that day. My lifeline. My sanity.

Odd behaviors and bad decisions continued to plague our home after we got home from Abilene, but Snuggles softened the blow.

Layla and Snuggles

Occupied my time. Calmed my fears. She played with me outside and inside. Slept with me. Ate with me. Shared my dislike of Sheri. Peed in Sheri's favorite chair whenever she yelled or struck me. A gesture I appreciated. Sheri did not.

Regardless, nothing anyone did could make Sheri behave. Could make her take her meds. Could pull her back from black. Whether I tried love, tantrums, begging, or punishments, Sheri's downward spiral already had wings. Momentum.

At times, she was hyper. She talked nonstop. Laughed loudly and uncontrollably. As she dressed, her insecurities poked holes in her reality. In her self-perception. In her looks. Standing in front of the mirror, she rambled on and on about her thinning hair. Her weight. Her clothing.

Other times, she acted paranoid. She thought everyone was out to get her. Get her man. Get her things. Get her child. She adamantly believed everyone she encountered wanted to harm her. She ranted and raged about plots and schemes. Talked incessantly. Convinced herself. Trying to convince me. She moved between reality and unreality, brown and black.

I didn't dare engage. Didn't escalate the situation. I listened. Shook my head. Continued cooking. As I stirred the premade mix in with the avocados one night, Sheri stopped talking. Focused on me. Grabbed the mix package. Read it. Leapt into a rage.

"You idiot! This is not the right mix! You fucking did this on purpose! Just to hurt me! Why do you *always* try to hurt me?" she screamed and threw the bowl at my head.

I ducked. Tried to get away. Tried to understand.

"Go get a belt! *Now!*" she yelled.

I ran to her closet. Found the belt hanger. Tried to locate the softest one. The kindest one.

"Hurry up! Get your ass in here!"

I yanked the best one down. Ran to the kitchen. As soon as the belt touched her hand, she hit me. Over and over. I refused to cry. Refused to show fear. I wanted her to see she couldn't hurt me. Couldn't break me. She hit harder. Became angrier. Screamed louder. I stood. Winced at times. Withdrew at others. But I didn't cry.

She tired eventually. Fell on the ground. Started to wail.

I retreated to my room. Confused. Hurt. Angry. I assessed the damage. Put a wet rag on my welts. Curled up in my sheets. Snuggles hopped on the bed. Licked my wounds. Walked to the living room. Peed in Sheri's chair.

In the midst of the chaos and paranoia, Sheri still snuck Mark in and out of the trailer. He lived with us between the hours of 1:00 a.m. and 5:00 a.m. His clothes hung in the closet. His shoes cluttered the floor. But he and I never interacted. We were apart.

The few times our eyes met, we quickly turned away. Each night, he faintly knocked at the back door. Wormed his way in. Smelled of BBQ. Showered. Spent hours with Sheri, fucking or fighting. Their sounds filled the trailer. Rocked the walls. Kept me awake. I often fell asleep praying for God to stop the sounds. Stop the movements. Stop the insanity. The sounds often ceased while I prayed. My prayers worked. We all finally slept.

At 5:00 a.m., Mark left, and a new day was born. Sheri never told anyone he lived with us. Lied to everyone. Lied to herself. Threatened me if I said anything. We all just pretended. She imagined Mark lived elsewhere. I imagined a life apart from him. Apart from Sheri. Apart from the trailer. One where Snuggles and I could walk away, unburdened. Over the levy. Across the field. Somewhere, anywhere, Sheris weren't allowed and black didn't exist.

Hot and humid, sixth grade was finally over, and summer came. Instead of staying with PD for the summer, I had a long visit scheduled with my dad. I was grateful Sheri arranged it, but I was still angry with her. I organized. Packed. Planned. I counted the days until my green arrived. I wrote down instructions for Snuggles. I attempted to review them with Sheri, but she just laughed. Seemed giddy at my departure. She and Mark could finally play house.

On the big day, I woke up early. Dressed. Collected my suitcase and Roni Rabbit. I sat at the front window with Snuggles and waited for my dad. Anticipated. Expected. Assumed. Sheri slept. I only left my post for a snack. For the restroom. For the phone. I checked the dial tone to make sure it would work if he called. By 1:00 p.m., he was officially an hour late. I brushed off all negative thoughts. Stayed positive. Listened to my Walkman. Stared out the window. Played with Snuggles. Waited. Another hour passed. Sheri woke.

"What are you doing? What time is it?"

I rattled off the time. Rattled off the plan. She looked shocked in return.

"Let me call him. Have you been sitting there all morning?"

I couldn't answer. Stared out the window with sadness. Shame. Tears formed. Fell. She left a message. *He didn't answer. He's probably on his way. Just a little late.* Sheri dressed. Made food. Relished my dad's shortcomings. Oozed pity.

I sat determined in the window. Prayed for his arrival. Prayed he would keep his word. Another hour passed. Sheri offered food. Drink. Words of wisdom. I sat. Stared. Waited. Fell asleep. Head in hand. Butt cheeks numb. Sheri woke me at 7:00 p.m.

"Is he here?" were the first words out of my mouth. They were also the last words I spoke for days. He never showed. Never called. When I attempted to call him, I found out he'd unlisted his number.

I fell into a deep, agonizing despair. I could only sleep or cry. I refused to eat. Refused to speak. Wanted to die. *He forgot me. He doesn't want me. He doesn't love me. He left me here with Sheri to rot.* She tried to help and pretend to be a mom. But I couldn't receive it. Couldn't accept it. Didn't want it.

The little girl waiting in the window haunted me. Became me. Was me. Every thought I had was filtered through that experience. It dictated my emotions. Controlled my behaviors. Warped my relationships. *I am forgotten. Dismissed. Left. Not by one parent but by two. My green. My hero.*

All I ever wanted was to belong to something. To anything. To a family. To a mom. But truly, I only ever wanted my dad. Being apart from him crushed me. Being left alone by him literally broke my heart. Changed me. Defined me.

After staying locked in depression for a few weeks, Aunt Jerry invited me on her family vacation. They took me to Disney World.

Showered me with love. Slowly pulled me back to reality. Saved my life. I will never forget their kindness.

Even though I started to feel better, the damage was already done. I was angry. Adults were broken. The world was cruel. I fought with authority. Battled teachers. Broke rules. Grew cold and sarcastic. Aggressive. Detached. I immersed myself in preteen life. Stayed with Debra. Partied. Played. Performed. Proved. I let Sheri spin out of control. I didn't save her this time. I left her in black. I stuffed my feelings down. Numb.

When Debra's mom died in a car accident, I couldn't feel it. Couldn't experience it. Couldn't deal with it. I let it pass like a putrid scent in the wind.

Between the trailer walls, Mark and Sheri fought. And fought. And fought. Their blowups were often triggered by her paranoia. They always ended with her aggression.

I no longer gave a shit. I packed up and left for the Melendys.

"You know, your mom was in jail. My mom just got her out," Keisha told me one afternoon after I'd been there for a few days. I ran to Karen.

"Oh, Keisha!" Karen sighed and began. "Listen, your mom got in a fight at Rollies with some woman. Mark called the police on her. I picked her up. She is okay, and she is home."

I tried to remember the last time I spoke to Sheri. It had been a while, but I'd stopped caring long ago. When I returned home, Sheri was laughing on the phone. She pointed me to my room, unaware that I knew the jail story. She didn't want me to hear. As I followed her directions, she laughed.

"I beat up an iron steel worker. Can you believe it? I told her I would whup her ass. I warned her. I would've gotten by with it, but Mark called the cops. He told them I had a gun in my purse. So they cuffed me. I was almost naked when they took me to jail."

I closed my door. I didn't want to hear anymore. Sheri cackled, thinking she was clever and cute as she retold the story several times to captive ears. It was like she believed I was clueless. That thin trailer walls blocked something. That people didn't talk. That kids didn't know a thing.

After the cuteness wore off, Mark didn't return to the trailer, and Sheri checked out of life. She rotted in her room. She slept. I cooked. She slept. I cleaned. She slept. I went to school. She slept. I fought with teachers and peers alike. She slept. I lied to everyone about everything. She slept.

When Sheri finally stirred, she spewed. She whined. She mumbled.

"Please let me die. I can't do this anymore. I just want to die," she begged God.

I tried to console her. Tried to feed and water her. I convinced her to go back to MHMRA. This time, we left with Valium, not lithium. I didn't know the difference for a few days, and she slowly slipped into a coma. I checked for breathing. Checked for signs of life. When she woke, she still begged to die, but her awake state was short-lived. I crawled into bed with black. Laid there until hungry. Worried about her. Worried about running out of food. Struggled with what to do.

After a few weeks, I searched for money. Searched in her clothes. Sheri had a habit of safety-pinning big bills into random pockets. After a successful treasure hunt, I walked across the street to the convenience store to load up on essentials. I contemplated running away. I thought about burning the trailer to the ground, Sheri and all.

The phone rang. On January 30, 1984, the day after Sheri's thirty-first birthday, our lives changed overnight and without warning. In some ways, the call was devastating. In other ways, it was a lifeline. Aunt Lottie was involved in a horrific car accident. A diesel truck plowed into her small car. Plowed into her life. And ours.

In an instant, she was robbed of the ability to live independently. And in an instant, Sheri regained her will to live. Found a purpose. Stopped taking Valium. Jumped out of bed. Rushed to her sister's side. The doctors explained the collision caused an extensive brain injury, leaving Aunt Lottie with severe mental, physical, and psychological impairments.

She learned to crawl, walk, and talk all over again as a middle-aged woman. And as her support system, Sheri and I drove to Dallas in the evenings and on the weekends. I entertained her while she drove. I wanted to keep her spirits high. To help her push depression aside.

I pretended to be a moving mannequin selling Pepsi or chips—whatever product was available in the car. I repeated the same movement with the same plastic smile until she laughed. I continued until we both fell out. My bit transformed my mom's depression into elation. Transformed our drive. Transformed our moods.

We arrived all smiles for Aunt Lottie, ready to help with her therapies. As Sheri taught Aunt Lottie to cuss again—a main concern of Lottie's—I rolled myself around the hospital in her wheelchair. Aunt Lottie was grateful for our company. Grateful to the doctors and her team. She worked hard to find herself again, and after months of struggle, she recovered. However, now she was a different Lottie. She was an independent, brand-spanking–new Lottie. Once she received her settlement, her marriage didn't survive. There was too much trauma. Too much distance. Too much reality.

To further support Aunt Lottie, my mom and her sisters planned a family reunion, which would turn out to be the last one I attended. Sheri sang and drank the whole trek to the lake. She was unbothered. I was worried. Her brown was pulsing.

With each mile, I grew more anxious. The siblings were incapable of problem-free events. I wrestled with various scenarios. Various escape plans. As we hugged and visited with Sheri's siblings and great-aunts and -uncles, I astutely observed Sheri and behaved accordingly. I watched for her signal to leave. Didn't get too comfortable.

After an hour or so, my focus shifted to the surface. My family's appearance gave me pause. Prompted speculation. Caused angst. Regardless of which family member I inspected, I immediately feared for my future self. My eyes moved from one aunt to the next. *Am I losing my hair? At what age did these women become bald? Are my eyes slowly turning crazy? Do I look poor and frazzled? Do I sound ignorant?* My heart raced. I fought the urge to chop off my head. It was too overwhelming to witness our gene pool all at once. I panicked and told no one.

"Look, Pat's here," Sheri said.

I was jolted back to reality. Dodged Pat's affection. Ducked her crazy-eye gaze.

Her kids were older than me, and I was intrigued. I followed their lead. Imitated their behaviors.

"Wanna go in the lake? Ride on a float?" Pat's oldest asked, just before the boredom settled in and got comfortable.

Grabbing a float was a reasonable, safe activity, so I hopped on. I welcomed the attention. Excited. I sat solo on the float as Pat's five teens swam beside me, pushing and pulling me further and further from shore. I noticed but felt secure. Said nothing.

A boat sped by. I realized we were in the middle of the lake. My eyes darted toward shore. I saw Sheri. She was a speck jumping and waving for my attention. I sensed her desperation. Received her signal. At that moment, the teens flipped the float. Forced me into the water. Confused and scared, I quickly swam underwater toward shore.

"Get her!" someone yelled.

I felt Pat's teens on my heels. I barely rose for air and refused to look back, swimming as fast as I could. When I arrived at the shoreline, the adults were fighting, cussing, and screaming. Everything was in complete chaos. Fists swinging. Everyone blaming.

Barefoot and wet, Sheri flung me into the car. With her middle finger erect out the window, we fled. Drove in silence. I sat scared, but still wasn't sure why.

"Why do they always try to hurt me? I can't believe they tried to drown you."

I stared at her in shock. Eyes wide. Mouth open. Breath gone.

"I overheard Pat and her little demons discussing a plan to lure someone into the lake. They planned to drown them. I heard it with my own ears. I was warning others when I looked up and saw you were with her kids. Layla, you were in the middle of the fucking lake. Why did you do that? You know they're insane. You have to listen to me."

She went on and on. Lulled me to sleep. When I woke, she was still ranting. We eventually pulled up to our trailer, tired and soggy.

Mark paced outside. I died inside.

10

Failed

It is sometimes an appropriate response to reality to go insane.

—PHILIP K. DICK, *VALIS*

We vibrated with excitement. Our energy transmitted throughout the school and probably across America. Our science teacher, Mr. Wilson, wheeled the TV to the front of the classroom. We smiled, barely able to contain ourselves. We'd studied the profiles of the seven heroes for weeks, planning and counting down to this morning. Our teacher, who previously had worked at NASA, had discussed the mission's importance at length. We understood the significance. And today was the day.

Even though I preferred being absent, I couldn't miss today. Couldn't miss my heroes. As anticipation permeated the room and filled our veins, whispers became shouts.

"Calm down. Lower your voices. It's only a few more minutes. Take out your profiles," Mr. Wilson said, shushing us.

As the clock ticked, Mr. Wilson turned the TV toward us and found the channel. As he adjusted the rabbit ears, the picture came into focus. All seven astronauts waved to the cameras in their blue jumpsuits. The commentator announced the name and occupation of the two women and five men. When the "first teacher in space" was introduced, we clapped while Mr. Wilson beamed with pride. In that moment, all Americans were one. The little guy, the female, the professional—they all mattered. We knew all of us could accomplish anything. All of us were superheroes.

On January 28, 1986, seated in our desks, we all collectively dreamed of leaving this planet. We imagined life in space. Quiet. Massive. Peaceful. Sheri-less. As they walked on board, fastened their gear, my heart beat faster and faster. Then the hatch closed. Mr. Wilson readied.

"10. 9. 8. 7. 6. 5. 4. 3. 2. 1. Liftoff," we whispered with the world.

All eyes glued to the TV, no one spoke. The space shuttle ascended gracefully. The spacecraft took flight. They were over the Atlantic. Heading toward space as calculated. As intended. As projected.

We cheered. I held my breath. I wished I was there. Wished I was them.

Then, after seventy-three seconds, it exploded. Mr. Wilson burst into tears. His tall stature doubled over. Limp. We stared. Confused. Silent. I looked from Mr. Wilson to the TV. The commentators sounded stunned. I wasn't sure if the explosion was planned or not. I wanted answers, but all the adults were speechless. Shocked.

Mr. Wilson stumbled to the TV. Turned it off. Addressed my class. Explained what we witnessed.

"The *Challenger* is gone. They are all gone."

My next two years were a blur. For months, I followed the Challenger investigation. I wanted to understand what happened to the spacecraft. To the mission. To my world. To me. When NASA failed, when scientists blew up my heroes, I lost all hope in our leaders. In our country. In adults.

The explosion became a self-imposed metaphor for my life. Sheri and I were traveling uncontrollably through space. Teetering on disaster.

Heading for calamity. Accelerating toward death. Mr. Wilson's words, "They are all gone," orbited around in my skull.

Overwhelmed with the fragility of life, I no longer felt comfortable. My stomach twisted in knots. Ached. Churned. Not only was my home life unsafe, but my world was unsafe. Everything smelled red. And wrong. I took it to the extreme. I obsessed over it. Felt lost. Acted out. Left God behind. Whenever Sheri practiced her crazy, I tested out mine. One spark of madness begot another spark of madness. We left zero room for sanity. For reason. For oxygen.

For two years, I answered her ridiculous behavior with an equally ridiculous behavior. Answered her bipolar with full-blown puberty. We fed off each other. Tit for tat. Quid pro quo. Whenever she hurt me physically or emotionally, I punished her. Wanted her to pay for lousy parenting. Wanted her to feel my hurt. Wanted her to experience my anger.

In some ways, without realizing it, I wanted her to pay for the Challenger. For the shitty scientists. For her fucked-up generation. But most importantly, I wanted payment for her mental illness. In my mind, she owed me.

I asked for payment daily, although it was a game I played alone. Sheri hardly noticed. Hardly cared. Barely acknowledged me. Rarely came home. A choice that possibly wasn't hers. Bipolar tended to take control. To insert itself. To become undeniable. Compulsory. Blind. Cruel. Though her madness seemed inevitable, mine proved spiteful. Deliberate. A cry for help. A cry for attention. I longed to be seen. Heard. Recognized. I longed for stability. Accountability. Decency. I longed for fucking parents. For competent adults. For heroes. I longed for something I never had. Never could have. Madness made my longings an impossibility.

After my heroes were dead, when my basic needs felt impossible,

I lashed out at everyone around me. I justified. I validated. I pillaged. I took what I could and did exactly what I wanted. I skipped school. Destroyed my room in anger. Slept all day. Stayed up all night. When I woke up, I had friends over. We watched MTV or horror films. Ordered Domino's. I hung out with Debra and the high school boys. Experienced my first kiss. Then several more.

When I learned boys found me pretty, I inhaled their attention. Flirted. Teased. Laughed. Cried. Instigated. I discovered my knack for talking friends into doing whatever I wanted. Talked a friend into stealing her parents' car. We rolled it down the driveway. Drove around town. Picked up boys. Stayed out all night. When we returned, her parents were sitting on the porch, waiting for us. She reluctantly retreated inside. I ran. Fast and on foot. I walked the neighborhood all night. Slept outside a friend's window. Went home in the morning.

Sheri knew nothing. Didn't care. Didn't ask. Completely unbothered. Weeks later, our crew decided to toilet-paper an older girl's house. I didn't know her, though I knew of her. We exited the car with several rolls and shoe polish in hand.

"Do y'all like this girl?" I asked.

"No!" several responded in unison.

I took that as a green light, grabbed the black shoe polish, and ran to the front door. I wrote *Fuck you* all over it. I released my rage and inhaled euphoria. We vandalized the house until her dad opened the door. Scurrying to the car, we screeched away. Laughed uncontrollably. Slept soundly.

I woke to Sheri's black fury the next morning. The police were there. Even though it wasn't my idea, and I didn't know the girl, the police reported, "Ma'am, your daughter was the instigator. She vandalized a home. The other girls just toilet-papered the property."

Sheri glared. Suggested they cuff me.

"You can take her to jail. I don't want her. But if not, I'll handle her."
I rolled my eyes.

"The parents aren't pressing charges. They just want the girls to clean up the yard and paint the house as soon as possible," the police responded.

When the police left, Sheri beat me and then grounded me. I laughed at the punishment. Sheri couldn't ground me. She was never home.

Blonde, stupid, and full of teen angst and anarchy, I recklessly ran the streets to the soundtrack of *Purple Rain*. I got my kicks where I could. Bounced between my house and Debra's. Lived in a hazy fog of revenge and rebellion. I attended every party. Guzzled alcohol. Streaked naked down the streets. Spent weekends at Six Flags. Met new boys. Cheated. Lied. Exaggerated.

I ripped apart sanity when I saw it. Discarded feelings when I found them. Laughed the loudest. Mouthed off the most. Annoyed everyone and backed down to no one. Almost.

And then there was the high school Roper boot chick who didn't take kindly to me dating juniors. None of the boys knew she existed, and none of us cared, until the bullying started.

"I'm going beat your scrawny ass! See ya after school. You better run!" she'd say on the phone. She left threatening message after threatening message. For the first time, someone other than Sheri scared the hell out of me.

I had good reason to be afraid. The high school was directly across from the middle school, separated only by one side street. And unfortunately, I walked home, so the bully could easily find me. Terrified, I confided in Sheri. Played her the messages. Detailed the problem. Sheri's response, however, just scared me more.

"We aren't scared of nobody. Do you hear me? If you don't deal with her, I'm gonna deal with you. You got that? And Susie? Take the first punch."

I couldn't sleep. Couldn't eat. I imagined and replayed the fight in my head. I was five foot three and weighed eighty pounds. The girl was huge. All my imagined scenarios ended badly and bloody. I stayed home in fear. Accrued more absences. Avoided school. Averted death.

Even with my avoidance, the phone calls continued. She either hung up, left messages, or screamed in my ear. One night after weeks of this, a drunk and annoyed Sheri snapped.

"Give me her number and address. I'm sick of this shit. I'll handle it."

I exhaled. Felt relief. Searched the yellow pages for my bully's address. Sheri called. The bully answered. I paced.

"This is Layla's mom. I'm on the way to your house. You and your mom better be outside. I'm gonna whip both your fuckin' asses!"

Sheri slammed the phone down. Grabbed her keys, her beer, and the address. Exited our trailer. Spun out. I felt every emotion at once. Anger. Pride. Fear. Gratitude. Anxiety. Sadness. Happiness. I sat with Snuggles, both nauseous and thankful for Sheri's help. I waited, paced, and waited some more.

Hours later, Sheri appeared out of the ether, full of adrenaline. Full of pride.

"You don't need to worry about her no more. That's done."

She grabbed another beer and left. And with no further explanation, my bully was gone. And so was Sheri.

On the days I felt bored, I attended school. I arrived half-cocked, surly, and sarcastic. As soon as the bell rang, I morphed into a class clown. Popped off. Took the teachers down. Corrected their lectures. Mocked them. Shrunk them. Enjoyed their frustration. Laughed at their tears. Relished in peers' attention.

I refused to participate. I refused to work. I intentionally failed every assignment, either opting for a zero or writing bogus answers. When report cards came, I bragged to my peers about my low grades. Laughed at my 13 percent average. Tried to beat my low scores.

Whenever the teachers intervened and sent letters home, I forged Sheri's signature. I could no longer see or hear reason. My inadequacies were too loud. My insecurities were deafening. And when I wasn't loud enough, Sheri was louder.

She and Mark proved a tragic backdrop for my pain. I spent weeks without seeing them in the daylight. Without their presence in the night. When they did appear, they fought. Then they disappeared for days. So, when I did show up for school, I showed up raw and broken. Tired and spent. Ready to riot. Waiting for an opportunity. Ready to pounce.

Teachers sighed at the sight of me. Shook their heads. Rolled their eyes. They hated me. And I didn't blame them. I hated me, too. They had no tools in their toolbox to deal with me, a fact I knew and exploited. Inevitably, after a few choice wisecracks to get the entire class belly laughing, teachers banished me to the hallway. I didn't mind, though. There really wasn't a punishment they could give me that felt like punishment.

Even my coaches were annoyed. Because of failing grades, I was never eligible to play in our volleyball and basketball games. Consequently, I was no use to them. No one knew how to help, and after months of sparring with me, no one tried anymore. I was a walking nightmare.

Eventually, my principal called me into his office after a long stint of absences.

"Sit down. I've been trying to reach your mother. I've left multiple messages."

I knew he did. I'd heard them. I'd erased them. But I said nothing. I looked right through him.

"Layla, I must speak with your mother. This is important. You were a straight-A student. Now, you're failing every class miserably. You're too intelligent for this. Listen, I'm trying to help you."

He poked and prodded but stayed gentle throughout his inquiry.

He tried to gauge my situation. My home life. My pulse. He acted concerned. He seemed sincere. I, however, was not concerned. I was of no help. I offered zero information.

He stared at me a bit longer. I looked at the floor. Wanted my trailer. Wanted my cat. When he finally excused me, I stood. Before exiting, I turned.

"If you find my mom, tell her I said hi!"

He was unamused. I wasn't kidding.

The school year closed with a bang and a white envelope. My report card. In black-and-white permanent ink, I read it. I failed the eighth grade. I froze in disbelief. Wrapped in teenage stupidity, I never thought they'd hold me back.

I can't believe they failed me, I thought. *Those bastards know I'm smarter than all those kids. Shit! What am I going to do? I can't deal with this. How can they fail me? They don't want me for another year! Those teachers hate me! All my friends are going to high school. Fuck, I'm not staying in this school. Sheri owes me.*

Just as she entered my mind, Sheri entered the trailer.

"What are you doing? What is that?"

I didn't know how to begin. She had no clue about my grades. My behaviors. My absences. I had forged her signature on every notice. Every report card. Every bad grade. Every teacher's letter. She peered at me, brownish-black, and I felt like I was falling. Struggling to breathe. Crashing into earth. Bursting into flames.

"Talk, dammit! What is going on?"

My eyes darted to the front door. Contemplated running away. Instead, my anger swelled. Multiplied. I saw red. I blacked out. When I came to, shattered glass surrounded my feet. I heard myself screaming.

"You fucking did this! I failed because of you! This is all your fault!"

Sheri snatched the paper from my hand. Studied it intently. Studied while I ranted.

"I'm not staying here. We have to move. I'll run away. I'll kill myself! You did this! Fucking fix it! You ruined my life! I fucking hate you!"

I braced myself. Waited for her rage. For a slap. For a body slam. For some wrath. Instead, Sheri sat down. Tried to absorb the news.

"What happened? You've always had good grades. The school said nothing."

I escalated when she played dumb. Threw a bar stool. Spewed. Sheri raised her voice.

"Stop it! Sit down now! Tell me what happened."

My tantrum turned into tears; then my tears turned into words. I talked for hours. Sheri listened. I came clean about stealing the car, forging documents, making teachers cry, and refusing to work. I even shared my anger toward her and Mark. Scientists and teachers. My dad and life. I cried and cried. Sheri promised to make it right. Promised to move. Promised to leave Mark.

With no money to relocate, Sheri got resourceful and requested a meeting with the Family, her wealthy employer whose home she cleaned. She then asked for a loan and presented a detailed repayment plan. For her final sales pitch, she used me. Informed them that I failed. Insisted Burleson had better schools. Better teachers. No bad influences. Since the Family had watched me grow and were invested in me, they agreed to the loan. Promptly, we celebrated and packed. Taped cabinets. Secured furniture. Readied the trailer for the move to Burleson, Texas. Thankfully, the city was closer to the Melendys and farther from Mark.

On our final day, Sheri drove me to Debra's. My best friend of four years. My rock. My person. As we inched closer to finality, I rehearsed my goodbye. Rehearsed my apology for failing. For disappointing her. For moving away. I needed her to understand I loved her and her family. How sorry I was her mom died. But once she ran toward me, all words vanished. We simply hugged. I couldn't stop crying. Couldn't let go. Couldn't face reality. It felt too final. The gravity felt overwhelming.

In a blink, our grasp loosened. Our arms fell away. I climbed into the car. My breath escaped me. I gasped for air as space and time expanded between us. I could only wave.

As the final touch, the driver hitched the truck to our trailer. I sat with Snuggles. Sad. Wrapped in adolescence. Wrapped in me. Dejected and lost. My thoughts hiccupped. Formed. Disbursed. *I should've tried harder. I should've cared more. I should've ignored Sheri. I've ruined everything. I'm such an asshole.*

Without warning, the trailer shook violently. Let off a loud boom. Snuggles bolted. Frantic, she fled my arms. Ran over the levy. I freaked. Yelled her name. Begged. Searched.

"Let's go! The driver's ready," Sheri called.

Sweating and panting, I tried to explain. But no one particularly cared. I could feel Sheri's stress and the driver's annoyance. I abandoned the search. I left without Snuggles. My lifeline. At thirteen, I was ill-equipped for such loss and disappointment. My fight fled. Words escaped. Emotions numbed. Senses died.

With my home on wheels, we drove to Burleson and our last trailer park. While I gazed out the window, the city morphed into the country. Streets bled into highways. Skyscrapers turned leafy and green. Sheri drove and glowed happily, singing along to Boston. As we weaved through our new park, each passing trailer ignited thoughts of my friends and then thoughts of Snuggles. I heard my teacher's voice on the morning of the *Challenger* disaster: *They are all gone.* It hit me. Hard.

As Sheri unpacked, I aimlessly walked around our lot. Scanned the woods. Analyzed my choices. I asked God for forgiveness. Then, something moved in my peripheral vision. From under the trailer, Snuggles materialized. Eyes wide. Body frazzled. Wild. She darted to and fro. I yelled. Grabbed her. And exhaled. Snuggles had ridden under the trailer from Fort Worth to Burleson. She refused to be left behind. Refused to leave me. Hugging her tight, I thanked God and vowed to be different.

New city. New faces. Same problems. Same behaviors. Same shit. Without any outside intervention, counseling, or meds, geography was the only difference. Mental illness still controlled us. Poverty still limited us. Poor coping skills still defined us. No matter my prayers or wishes, there was no magic wand. No off switch. No quick fix. We were at the mercy of Sheri's cycles. Doctor's prescriptions. State funding.

We arrived to register on the first day of school in all our dysfunctional glory. Sheri glowed golden brown as she played the doting mother. She made excuses. She lied to control their perceptions of us. She wanted a fresh start. I, however, couldn't pretend. I grew more and more embarrassed as the admin inspected my grades and absences. I was ashamed of us. I wanted her to stop talking.

Well into the morning schedule by the time we were done, I joined my new English class. Within minutes, I met my new best friend, Jessie. We were both blondes. Both listened to Beastie Boys. Both possessed a warped wit. We were a perfect match.

By midday, all my peers grew curious and interested in the new girl. And by the end of the day, everyone had introduced themselves and made me feel at home. By the end of the week, my popularity soared. Guys asked for my number. Girls either befriended me or hated me. I lapped up the attention, which stroked my ego.

By the beginning of the second week, Jessie and I ruled our grade, while Sheri and I were the talk of the town. Sheri's looks and single status were a topic. A thing. A consideration. Sheri caught the eye of our football coach and other women's husbands, which was mortifying. "Your mom" jokes became a constant. To be clever, when my guy friends called the house, they'd ask, "Can I talk to Sheri?" I hung up in response.

One day that week, friends gathered at my locker, and a tall, long-haired, blonde guy approached. As he spoke, I felt a sense of familiarity. A glimmer of recognition.

"Layla, it's Joey! From the third grade . . ."

I dropped my books. Leapt into his arms. I was home.

The doting mother routine quickly turned into the more familiar absent mother routine. Only vaguely bothered by it, I immersed myself in social drama. I narrowed my focus to weekend fun, when I joined either Robby on excursions or Joey on adventures. Parties in the country with Texas boys were magical. The warm dark nights proved massive and hopeful. Gatherings sprung up in backyards, the FasTaco parking lot, or empty cul-de-sacs.

As always, I gravitated toward the boys. I loved their wit and one-liners. I basked in their laid-back ways. Felt special by their side. Laughed the night away. A million stars observed our fun as the hours passed. They danced and blinked as we drank, and they smoked pot. I never smoked. Though Joey and his best mate often passed me the joint, I would smile, decline, and pass it to the next person. One evening, after I declined a joint for the two hundredth time, the guys burst into laughter.

"What's so funny? Tell me!"

Joey collected himself.

"Well, Lulu, they're laughing because your mom smokes pot and you don't."

"How do y'all know that?" I asked, shocked and a bit embarrassed. Another guy friend interjected.

"'Cuz she buys it from my older brother."

The "your mom" jokes ensued, and everyone had their fun. But I went inward. I understood what her smoking meant.

I braced myself for Sheri's next ride. But before it all went to hell, I decided to take a ride of my own. Have fun. And I took Jessie along with me. Before long, our principal summoned us to discuss our weekend of drinking. Informed us that a peer ratted us out, a redhead who drank with us. Her lecture about drinking around others droned on.

"If you drink and don't want to get caught, then do it alone and in your shower. If not, this is a small town; it'll get out. And you'll be in trouble."

Our principal informed our parents. Except she couldn't tell Sheri— no one could find her. She called our coaches. Our consequence was sprints every day after school for weeks. Still, these punishments failed to curb our behavior. In fact, they were a joke to us and the boys. On the days I didn't want to run, I stayed home. Ignored the bus driver's honk in the morning. And so Sheri and I reprised our roles.

One Saturday, Sheri unexpectedly burst through the door. Giddy. Silly. Overcome with joy.

"Wanna learn to drive? You should know how to drive a stick in case of an emergency."

I inspected her. Gauged her mood. Took note of her color. Soft brown. Once I determined she was sober, I agreed. After a bit of yelling and hurt feelings, I got the hang of it. I drove up, down, and all around the frontage roads. Sheri had one foot out the window and one on the dash. We loudly sang "Born to Run" by Bruce Springsteen the whole time. A sweet moment. A memorable moment. But a fleeting one.

Within days, she crashed. Turned black. She couldn't move. Couldn't talk. Couldn't wake. Karen eventually convinced her to visit

MHMRA. And once again, she returned with Valium. Returned to a coma. I wanted to crash, too. To break into pieces. To cease to exist.

At school, if I went at all, I was unable to ask for help. Unable to cope. I fought with bullies. Lashed out at authority. My science teacher, who doubled as my bus driver, took the bait.

"You will call me 'sir'!" he ordered with aggression while he argued with me in class one day. I laughed.

"No, I won't. I don't call my dad 'sir'! So I'm not calling you 'sir.'"

The class fell silent. No one ever challenged him. In shock, I felt their eyes move from him, to me, and then back again.

"You aren't leaving this class until you address me as 'sir'!"

I rolled my eyes. "Then it looks like I'm living here."

The bell rang. My peers left for lunch. I remained in my seat. Acted unaffected. Doodled. Fifteen minutes passed.

"Say 'sir,' and you can leave. I know you're hungry."

I ignored him. I had nothing to say. After thirty minutes, our principal joined us. Reprimanded us both. Apparently, teachers couldn't withhold lunch. She dismissed me. I didn't see him until the awkward bus ride home.

Sheri slept as I finished my homework. As I dressed for the Witnesses's Bible study, I heard her call for me. I hurried to her room.

"Where are you going?" she asked, agitated. She'd forgotten about my plans.

"I'm going to book study."

"I'll be right back." She darted to her drawers and snatched out a piece of paper.

"I wrote it down. When I die, you're not going to the Melendys. Oh no! You're going to foster homes. Just like me. You think you got it bad now. You'll be in hell when I'm gone."

"Mom, I'm just going for an hour. I'll be right back. It's okay," I said, confused and scared.

She begged me to stay. Threatened suicide and foster care. Pleaded. Ranted. But I kept my plans. We needed to be apart. She needed to calm down. The car honked. Sheri screamed something as I left. I said nothing to the friend who was picking me up.

We enjoyed the meeting. Socialized. When we returned, Karen, Keisha, and another friend were banging on our trailer door. I jumped out of the car. Unlocked the trailer.

Karen gently called Sheri's name as she walked toward her room. There was no answer. Sheri lay unconscious on her bed. Lifeless. Peaceful. We rushed her to the ER. She had overdosed on Valium. They pumped her stomach. I sat in the waiting room angry. I refused to visit her. I wanted answers.

"A sheriff drove up to my house tonight. Winona called the police because Sheri was having serious problems. Winona tried calling me but couldn't reach me. Maybe she had the wrong number. She gave the police my name. They found me. I promised to check on her," Karen tried to explain.

After several hours in the waiting room and a positive prognosis, Karen took me home. I gathered my clothes. We searched for Sheri's makeshift will of her dying wishes. The search was in vain. While Sheri healed in the hospital, I stayed with the Melendys. It was good to be home, if only for a short time. Black and withered, Sheri was released after four days on suicide watch. We both returned home. Damaged. Weary. Lost.

I confided in no one. Sheri revived her relationship with Mark. She confided only in him. She moved him back in with no concern for the consequences. With that one decision, Sheri lost our entire support system. The Witnesses disfellowshipped her. None of them, including the Melendys, could associate with her. She was deemed a bad influence. Immoral. Unrepentant.

With that one decision, I was left alone in the fight. This time, they really were all gone. My whole life was a space shuttle explosion. I adjusted my mindset. Adjusted my calculations. Stopped pretending. Stopped hoping. Stopped trying. Stopped sifting through the wreckage. I abandoned the mission.

11

Isolated

I'm lonely. And I'm lonely in some horrible deep way and
for a flash of an instant, I can see just how lonely, and how
deep this feeling runs. And it scares the shit out of me
to be this lonely because it seems catastrophic.

—AUGUSTEN BURROUGHS, *DRY*

How do I eulogize a place, a thing with more meaning and worth to my childhood than my family? How do I praise something society deems vile, trashy, an eyesore? How will anyone understand our complicated relationship or the depth of my appreciation before looking away in disgust?

In my quest to convey such a delicate situation with accuracy, in my intent to pull away and bid farewell, it is crucial I dissect, categorize, and quantify each detail. Each memory of my childhood home. Each mangled feature of my trailer. Understanding our intimate, complex bond can only be developed over hours, days, and weeks of time together. Alone.

To the observer, my trailer represented poverty. Trash. Lack. To me, it felt like a warm, tattered blanket. Depending on the situation, day, or age, the trailer presented itself as an annoying sibling. An unpredictable babysitter. A kind, toothless grandmother. To ward off loneliness, my trailer became essential. It listened as I spoke to myself. Watched TV with me. Discussed the characters and plots of *I Love Lucy*, *Cheers*, and *Happy Days*.

The trailer was there. The only consistent aspect of my childhood. There when I woke. There after school. There for homework. There for meals. There for hunger. There for heartache and laughter. There when I closed my eyes. There when all I needed was someone or something to be there. My trailer was there.

Before the age of five, I'd never lived in anything quite like it. But now I couldn't imagine my life without it. Though I was not accustomed to luxury, I was accustomed to sleeping in a sturdy structure. A house. An apartment. A guesthouse. A solid building. Made of brick, mortar, Sheetrock, wood, and concrete. Immovable.

I never wanted to live in a trailer. But Sheri received it in the divorce settlement, and we were poor, so we took what we got. We made the most of it. We dealt. From ages five to fifteen, a white single-wide trailer adorned with three gray birds was my home. Even as a child, I knew a house on wheels with no hallways or twists and turns was unusual, if not embarrassing. But it was home. My home. I was grateful to have one. Even an ugly one.

The trailer was not new at our acquisition. Well on its way to being worn and dog-eared, it consisted of three small bedrooms, a living room, a kitchen, and two bathrooms. Nothing more. Nothing less. My room was in the front. Sheri resided in the back. It took seconds to walk the entire square footage. I could stand in my room and see straight to the end of the trailer. Therefore, I was privy to all comings and goings. All information. All deeds.

I never felt completely secure within its walls. They felt thin, flammable, and held no secrets. Hanging anything required thought and intention. Sheri and I feared hitting electrical wires with nails and having them catch fire. Become ashes. But the real tragedy existed in the restlessness of objects that lived on them. Nails couldn't hold firm in the thin wood paneling, often falling straight through into the unknown.

With each door slam and foot stomp, our walls shook. Our pictures and memorabilia clung for their lives. At times, they fell to their deaths. I hated the sound of their movement. Each object seemed in perpetual motion, as if we were toppling over speed bumps. The fercuckted way each object hung caused me great anxiety. I always noticed their inadequacy. I always straightened. Exhausted, after years I stopped straightening and obsessing. Instead, I took to ignoring.

Our doors to the outside confused me. Why an eight-hundred-square-foot space needed three doors was lost on me. One door would have done the trick. Two might have helped with safety. But three was ridiculous. The doors appeared to be randomly placed around the rectangular shape. The "front door," situated in the middle of the trailer, was marked by three handmade wooden steps leading up to it. The steps signaled to guests, "Hey, this is the front door. Come this way." The "back door" was positioned approximately twenty feet closer to my mom's room, still on the front. It was her personal door, used to sneak herself and Mark in and out. The second "back door," located on the right side of the house, was worthless. Never used. No steps. If a guest unknowingly opened it, they fell.

Doors in appearance only, they were made with a flimsy mystery material, like a cousin to the shed door. I developed a love-hate relationship with them. I am quite certain my first curse words were hurled their way. They knew I knew they couldn't do their job. They were worthless and hollow to the core. The idea of security was lost to them. They couldn't keep anyone or anything in or out for too long.

To open and close the doors, we had to muster all our energy, push, pull, and then kick—a sequence I mastered over time. It was impossible to hold objects while closing or opening them. The metal frame encasing each door was bent for reasons unknown and made a good seal unattainable. Unwanted elements and air hot and cold freely came and went. For ten years, I cursed them. For ten years, I also prayed for their compliance and protection.

The floors weren't trustworthy, either. I often imagined the furniture dropping straight to the ground if I jumped or flopped too hard. I believed this to be an unrealistic worry until Sheri killed that fantasy.

One day, she discussed how her floor was caving in under the weight of her toilet. After she showed me the spot where floor was separating from the wall, I immediately ceased using her restroom. I sat lightly on my toilet. Tiptoed through my bathroom. I became acutely aware of the thin layer of material between me and the outdoors.

From then on, I worried about the floors with an all-consuming dread. I chewed on it frequently. The thought that we could lose our floors evoked deep shame in me. Made me hate poverty. Made me mad at Sheri. I took to gingerly navigating from one room to the next. I frowned when overweight guests stayed too long. I began to side-eye every heavy appliance. I often attempted to calculate the effect of their cumulative weight over time to determine how much longer we had until we lived on dirt.

I feared the floors might collapse while my friends stayed the night. *What do I say? What is my excuse?* I resolved to blame it on them. "Your bags are too heavy" or "You walk heavy-footed!"

At some point, we realized wild animals were contributing to our floor problems. Critters were eating holes in our floors. Tunneling their way inside. Devouring our home.

Once while watching TV, I opened a drawer to retrieve a fork.

Heard a hissing sound. I recoiled my hand and looked down to find a scared baby possum sitting on our silverware. Mouth open. Teeth at the ready. I did what any child would do without an adult. I closed the drawer, cleaned a fork from the sink, and continued watching *Cheers*.

Some elements of the trailer amused me. For instance, we needed a specific metal tool to crank open the windows. After just a few rotations—*bam!*—a breeze filled the room. It was a novel and pleasurable concept until all the metal tools were lost. The windows were permanently closed. Sealed tight. This realization cued immediate claustrophobia. I attempted to pry open the windowpane. But this left the window mangled. Still tightly closed and now disfigured.

For years, this experience prompted anxiety and a need to escape. I tried not to think about the windows, which, of course, caused me to think about the windows. Claustrophobia set in. Once a window-related thought entered my mind, I grabbed Snuggles and exited the trailer. We stayed outside until the thought vanished—or until we stored up enough oxygen to reenter the box.

I also took great comedic pleasure that our trailer wore a skirt—a logical upgrade for the trailers of the lucky. The tin panels installed from the trailer to the ground hid the underpinnings and provided a natural storage area for crap. A trailer without a skirt was like a lady caught with her pants down. Though ours was bent and detached in places, we possessed one of the few skirts in our trailer park. I secretly took pride in this fact.

My final comedic point was saying to others, "I live in a two-story house." Our third bedroom, a space the size of a twin bed, had three steps leading to it. An upstairs level meant an upstairs room. And up those stairs was a loft-like platform with exactly one twin mattress and two windows.

For a short-lived period, this room was considered Judah's. For a much longer period, the room and its bizarre, sad history was ignored. Never discussed. Sheri and Mark tore it out when I was in ninth grade to create one big room for me. The three steps then led to my bed.

In a trailer made of all rickety materials, safety was elusive. Living in a tin box required us to suspend reality to feel secure. For us, something like the weather was never an inconsequential factor. It was a daily thought. A source of stress. A consideration. From a young age, I feared and dreaded the weather like an abusive uncle staying the night. Weather—specifically the wind, and more specifically tornadoes—terrified me. The mildest rain was magnified by our tin roof, so anything beyond mild incited great anxiety.

When Sheri and I were together under an ominous cloud, significant, though different, responses were triggered in us. She immediately called friends to discuss our course of action. Searched for a safe house. One with brick, concrete, and a roof. I immediately shook with fear. My heart raced. My pupils dilated. Severe anxiety riddled my bones. Glued to the TV for weather updates, I thanked God for our illegal cable box. I needed the 24/7 weather channel. I needed to hear about my city. My problem. My fate. I needed to know. I needed a plan.

Depending on the forecast, one of many well-rehearsed drills was set in motion. A rainstorm meant a sleepless night. A night of TV, Sheri's bed, and eyes wide awake. If the weather reached severe thunderstorm status, the wind mattered. A wind speed of seventy-five miles per hour will be forever seared into my brain. High-speed winds meant we must prepare to leave. Start packing our bags. We would soon be gone. A tornado watch or warning meant leave immediately. No bags. No shoes. Go.

As the wind whirled and rain spit, I cried. Leaving Snuggles, my best friend, inside the trailer with a tornado approaching killed me. Escaping the trailer was often paired with Sheri and me fighting. Our forecast was high anxiety with low sympathy. My thoughts and emotions were confused. I wanted safety. I wanted an escape plan, but I detested the thought of leaving Snuggles. Alone. Scared.

Sheri never understood. Never attempted to care. She despised my cat. Jealousy consumed her. I never hid that I loved Snuggles more than her. But it was never more apparent than in times of escape. The game of "Who would you save?" became all too real in these moments. Truly, I just wanted to save my cat and myself. I craved an escape plan for both of us.

"What? You want us to die over this fucking cat? What is wrong with you? Stop crying!" she screamed when she realized my thoughts.

In some ways, I was grateful for Sheri's unexpected presence during these times. With her car in the driveway, I could leave the trailer. However, Sheri was never easy. Never helpful. She was horrible at reassurance. Horrible at calming nerves or being a soft place to land. Horrible in moments of crisis. She possessed zero patience. Zero coping skills. Zero sympathy.

"You want to stay here? Fucking stay! Either get your ass outside *now*, or I am leaving you!"

I knew she would, but I didn't care much. Being left alone with Snuggles in any type of weather was not foreign to me. But her hysteria, her brownness, suffocated my thoughts. Stifled my decision-making. While trying to contemplate my options, while in my pause, she grabbed, pushed, and hurled me toward the door. Slammed the car doors. I bawled. She screamed. And we sped off toward safety. Drama made up steps one, four, and six of our escape drills.

Being home alone during any storm, literal or figurative, prompted a completely different course of action from me. Of course, I was still terrified. But without Sheri, the scenario was less stressful in some ways. No screaming. No aggression. No demands. Being alone meant fewer options or even the possibility of death. However, if she was gone, I couldn't make her return; nor did I know how to find her. I had to deal. I had to protect Snuggles—and myself.

At the first sign of impending doom, I gathered pillows, blankets, snacks, and Roni Rabbit. I made us a huge pallet in the living room. I placed the blankets over the floor vents so that the AC or heater filled them. A comforting feeling. A calming sensation. Snuggles and I glued ourselves to the weather radar. Listened to the rain pound the tin roof. Felt the trailer rock this way and that. The sounds alone highlighted the fragility of our shelter. Over and over and over, windows cracked. Doors buckled. Skirt smacked.

With each rock and sway, we were at the mercy of the storm. Helpless. Vulnerable. Bare. Even if the trailer intended to protect us, it was unfit. Incapable. But it was all we had. As the red approached us on the radar, I trembled. Snuggles hid. I wanted to reach for the phone. Call for help. Call someone to rescue me. But I was not allowed. Sheri would not approve. No one could know I was alone.

Questions whirled in my mind as the wind raged. *How long do I wait? What time is it? Is anyone awake? What day is it? Do I have school tomorrow? Have I waited long enough to call for help?*

"Hold on. Don't call. You'll be in trouble. The storm will pass," I repeated aloud. A mantra.

Out of fear, Sheri's secrets became my secrets. I knew her wrath. Her inner workings. I wore her mental illness, her shame, like a heavy, dark cloak. I refrained from calling for help.

Instead, I played a game with myself. It was an extensive one I used to weigh my options. It helped me focus my attention on something— anything other than the storm. Anything other than fear.

First, I determined how long I'd held out the last time before calling for help. *Did I wait three days? A week? Did I call too soon? Was it serious enough to involve an adult, alert outsiders, and prompt punishment for all involved? Did I have food? Was I okay?*

Once the answer was clear, I tried to recall the severity of the punishment I received for being rescued. Telling her secret. Exposing her. *Did I get a spanking, a beating, or did the adults get in trouble? How long was I forbidden to visit them?* I weighed the pros and cons to determine if this storm was worth the scene. The pain. The scars.

Finally, I listed aloud all the situations I had survived alone in the trailer. I wanted to remember my strength. My courage. My willpower. I typically reached around eleven fingers before inevitably homing in on the "Footstep Man," the scariest character in all my alone moments.

Don't focus on him, I told myself. *It doesn't count. That was terrifying. I had to call. I was younger. It was a different trailer park. It was more serious than this storm.* I attempted to erase the thoughts of him. I focused on the TV. My cat. The storm. For some reason, though, when I was alone and scared, I sought out fear about past situations. Different situations. A different time. A different me. I avoided this situation. I avoided the now.

While I stared at the screen, my mind drifted to the past and the man's slow, methodical footsteps. I heard him move from one end of the trailer to the other. The faint steps growing louder. He stopped when he reached the front door. Snuggles flattened her ears against her head. She turned toward the door. My eyes darted from the phone to the door. All the locks were secured. I exhaled.

God, keep the door closed! Protect us! I prayed he would leave. I prayed the door worked. Mid-prayer, the handle turned. He shook it again and again. I dashed to the phone. Snuggles bolted. The phone trembled in my hand. His footsteps moved to the back door. *Was the door locked?*

The thought of him coming in the trailer was more than I could bear. I called the Melendys. My family. My saviors. Their phone rang.

He stepped. Determined. Deliberate. No one answered. I called the police. The back door handle turned.

"I need help! Someone is breaking into the house! Help!" I yelled as loud as I could.

The footsteps moved faster and in my direction. He aggressively pulled on the front door several times. I begged the police dispatcher to stay on the phone. Silence. No steps. He left. The "Footstep Man" returned to my trailer periodically for a year.

The night of his final visit, my mom was home. He followed the same scheme. But this time, when he turned the handle, my mom retrieved her gun. She was ready and unafraid. She loved a fight. She couldn't handle storms, but she could handle people. Hiding behind the couch, I almost felt sorry for him. She slowly pulled the curtain back. Placed the gun in position. Methodically aimed.

Then she jumped back, alarmed. The curtain fell. The male figure was a police officer, an officer she recognized. One she previously had asked for help. He knew she was single. He knew I was home alone. He noticed her and the gun. He ran. He never returned. If I ever decided to call for help in the future, I would call civilians, not the police.

On those alone nights, once the nightmares ceased and the storm passed, I remained awake. Drunk on adrenaline. Shaky. Exhausted. A bad night in the trailer meant no school the next day. Even when I was more responsible with grades and teachers, I simply couldn't wake for school after a hard night. I heard the bus pull up, the honk, and the sound of the bus leaving. But I couldn't move. My bus driver knew I wasn't going to school those mornings. He stopped at my trailer as a formality. Without a proper parent, I saw school as an option after restless nights. A mere suggestion. A place to go. A place to socialize. A place to eat. A place to not be alone.

By the ninth grade, however, I knew I needed to be in school. I knew the consequences. I had failed eighth grade because of eighty-nine unexcused absences. Eighty-nine days with no learning. Eighty-nine days of watching TV. Eighty-nine days spent within the feeble trailer walls. Eighty-nine days without an outside voice. Eighty-nine days without a parent. Eighty-nine days alone in my trailer. Eighty-nine absences in a single year.

Over the fourteen years of my life so far, a ridiculous number of school days were sleep days for me. I had plenty of bad nights in the trailer for one reason or another. Alone and scared. Alone and hungry. Alone and lonely. Alone and sad. Alone and mad. Alone with my mom. Sad with my mom. Hungry with my mom. Angry with my mom.

Countless nights, Sheri returned unexpectedly. At random times. In random states. With random strangers. Loud. Drunk. Free. Beautiful. Deep brown. Disturbed.

One night, she snuck in two strange fellas from the bar. As with all drunks, they underestimated their obnoxious ways. Jessie and I woke up. Startled. Confused. Embarrassed. At 2:00 a.m., my mom made drinks. While she mixed and laughed, she charmed us into the living room. The men relocated to the couch. As Sheri played her favorite Rod Stewart album, she requested that we dance for her. For the men. We reluctantly agreed but switched to our music. Beastie Boys. Two self-conscious, sleepy fourteen-year-olds, we moved to the beat and entertained three disgusting barflies.

My nights were at her mercy. My life was disrupted at her every whim. Instead of attending school, I needed to rest. Needed time to process each night's events. Needed time to heal my bruises. Needed time to grieve my life. I needed time.

During Sheri's mania and in her absence, I learned the many levels of loneliness. Mine became a tangible entity. Became something I felt. Something on which I depended. Something I understood. My mind adjusted to each level. Each depth. I created a world where loneliness was commonplace. Normal. Expected. I found comfort in ordinary sounds. Water dripping. Cat purring. My own chewing. Appliances humming.

I conversed with myself. I confidently answered my own questions. If I didn't, Snuggles did. We entertained ourselves for hours with good stories. With the day's plans. While we talked, I taught Snuggles to sit, fetch, and lie down. Each successful trick was celebrated with raw bacon or turkey slices.

When Snuggles napped, I imitated Steve Martin in the mirror. I was both the stand-up comedian and the audience. I belly-laughed at my own jokes. I harshly critiqued my material.

As the audience exited and I slipped into deeper aloneness, I made prank calls to random numbers. I dialed numbers from the phone book. Requested the person by name when they picked up. I pretended to be a friend. We talked for as long as they would have me. If no one answered, I left lengthy, dramatic messages. Sometimes I called my Aunt Rebecca. I asked the operator to conduct an emergency breakthrough when her number was busy. I annoyed her until I was bored.

On a deeper level of loneliness, my brain created imaginary friends. They had imaginary problems with imaginary solutions. When those friends tired of me, I turned into a preschool teacher. I reigned over a classroom of unruly children into the night. When my students finally went home, I focused on the TV. I visited my other families—the characters of various shows. I intertwined myself with their situations. Their storylines. I cried at their closing songs. Shed tears of sheer loneliness.

At this level of loneliness, I prayed. Socialized with God. Depended on Him for relief. Called out to Him from the lowest levels of despair. Stayed with Him until He slowly pulled me to reality.

I didn't realize the effect of isolation until I mingled in the company of actual humans after days of being alone. I startled easily in their presence. Skittish, I jumped at the sound of others' voices. I was provoked by their shrillness. Agitated by their behaviors. Reacclimating to people took me a day or two. And depending on the company, I craved my trailer. I craved my loneliness.

Even when Sheri surfaced, I required an adjustment period. It felt odd to have her home. When she walked through the door black and broken, she felt like an intruder to us. Snuggles moved differently. Cautiously. The trailer sat tight. On guard. I struggled to act normally. Engage. Stop talking to myself.

After I adjusted to her sounds and behaviors, I tried to socialize with her. Gauge her temperature and shade. Determine her level of lucidity. But soon, the song to accompany our too-familiar dance began to play. The dance of depression lulled me to the cruelest level of loneliness. A loneliness I only felt with Sheri by my side. Whenever she returned, usually after a breakup, so did the cruel, cyclical realization that her illness followed her home. Black engulfed the trailer.

At this level of despair, I transformed into an angry, bitter daughter. After a few days, I wanted the trailer to myself. Just me, my cat, Roni Rabbit, and the TV. I longed for my typical levels of loneliness. I understood them. They were familiar.

I hated watching Sheri sleep. I hated the smell of her breath and sweat on the sheets. I hated her depression. I hated her. I didn't want to take care of her. *When did she take care of me? When was she my mom?*

I despised the adult responsibilities Sheri thrust upon me. The mundane tasks of bookkeeping and housekeeping. The task of paying rent and bills. I resented writing checks from her checkbook. I loathed signing her signature perfectly. I detested delivering our rent check to the trailer park office. It was all unbearable. But I had to do these things. I couldn't lose our lot. Our trailer's space. The office secretary never missed an opportunity to spew shame my way. "My mom is busy" or

"My mom is out of town" were my excuses as I left the office. Something, anything, to stop her pity. I knew she hated Sheri, but who didn't?

As Sheri's slumber settled in with no end in sight, I took her car into town for groceries, another task I hated. We needed the basics. Milk. Food. Anything other than instant mashed potatoes or mayonnaise sandwiches. I hated the stares. The eyes and ears of small-town Texas were on me. The loathing was palpable. Everyone knew our business. Everyone knew we were incapable. Trashy. Ill.

I attempted to bop around the store with blissful steps. I wanted onlookers to believe my mom was home baking. We needed a few things. Nothing to see here. Nothing wrong with us. Unfortunately, my friend's parents owned the store. They knew differently. They knew our patterns. They whispered. Others shouted. Sheri's illness was airborne.

With her depression and weeks of sleeping came MHMRA. This time it came sooner than usual. Just six months ago, we were in the same position. Typically, I opted out of joining her. I preferred the trailer. My sanctuary. My safe place. But I needed the doctor to understand. I needed him to hear me. Sheri's cycles were accelerating. Speeding up.

I got her out of bed. Got her dressed. Got her to the clinic. After hours of waiting and a few minutes with the doctor, I gave my best account of the situation. Despite my story and regardless of the doctor's education, he prescribed Valium. For some unknown reason, all Sheri's psychological interventions involved Valium. Always Valium.

Why did doctors prescribe a sedative to someone who couldn't get out of bed? I never understood. But what did I know? I was just a teenager. Over the years, I learned a valuable equation. Doctors equaled Valium, Valium equaled hopelessness, and hopelessness equaled suicidality.

With each cycle, I blindly navigated life inside my trailer's walls. Confused. Alone. Scared. So confused and scared about suicide. *What if she succeeded? What if it happened while I was home? What was my role, my plan?* Typically, her suicide attempts were just that—attempts. Attempts to stop the pain. Attempts to gain attention. Attempts to get actual help.

I understood that she was hopeless and wanted to die. I understood that our life was no life. I witnessed her despair. I understood that suicide was a viable option. An immediate option. A permanent option. Possibly the only option. It was a fair, just ending. I was practiced in her mental illness. I was clear. I understood. I wondered if this time her suicide talk would lead to suicide. I wondered if this time she would pull it off.

Some days I dragged myself to school but was present in body only. I walked the halls unfocused. Removed from reality. I acted fine. Laughed with friends. Slept in class. Pretended to be a teen. Imitated a human. Still, my mind remained in the trailer. I anticipated what came next. I waited for disaster. I waited for death.

When I arrived home on these days, I pried the door open and looked toward her room. If Sheri was awake, she greeted me with grogginess, slurred words, crazy hair, and googly eyes in a confused state. If she was asleep, silence, stillness, and a horrid smell greeted me. I administered my breath test. When she breathed, I exhaled and got busy being busy. Busy being anxious. Busy waiting.

I nervously, anxiously redecorated the trailer. Moved furniture around. Set the table with wine glasses and napkins. Adjusted the figurines on the glass shelves. I checked on her periodically. Sometimes I tried to wake her. I tried to give her food and water. Tried to provide warmth and comfort. I felt like I was sharing space with a corpse.

On one of these mornings, Sheri startled us awake. Snuggles hid. The trailer shook. Sheri yelled and stomped around. I walked closer but not too close. She looked crazed. Irritated. Hostile. Insane. Black.

"When I'm six feet under, it is going to be your fault. Do you hear me? *Your fault!*"

I stood there, paralyzed. I stared. And. Did. Not. Move. She continued for a few slurred, inaudible minutes. When she moved to the bathroom, I scurried to my room. Threw clothes on quickly.

"Bring me some water! Now! This is on you!" she yelled.

I knew what she meant. In her stupor, she blamed me for her pain. She blamed me for her suicide. She wanted to place the blame for her actions on someone. Anyone but herself. She hurt so she wanted me to hurt. I, too, wanted her free from pain. I wanted *me* free from pain.

I complied with her request. Poured her water. I grabbed my shoes. The bus honked. Cautiously, I entered her room. I placed the glass on her dresser. I felt her glare. I refused to meet her eyes. I bolted. I pushed the front door open. I kicked it closed. She screamed from her dark, primal abyss as I walked to the bus. The bus driver was shocked to see me. And I, him.

I failed to alert anyone. I failed to call for help. I failed her. I knew exactly what she was doing. This familiar pattern. This familiar emptiness. I sat in class, but I was hollow. I placed my head on the desk. Prayed to God. I asked Him to handle the situation. I prayed for no specific outcome. I just wanted God to carry my weight. Remove the gravity. Remove the pain. *I'm a kid. I'm just a kid*, I repeated silently.

I knew He knew I wanted her gone. Removed. Out of my life. Gone from this world. Free from torture. I wanted forgiveness for my feelings. For my hatred. For my silence. For my inaction. I wanted forgiveness for the fucking glass of water. Tears rolled down my face. I excused myself from class. My teachers acted unfazed. They'd stopped asking about my behavior and home life long ago. I muddled through the day. Smiled when I needed to smile. Spun tales. Gave bullshit answers. Talked on command. Ignored most.

With the last bell, reality rang. I walked to the bus like a zombie being pulled through life, by life. On the bus ride home, I stared out the window. Blank. I wished for an empty trailer. I longed for the days of Snuggles, Roni Rabbit, and me. But I knew this situation was in full motion and on repeat. It was a recurring nightmare. A recurring scene.

As the bus turned my corner that afternoon, the penetrating sound of an ambulance filled the trailer park. I refused to react. The bus stopped. The students fell silent. I reluctantly moved forward. The bus driver peered at me with pity.

My heart burrowed in my throat. My only thought was, *She did it*. As I walked to my trailer, unidentifiable emotions filled my cells. I hated strangers in our trailer. Hated the blind sense of urgency. Hated the paramedics' hurried tone. Their breathless explanation made my skin crawl. Little did they know, I was versed in suicide.

"Sweetheart, let me explain," I wanted to say, but I allowed the paramedic to drone on. I declined to ask if Sheri survived. Whatever the answer, whatever the outcome, the damage was done. I remained stony. Detached. Pissed. Continued walking briskly to my room.

"She's alive!" another paramedic shouted.

From my bones, I wanted to scream, *Let her die! She wants to die! Please let her die!* with everything I had. But I refused to bend. Refused to let them in. I hid from their unsolicited concerns. They knew nothing of us. Nothing of our situation. I felt sorry for them. Sorry they used their resources and skills on us. *What a waste! Don't they know this is what she does? Her coping skill. Her hobby. Her destiny.*

I retreated to my room. Waited for them to hurry me out. They wouldn't leave a minor in the trailer. They felt compelled to rescue me. Compelled to be my heroes. I supposed poverty and children evoked pity in others, but I needed to talk to myself. Needed to hear the walls' opinions. Snuggles's feelings. I needed my trailer. My friend.

Since staying wasn't an option, I called some adult and left. I refused a hospital visit. I opted out of pretending. Opted out of caring. The days of feeling excited for her survival were over. Long. Over.

After this hospital stay, after the drama waned, I assume Sheri returned as she always did. Defeated. Agitated. Embarrassed. Pissed to be alive. I assume she apologized. But whether she did or not, I no longer heard her. My brain was too tired. With every suicide attempt, a hush fell over us. Shame silenced us.

At some point, shame and trauma blocked my memories, emotions, and thoughts. I was left with a void. I don't recall anyone processing these situations with me. I don't recall any conversations about these events. I don't recall the details of each episode. I don't remember where I stayed, what hospital admitted Sheri, whether I went to school, or what method Sheri used in her attempt to off herself. Life simply moved on.

We shoved situations into the past as quickly as they happened. It was almost as though they never existed. Never occurred. Over the years, when I tried to recall the details, a brown fog formed. My memories were jumbled, scrambled, or nonexistent. No matter how hard I tried to remember, I couldn't.

But why? I wondered. *Is my brain protecting me? Is God protecting me? Was I taught to ignore it? Did it even happen? Maybe Sheri was just sick and called an ambulance. What did the paramedics say? Did I ask? Did I assume the worst? Did I fill in information? Do I have a heart? Am I going crazy? Where are my memories? And why are some memories clear and others lost in space? Did anyone know how Sheri and I existed in the trailer? Is there anyone I can ask about my memories? Does anyone care?*

As the weeks passed, we stayed in the trailer, only feeding and moving around zombielike. We did not talk. We did not sleep.

One night, a choking sound snapped me into reality. I ran to the living room. Snuggles was suffocating. Something was caught in her throat. I hurried toward her. Before I could help, before I could intervene, Sheri began to hit Snuggles over and over with the broom.

"Stop! She is choking! Fucking stop! You're hurting her!" I screamed.

I tried to stop Sheri. But with one swift push of the broom, Sheri swept Snuggles out the door. Snuggles bolted into the dark. She ran far away from Sheri. Far away from me. I searched late into the night. Continued for days. Cried while I walked the streets. I called her name repeatedly. Begged for her to come back. Awaited her return. When the realization that Snuggles wasn't coming home hit me, I burst through the trailer door.

"You killed my cat! You wanted her dead! You hated her! Well, I hate you! I will never forgive you! *Ever!*"

Sheri started to talk. Started to walk toward me. Then, she abruptly stopped, still and silent. Retreated to her room instead. This attempt and Snuggles's death marked the end of my life in the trailer. My life with Sheri. They didn't mark the last storm between us, but they incited change. These resounding wake-up calls prompted me to move in another direction. Any direction.

I knew if I stayed, I would drown in her wake. Drown in brown. There was too much Sheri in Sheri. Too much Sheri in our lives. Too much Sheri in me. I started looking for another home. Another life.

12

Adopted

Two roads diverged in the woods, and I,
I took the one less traveled by, and now I am lost.

—ME, IN MY SENIOR YEARBOOK

As the summer before my sophomore year came to a close, I left the trailer for good. Without Snuggles, love would never visit the trailer again. And I wanted to be loved. Wanted to be wanted. After I moved out, Robby helped me sneak out my belongings while Sheri worked one night. Our hearts pounded as we pulled in the driveway with headlights off. Our adrenaline pumped. On the edge of hysteria, I pulled and kicked the door open while Robby kept watch. I ran to my room. Wild, I grabbed my essentials. Pulled my clothes from the closets. Emptied my drawers.

"Hurry up!" Robby yelled. When I finished, all my life's possessions filled a trash bag. I scanned my trailer one final time. Tears fell from my chin. I refused to look toward Sheri's room.

"Let's go!" Robby pleaded.

I pushed and kicked the door closed. As Robby peeled out, I gazed at my trailer. My friend. My past. It looked dejected. Wrought with grief. And for the first time, I saw its ugliness. I wanted to burn it to the ground. Turn it into garbage. Put it down. Instead, I blew it a kiss and waved goodbye.

Properly dressed in Laura Ashley, I moved toward the federal building in a haze. The day I could petition the court to revoke Sheri's custody had finally arrived. My senses flooded. Overwhelmed. Stressed. Hurried. I felt like I was drowning. Even for a teen wise beyond her years, the experience was too adult for me. Oak wood engulfed my view from floor to ceiling as far as I could see. Oak wood and powerful white men.

The father of my adoptive family was an attorney. He knew everyone present and was versed in the "good ole boy" ways. The judge was his old roommate from college. They were old pals with old favors.

Our case was airtight. A fact that I'm sure Sheri realized. While the legal men drafted, patted, and reminisced, my dad and I jumped each time the heavy wooden doors opened or slammed. Without speaking a word, we shuddered at the mere thought of Sheri's presence. We were unaware of her arrival time. Unaware of her intentions. Unaware of her state of mind.

We sat paralyzed. Still. Submissive. Neither of us was prepared for a confrontation with her. We knew more than anyone what the wrath of Sheri entailed. We both remembered Judah's custody battle. We both possessed her scars. We both were done with her. Consequently, we sat silent. Silent while the judge and attorneys paced, signed, and congratulated one another in front of us. Even though my dad and I had plenty to say and years to discuss, our anxiety kept us quiet. My dad stared into space. Glued to his seat. Weighed down by his history. I stared, too.

On the outside, I appeared calm. Soft. Young. Grateful. Confident. On the inside, I felt sick. Insecure. Hardened. Old. Discarded. Dazed. Eventually, my dad spoke, pulling us back from turmoil.

"Are you sure you want to live with these people?"

It was a valid question. "These people" were strangers he met moments before.

"I am sure."

And I was. I was as sure as any other fifteen-year-old is sure about serious life decisions. Secretly, in my heart, I wanted my dad to halt the procedures. Tell everyone to go to hell. Take me to Taco Bell. Then home. But his anxiety, male ego, and parental guilt inevitably bottled up his emotions and paralyzed him. He proceeded on autopilot. Stuck to the basic parental questions. Battled a lifetime of disappointing me. A lifetime of a life without me. A life he built with a wife and two other children. He wanted to grant the only serious request I ever made of him. Once it was evident Sheri wasn't going to show, my dad signed over his parental rights. He hugged me. And then he exited stage right.

I returned to my new home. My new family. Everyone seemed thrilled with their "brave" new daughter. As soon as night fell, the reality of my mistake laid heavily on my skin. Flashes of sadness and anger at Sheri jolted my senses. Swam through my veins. They came and went throughout the night. To stay in my bed, stay in the house, fight the urge to leave, I silently repeated, *You are safe. Food is in the pantry. Caring adults are down the hall. You are okay. Breathe. Nights alone in the trailer are over.*

My life in that trailer was gone. Dead. Nothing. No things to return to. If love ever resided in that tin box, it left long before I could remember. *You are good. Breathe,* I thought. The decision to leave Sheri was right. Long before she cleaned house for the Family. Long before

George or Mark. Long before her disappearing acts or suicide attempts. Long before I realized I never truly had a mom. *Breathe.*

She left me with no choice. In fact, she left me first. Multiple times. I wasn't actually leaving her. I wasn't leaving. *You are okay.* I was creating a new life that did not include her. Did not include waiting on her.

Still, the feeling in the pit of my stomach told me this family was wrong. *You will be fine. Calm down.* All wrong. They were not a good fit. The size was off. They were suffocating. *I can't breathe.* I couldn't explain why, but I knew they were the wrong family. The wrong home. Completely wrong. *Breathe.*

While the rest of the family slept, I remained mixed up. I fixed my eyes on the tree outside. I felt like the little girl waiting in the window for my dad. I contemplated running, but I held myself back. I soothed the urges as my rolodex of fleeing fantasies rolled through my mind. Rolled along a well-worn mental path.

My fantasies inevitably started with my dad rescuing me. I knew, however, this would not occur with 100 percent certainty. That fantasy had died in elementary school. I should have chosen the Melendys. They raised me as one of their own. Their sixth child. They wanted me. They broke down when I did not choose them. But I didn't want to add to their life. I didn't want to be another financial burden. Another child. Another responsibility.

Even so, the deciding factor was their religion. At that time, the Witnesses discouraged education on any formal level. Many of the Witnesses's children, including the Melendys', were home-schooled. I feared being uneducated. Feared being Sheri. But I also worried about how sheltered they were, especially compared to my feral existence. I didn't want to corrupt them or hurt them in any way. I didn't want to bring my worldly ways into their godly home.

As I lay there, failing to find sleep, a multitude of feelings bubbled up inside me. *Maybe it was better that I never settled on their house. Maybe they were glad I moved in with the Family. Maybe, just maybe, I have to repeat these tales to stay sane. To stay in this house, with these people. How stupid could I be? How selfish? Because of their religion, I chose strangers. How ridiculously fifteen of me. I threw away a family. A family who loved me. My family.*

I hated being in this situation. I hated Sheri for putting me here. I tried to recall the reasons for my decision. I needed to remember why and how my plan meticulously unfolded. *How did I get here? Why am I in this home? Why did I choose this family? Why not my grandparents? Why not my own blood?*

The painful, arduous decision fizzled down to two reasons. Growing up poor with zero resources would mean continued poverty, and I understood the importance of education from a young age. Sheri often told a story of me after my first day of kindergarten. I returned home crying, almost inconsolable, after overhearing my teachers discuss the cost of college.

"What is wrong?" Sheri asked.

"We can't afford college. We have no money!" I blubbered through my tears. Sheri laughed hysterically.

"Can't we get through kindergarten first?" she quipped.

Education was my primary concern, and after failing the eighth grade, I was behind. The Family valued education. They funded summer school programs to fill in my academic gaps. Both their boys graduated from high school followed by good universities and law schools. I craved the same. Neither of my parents graduated from high school. The cycle of poverty, like an ugly birthmark, would stain me. Define me. Hinder me. Chain me to my trailer.

Second, and most importantly, I needed absolute assurance that Sheri could not reclaim me. She could not whisk me off into the night air. Beat me the next day. After leaving her and exposing our secrets, if she ever got her hands on me, she would kill me. She would literally bury me. In the woods. Behind our trailer. Alongside Snuggles.

Legally, the Family could keep Sheri at bay. Far, far away. Neither my relatives nor the Melendys possessed the ability, the means, or the strength to fight her. For fifteen years, family and friends had attempted to compassionately raise me with her permission, to no avail. They held zero power over her. Zero control over her cycles. Zero claim to me. I was Sheri's property. Therefore, I was ever at her mercy. Ever hers. The Family proved to be viable, willing participants in my absolution from her grasp.

In the ninth grade, I set out to acquire the Family as my own. I knew my mom feared her employers. As their housekeeper, she cowed and deferred to them. She presented her best behavior to them. All smiles. All charm. All professional. She made her best, and only, attempt at a modest, demure woman in their presence. She remained defense-less against them. I watched it time and time again. As I observed her behavior, I believed she would never attempt to bring me back should they take me. They were her kryptonite.

So I got busy. While cleaning the father's law firm on the weekends, I wrote on Post-it notes to hide around his office. They read *Help me!* or *Please help!* I didn't sign my name or make any identifying mark. I left them on legal documents. Under books. In drawers. I carefully chose spots he would find at the right moment. Though I'm not even sure the notes were discovered, I lived frightened while cleaning. Frightened my mom would detect or dust a note. She would know they were mine if she found them.

I dreaded the times she worked in his office. As she dusted his desk and straightened his life, my heart raced. My pupils dilated. I paced. It's possible his messy desk saved my life. My Post-it plan never panned out, so I brainstormed other options while life continued.

Weeks following Sheri's last suicide attempt, she failed to pick me up from school. No call. No note. She simply did not come. I waited inside the school, then outside. I walked to a pay phone. Not foreign to this routine, I was not shocked or worried. I set out to acquire a ride. With a predictable, last-minute request, Jessie's mother fetched me and dropped me off at home. An hour or two later, my mom's car pulled up. I opened the door.

"Where have you been?" I shouted with sarcasm.

She burst into a black rage. Ran up the porch.

"Where have I been? Where the fuck have you been? I've been look-ing for you at your fucking school! Don't ever do that to me again!"

She pushed me into the house.

"Go get a belt! Now! You little bitch!" she shrieked.

I attempted to plead my case. But she planned to beat me. Planned to teach me a lesson. She aggressively followed me to the closet. Screamed various profanities with her alcohol breath. As I reached for a belt, she ripped it out of my hand. The sting caught my attention.

As fast as her arm could move, she repeatedly whipped my body with the belt buckle. Over and over, the metal stung my legs. The beat-ing lasted longer than normal. But the fire and fury were familiar. With each lash and welt, my temper rose. I became aware of my repressed feelings. Courage pushed my fear aside. My right hand balled up into a tight, angry fist. As my awareness shifted to my hand, so did Sheri's.

She dropped the belt. Stepped away. Yelled down the hallway to Mark. In shock, my head darted in his direction. I'd been completely unaware of his presence.

"Mark, come look at Layla! She's going to hit me! Mark, come here! Look!"

I held my pose. Adjusted my weight. Steadied myself for impact. Either my hand hitting her or her hitting me. I was unaware of the next step. This was a new dance. A different tune. Out of fear, I'd never fought back in the past. I silently prayed. I begged God to stop her. I never showed tears or fear. Never gave her satisfaction. But I also never fought back. I lived in terror of her, as did most people in her space.

"I told you to leave her alone!" Mark yelled from the other end of the trailer.

With that, she retreated to her room, and I realized someone knew that Sheri beat me. Mark knew. Mark witnessed it. I held my stance and clenched my fist for several minutes. Then I fell to the ground. Gradually, I shifted my attention to the gash in my leg. A long, metal stem from the belt buckle had broken off in my right shin. The wound scared me. My bone and tissue were exposed. Blood flowed and flowed. I needed stitches. But history had taught me the hospital was not an option.

While I compressed a blanket to my wound, the phone rang. Sheri entered my room. The phone shook in her hand. Though the phone was on mute, her voice was almost inaudible, desperate.

"The Family wants to speak with you."

Her eyes pleaded for my compliance. Pleaded for my pretense. My voice quivered, but the mother and father did most of the talking. They thanked me for the engraved silver platter I gifted them. This was a thank-you for a past kindness. I listened while fighting back tears. I wanted to scream, *Help! Come get me! I'm hurt!*, but Sheri's glare intimidated me. Once again, I felt helpless. I eked out a sufficient response and returned the phone.

I carried many scars from that evening. None of them killed me. None defined me. But I learned a lot about myself. I learned my breaking point. I saw my courage. My ability to fight back. Most crucially, I learned I had to leave. I had to leave fast and never return before one of us ended up dead. After this, I wasn't sure which one of us it would be.

In a final act of remorse, Sheri arranged for me to attend summer school in the Family's neighborhood at their expense and under their roof. Of course, I agreed. I needed academic help. I was tired of feeling like an idiot. Tired of being behind in school. But really, I needed to be away from Sheri. I also needed to be around them.

As my plan unfolded, I vacillated between excitement and terror. The mere thought of staying with them caused me intense anxiety. Even though I wanted to live with them, I was petrified at the prospect. They were relative strangers from a completely different world. While I busied myself with worry, Sheri busied herself with personal plans. The summer arrangement satisfied not only my immediate educational needs but also Sheri's ongoing plot to place me somewhere, anywhere, away from her.

In the weeks leading up to summer school, Sheri and I were eager for a break. We engaged in conversations about what to pack, how to behave in their home, and the expectations of summer school. Many conversations ended in unexpected motherly advice.

"Take advantage of this educational opportunity that I never had. Listen to them. Behave," she said.

I made lists and piles. Informed friends and teachers. As we inched closer to the date, my anxiety intensified. I didn't dare show it or voice it, but my insides danced with concern. *What if I failed? What if they didn't like me? What if Sheri didn't return? What if I never saw my friends again? What if my white trashiness dirtied their home?*

As Sheri pulled in front of their house, a palpable finality whirled around the car. It was unspoken, but the feeling permeated the air. I hugged her a little longer than normal. I used a softer, kinder tone. I tended to my bags. As the father talked with Sheri, she cried. Her brownness dimmed. As she pulled away, I panicked. For a moment, I was in preschool. I wanted to run after her, fast and chaotic, down the carpool line. I wanted to snot and cry. I squeezed my eyes. Took a deep breath. Steadied my feet. Then I walked into their warm, clean home.

The Family acted giddy. I anxiously mimicked their emotion. During the day, I attended classes. In the evenings, we ate together. I enjoyed the companionship. Savored the warmth. Appreciated their kindness. To my delight, summer school went off without a hitch. But my time with them was running out.

Though I have no recollection of how the conversation began, at some point I found myself outlining my life with Sheri to a captive audience. They pressed for details of the abuse, neglect, attempts. They wanted to hear about the days and nights alone.

The last abusive incident was emphasized. I recounted, answered, and offered information for hours. Once my stories were sorted and after a closed family meeting, they asked if I wanted to live with them. Of course, I agreed. My plan had worked.

The Family promptly asked my mom's permission to take me with them to Angel Fire, New Mexico—a last-minute summer vacation. Sheri agreed, though she was not in the dark. Astutely suspicious by nature, she always thought people were stealing her children. Her stuff. Her man. The Family placed miles, time, and space between Sheri and me while Sheri was served with legal papers. The moment she was served, she called. On cue, she acted like the insane woman I knew. Loved. Hated. My sweaty, emotionally exhausted body trembled as Sheri tantrumed. Her blackness poured through the receiver as she screamed and cussed at me. Then she screamed and cussed at the Family. Then me. She ended with the Family.

While the Family listened in, the eldest son's wife cried. They experienced Sheri's illness. Her rage. Her dark side. The trauma. My transition from her daughter to their daughter was quick but painfully sensitive for all involved. There was no turning back. Sheri would kill me not because she lost me, but because I outsmarted her. Exposed her.

Upon returning to Texas, after Robby and I visited the trailer and removed my belongings, I nestled in their nest. By then, all aspects of my decision to live with the Family felt ill-advised and horribly off. I stuffed these feelings down and focused on my future. Pushed forward. Pretended. At times, I felt special. Wanted. Loved. I believed they chose me as much as I chose them.

I reciprocated their kindness and focused on my gratitude for their home and family. Gratitude for the resources they used to rescue me. Gratitude for home-cooked meals and sibling banter. For the "Buttly" nickname. For a mother's presence after school. For parents at night.

To repay them, I attempted to be everything they wanted. A good student. A loyal Christian. A perfect daughter. But when I refused to call them Mom and Dad at their request, I felt a shift. A break. A rift. No matter how hard I tried, I could not form the words in my mouth. For better or worse, I had parents. The term "Mom and Dad" had history. Had memories. Had faces behind them. No matter how hard we all pretended, they were not my parents. It was like a neon sign hung above us.

Disappointment was planted on both sides. After they consulted with a psychologist, they promptly stopped all communication between my family and me. They believed that for me to bond with them, I had to sever all bonds with others. When I returned from the Thanksgiving holiday with my dad, they told me it was my last visit with him. My stomach churned. I cried in my sleep and woke up mad at myself. They allowed me to visit the Melendys for a final goodbye a few days later. We all cried. We all felt duped. Disheartened. Dejected.

When I returned, the Family's campaign began. The brainwashing commenced. They told sordid tales of my dad. I didn't listen to them.

I will not repeat them. They outlined how Sheri and Mark attempted to sell me. To them. Before the custody hearing. When the Family declined to pay, they failed to show up in court, got hitched, and fled to California.

After disparaging my parents, they tackled the Melendys. The Family played videos of former Jehovah's Witnesses outlining cult tactics and internal abuse. I ignored. I recoiled. But mostly, I was disgusted. Anger was planted inside me. And unbeknownst to me, my stomach ulcers bled.

Within the year, the Family's energy toward me soured. I felt like I was traversing across a foreign land and never learned the language. I was never accepted by the locals. As I walked through their house, ate their food, and attempted to communicate, they saw a foreigner infiltrating their family. I was not like them. I was not them, and that fact would never change. My attempts to dress as they wanted, talk as they wanted, and believe as they wanted would not change the fact that *I* was not what they wanted.

When alone, I let my mind flow, and I often wondered why they had wanted me. *Why would they take in a teenager when they were retirement age? Why would they adopt once their kids were successfully raised? When grandkids were on the way? Was I too old for them? Were we all caught up in some emotional haze?*

Shortly, I learned their motive and their intent. They needed me. They needed me to repair their infamous status in the community. They needed me to erase their racist reputation, which had been exposed in 1985 by their son's sins. Heavily documented in local and national papers. Reported on during the evening news. Discussed in Bible classes. Whispered throughout communities.

The Family desperately needed others to know that their son's transgressions were not their transgressions. They needed people to believe they were Christian, and I symbolized their Christian values. By adopting me, they showed their friends, family, and foes how compassionate, loving, and accepting they were. For months, a cavalcade of onlookers came to view their "pretty new daughter."

I grew to resent the pity-filled phrases the spectators professed to my face and whispered as I walked away. *Poor girl. How sad. Well, aren't you lucky to have this family?* I felt like a strange zoo animal on parade. While the Family puffed up with pride at each compliment and each slap on the back, I became clear about my place. Clear about my purpose. Clear about my role.

As months turned into years, my desire for a loving, safe home with an education shifted to craving a typical teenage life. My situation was nothing more than a means to an end. It was a way out of poverty via education. I walked a tightrope. I desperately wanted to be a typical teenager with a social life. But I also needed to keep the Family happy.

After a few months in their home, this dual goal proved impossible. The Family governed with complete control. Absolute rule. A tight rein. No room for differentiation. No room for individuation.

Being raised as a feral child until I was fifteen allowed me the luxury of forming my own opinions. I'd established my own rules in the absence of authority. Suddenly living with strict rules and a belief system outside of my own felt like a too-tight wool sweater. I itched and scratched at each rule. Each explanation. Each lecture. I failed to step in line. Failed to assimilate. Failed to comply. I sucked at adoption. As did they.

The Family demonstrated a bottomless pit of insecurity and dysfunction. Demanded constant appreciation for saving me. Expected gratitude through my behaviors, grades, expressions, beliefs, appearance, choice of friends, and boyfriends. My gratitude proved to be a never-ending, exhausting task.

Love was measured with a Gratitude Ruler. Everything was funneled through the lens of "gratitude." Everything was conditional. Any "bad," or "typical teenage" behavior demonstrated my ungratefulness. I lied, so "You are not grateful for our family." I dated the wrong boy, so "You aren't grateful for this opportunity." I broke curfew, therefore "You aren't appreciative of this house." With each act of noncompliance, no matter how insignificant or age-appropriate, I was viewed as an unappreciative ingrate. A loveless daughter. A mistake.

They lectured me with the Bible. Grounded me. Then they ignored me. On one occasion, the father angrily shoved me on the bed. Yelled in my face. Once again, I was both disappointed and a disappointment.

No one took the time to know me. My thoughts. My beliefs. My behaviors. No one cared that I just wanted to be a typical teenager. No one wondered why I had bleeding ulcers. Once they realized I was not a mindless soldier singing their praises and beliefs, nor was I ever going to be, we were at a standoff. Under the weight of gratitude and guilt, disdain and resentment grew on both sides while the Family plotted my extraction.

Though Sheri's parental rights had been removed by the Texas courts, my adoption by the Family never occurred. For my eighteenth birthday present, and possibly as an olive branch, the Family legally changed my name to theirs. But the gesture was in name only.

By Christmas 1990, we all simply ignored one another. I spent my final holiday with them locked in my bathroom. I nursed stomach pains. Popped pimples. Applied a mask. Dressed for the day. They opened presents with their married sons and their grandchild. Not one of them walked down the hallway to request my presence or announce the start of Christmas.

I sat paralyzed in the bathroom. Stared in the mirror. Listened to sounds of family and holidays. Rustling paper, clinking glasses, talking, and loving embraces filled the morning and wafted under the bathroom door. I could not make myself join them. I felt gross and out of place. My presence stained their holiday. I wanted to be nowhere. The phone rang. The mother answered.

"She is in the bathroom. I'll have her call you."

In that moment, I realized they knew where I was. They remembered me, but they simply chose to exclude me. They couldn't be bothered to summon me to the phone. They spent their holiday exactly as they wanted to: without me. I sat stunned. In disbelief. Outside of reality.

Without forewarning and with no conscious thought, I rose from my bathroom chair and emerged into their presence. The room fell silent. All eyes were on me. No smiles. No teeth. Just confused eyes. They removed me to another room, swiftly extracting me from their family and Christmas. Blamed me for my absence. Blamed me for avoiding. Blamed me for ruining Christmas. I accepted. Moved inward. Everything turned strange. Prickly. Unbearable. I wanted to run. Wanted to spew all my grievances. But the lecture sucked my energy. Sometimes I wished for beatings over lectures.

As the father ceased his inane prattle, I sat lifeless in their presence. Anyone who cared would know I was dying inside. However, anyone who cared was long gone. All removed. All with my permission. All with one decision.

Two weeks later, the father entered my bedroom. Announced that someone wanted to speak with me and left. Their pastor sauntered in. Failed at introductions. Barely looked my way. With a Sunday-pulpit inflection, he began a long-winded sermon. Even though his audience consisted of one, he postured as if he spoke to many. He spoke over me. Through me. Above me.

In my confused haze, the pastor unfolded a compelling plan: "God's plan." A plan to remove me from their home and enroll me in college a semester early.

"God is releasing the Family of their obligation to you. The Family tried everything to salvage this relationship and include you," he proclaimed.

I was so ungrateful and unlovable that God himself had to intervene. A child stain that only God could cleanse from their Christian home. Our eyes never met. The pastor never asked my opinion. Never included me in God's decision. All was decided without me. Before me. For me. In all his expensive glory, the pastor exited my room. His work was done. God's message delivered. A divine edict. An indisputable proclamation.

I sat on my bed. Confused. Ulcers bleeding. I attempted to absorb his words. But the realization that once again I had no home or family made me nauseous. Dizzy. Lost. Questions swirled in my mind. Questions filled my head. Questions with no answers. And no one to answer. *What is my next move? Can I stay one more night? Do I start packing my bags? Do I show up for breakfast? How do I act toward them? Do I thank them for three years? Do I hug them as I leave? When do I leave?*

I did not see another human that evening. Left to my own thoughts, my mind skipped from one random topic to the next. I grabbed Roni Rabbit and curled into a tight, scared ball. My attention settled on one, salient story Sheri had told often.

"You'll never believe what the Family did. You know how they got a new dog? Well, I just found out they got rid of their old dog to make room for the new dog. Who does that? Who gets rid of a family dog they've had for many years for a new dog?"

I burrowed in the covers. Cried at the injustice. Cried about the discarded family dog. The discarded daughter. The discarded life. As night descended, I closed my eyes. The house and humans turned sterile. My stomach ached. I returned to the little girl in the window waiting for her dad.

I resumed high school for a few days to complete any final requirements the Family negotiated for me to complete my senior year. I never will truly know what occurred between the Family and my school, but I somehow graduated second in my high school class in January instead of May—although I would still come back to walk the stage with my classmates. My friends, my boyfriend, and my teachers were stunned. Speechless. Those on the outside whispered and gossiped. A few caring adults offered solutions. Ways to change the Family's course of action. All were kind gestures. However, nothing was substantial. Nothing changed my fate.

With all my belongings securely stowed in a packed car, the mother and eldest son picked me up from my last day of high school. We drove four hours to Nacogdoches, Texas. The Family enrolled me in Stephen F. Austin State University (SFA)—a far cry from my other college offers. I sat in the back seat, invisible. The mother and son rattled on about the grandchild, court cases, and family members. The mother and son gossiped about their own for hours. No one was immune to their judgments. Their assumptions. Their criticisms. I sat while my ulcers pained me. While my anxiety escalated. With a flat affect, I gazed out the window at passing strangers. Strangers living lives with unimaginable possibilities. I envied each one. I craved any car but mine. I wanted to be nowhere.

Once we arrived, they unloaded my belongings and promptly left. I stood alone in the strange, cold dorm room, suspended in reality. My high school uniform awkwardly clung to my body. I was out of place. Contagious. Gross. Numb.

13

Collapsed

The person in whom Its [depression's] invisible agony reaches a
certain unendurable level will kill herself the same way a trapped
person will eventually jump from the window of a burning high rise.

—DAVID FOSTER WALLACE, *INFINITE JEST*

With luggage in hand, I checked my mailbox. I'd received
six letters from my boyfriend, Chuck. Each day I
received another batch of notes with only three to five sentences.
Goofy phrases. Stupid doodles. Hardly worth the time. Barely worth
the stamp. But they completely warmed my insides.

The first one read, *Have I told ya I loved ya today?*—a rhetorical question Chuck often posed with his dimples gleaming. His eyes glistening.
I saved the other five letters for the bus. With only one hundred dollars
each month from the Family, I stood in line to purchase a thirty-dollar
bus ticket. A ticket that would take me from Nacogdoches to Dallas. A
ticket home. A ticket to Chuck. A ticket to my first love.

As I boarded, I eyed the driver. Gauged his competence. Sat quickly
in the first available seat. Talked to no one for six hours. While being
jostled about, I slept a bit, but I woke and stared out the window at
every stop. I inspected each small town and the newcomers. As the bus

moved closer to orange, I read my letters. Sweet phrases in boyish hand-writing quieted my childhood fears. Quieted my anxiety.

When I finished reading, I daydreamed of Chuck. His curls. His jokes. Him. Then I returned to slumber. I had plenty of boy-friends before him, but I'd never experienced the all-consuming, heart-wrenching feeling of being in love. Of being best friends. Of being enmeshed. Of being wrapped in orange. It blurred my per-ceptions. Fucked up my decisions. The fallout was being homeless. Family-less. Penniless. Technically, I had no home. I lived like a gypsy. A beggar. My address was c/o Stephen F. Austin, but my belongings were scattered here and there. Some were at SFA, some were with the Family, some were at Chuck's.

As the bus neared Dallas, I freshened up. Butterflies filled my gut. I missed him terribly, though we were accustomed to being interrupted. A month into our relationship, the Family forbade us to date because of a false rumor—mere gossip that circulated the school following our first date. After a few months, they allowed us to date again. Then they kicked me out, sent me off to college, and removed me from his life.

Each disruption only bonded us more. Glued us. Solidified us. Bred an "us against them" mentality in us. Unfazed by the disruptions and the distance, Chuck smiled wide in his orange sports coat while the bus parked. My body vibrated. As soon as my feet touched the pavement, we hugged, we kissed, and off we went. Our song, "I Would for You" by Jane's Addiction, serenaded us home.

Each weekend was planned out. When I rode the bus or hitched with friends to Dallas, I stayed with Chuck. When he came to SFA, we stayed in motels. By March, I'd lost my virginity to "Sweet Child o' Mine" by Guns N' Roses. After this, I refused to return to school. Refused to get on the bus. I couldn't bear college. My days at SFA were spent curled in a ball while blaring Enigma throughout my dorm room.

I failed to attend my classes. Failed to engage with others. Failed. I was in no mental place for homework. Papers. Tests. Deadlines. Expectations.

The weight of my past and present pushed me into a depression. A state that settled in. A state that changed my personality. A state that turned all things black. I cried often for no reason. For all reasons. I had Chuck, but I didn't have much else. I hated SFA. It was not my scene. Not my people. I hated the distance from Chuck and the Melendys. I hated being alone. Hated all of it.

Full of bad decisions and secretly engaged, Chuck and I moved into his father's home. Within days, he collected the rest of my belongings from the Family. During the week, Chuck finished his senior year of high school. His father worked. I remained alone in the house.

I slept. I cried. Paced. Prayed. I brainstormed how to transfer colleges. Brainstormed ways to improve my situation. Brainstormed until my brain hurt. Until I dug a deeper hole from which I couldn't escape. Couldn't cry for help. Couldn't light my way. I failed to eat. My stomach bled. My weight plummeted to eighty-seven pounds.

I tried to keep my depression from Chuck, but ultimately, I pulled us both into the hole. As we navigated in the dark, we fought. On weekends, we partied. Drank. Laughed. Wrestled. Loved. Then we fought some more.

Eventually, I moved in with the Melendys. Robby and I landed jobs at Olive Garden. Rode together. Waited tables together. Chuck and I started dating again. He drove to the country to retrieve me. Sometimes I stayed with him; sometimes he returned me. But orange never quite reappeared with the same hue.

As I tried to form order from chaos, friends informed me that Chuck was cheating on me with a junior from our high school. In shock, I confronted him at his mom's house. He didn't deny it, and we promptly broke up two weeks before prom.

Life turned ugly. Whatever my dad and Sheri didn't kill, Chuck gutted. I cried from sunup to sundown. For days. For a week. When tears dried up, I lay lifeless on Keisha's bed. My will to live vanished. Karen and Keisha attempted to console me. All their attempts were futile. I believed I was nothing. Worth nothing. Possessed nothing. No parents. No home. No education. No money. No one. My history with abandonment was too real. Too deep. Too dark. Too piercing. And I indulged in it. Wallowed in it. Absorbed it. Embraced it.

A week of emotional agony with no end in sight prompted Karen to call my dad. He offered to take me in. I agreed. Ordinarily, the thought of being with him, much less living with him, would've summoned immense elation. Summoned visions of green. But I was numb. Dead inside. I was a zombie walking into my dad's house. I felt foreign and foul. Unwanted and unkempt.

I skimpily hugged everyone. Met my little brother. Sat silent on the couch. Envied the wallpaper. Wrestled with demented thoughts. Nothing felt like my dad. Like the dad I knew. Like the dad with whom I explored life. With whom I encountered green.

After all the awkward moments, I retreated to my assigned bed. Roni Rabbit and I lay limp. I felt invisible and morphed into a black hole. In the morning, my eyes opened to an empty house. A strange house. A house inhabited with strangers. Within seconds, my disturbed mind tossed about. *I don't belong here. I don't belong anywhere. I want to disappear. No one would care. They would be relieved.*

Sad mornings were the low point of my day. I woke to the realization that life continued regardless of my troubles—a concept I could never grasp. I needed life to stop. I needed a moment. I needed time to process and understand why life happened to me. Why life shit on me. Without a moment, without coping skills, I simply stuffed all my emotions down. All concerns. All colors.

My dad checked in periodically. Unaware of my suicidal thoughts, he tried to offer fatherly advice. "You know, Layla, I could plant you in any city in the world, and you would fall in love again."

I appreciated the thought, but my reasoning was turned off. My ears were muted. I was too gone. Too hurt. Truthfully, there were too many years between my dad and me. Too much unspoken. Too much heartbreak. He continued to father me, but I continued to move inward. I stuffed green, too.

After a few days, I met up with friends. We talked about all things prom. Gossiped about everyone. Stayed up too late. Drank too much. Ran the streets. Never returned to my dad's. Never even called. This choice crushed me if I focused on it too long, so I stuffed that down, too.

Prom day, I was giddy but anxious. My friends thoroughly briefed me. "Are you sure you want to go? Chuck is bringing *her*."

I nodded and stuffed it. Pushed forward. Switched to autopilot. Dressed. Joked. Drove to our meeting place—a predetermined spot several of us were to meet before prom. However, Danette, a beautiful blonde from Mansfield, Texas, was the only senior who showed up. Though we attended school together for two years, she and I had never hung out. We didn't share classes or friends, but there she sat in her car, waiting for her crew. Eventually, I left my ride and hopped in with her. We laughed about being jilted. Laughed that we would be each other's prom dates.

We headed to the venue, where the dinner and dance proved an uneventful mental obstacle course. I greeted all my teachers and administrators. I spoke to estranged classmates and acted unaffected. Dressed in black and shame, I avoided talking about college. I avoided talking about family. Home life. And Chuck. My conversations were short. Shallow. And false.

Randomly, I glanced at Chuck. I never met his eyes. We never connected. But I did realize I still wore Sheri's engagement ring, as I had for seven months. Subtly, I removed it and asked a friend to put in his tuxedo pocket. I continued, composed. I worked the room. I laughed on cue. I never saw the diamond ring again.

Eventually, Danette and I headed to the after-party, which was just what I needed. Loud music. Lots of booze. The perfect escape. I danced on tables until I noticed a commotion at the front door. Chuck's fellow male seniors wouldn't allow him and his girl to enter. Chuck, angered, pleaded his case.

"It's my party, too!"

I stopped dancing and told the boys to let him in.

"It's fine! I'll be okay!"

Chuck thanked me and introduced his girlfriend. Within minutes, I realized I wasn't fine. Within minutes, Chuck and his girl exited. I downed drinks one after the other. Stuffed feelings one after the other. I retreated to a friend's SUV and cried in the passenger seat. Tried to call Chuck. Passed out. Woke up at a friend's house. Sad. Confused. Lost.

Hungover and barely conscious, I called Karen for a ride home to wherever home was from wherever I was. Relieved to hear from me and afraid I might bolt again, she shared her recent conversations with my dad and the Family. Apparently, my dad was disappointed. He didn't want me to return. He had young children to protect. On cue, the Family refused any future financial support. They washed their hands of me.

I listened, nauseated, and grew angry with myself. Karen told me to collect all my items and return to her house so we could create a game plan. Stupidly, I started with Chuck.

"I need to collect my things from your dad's house, and I need a ride to Karen's."

He agreed. Before he arrived, I attempted to clean off the prom.

Clean off the hangover. Clean off the crazy. Within thirty minutes, orange honked outside. Within an hour, we were drinking and driving. Like a train wreck in motion, we propelled ourselves with great force through the morning. But within two hours, our laughter and love turned to resentment and rage.

Instead of driving to his dad's, he swerved in the direction of my friend's house. Flew into a parking lot. I screamed something. Jumped out of the car. Slammed the door. Chuck sped away. Within seconds, orange disappeared into the horizon.

My nerves short-circuited. I screamed. I trembled. Thoughts and feelings surrounding the breakup, my dad, the Family, Sheri, SFA, and my fucked future exploded. My stuffed emotions and colors poured onto the pavement. Everything I worked for. Everything I planned for. Everything was gone.

All the colors that caused me so much pain swirled and spilled around me. Browns, greens, oranges, and reds. My field of vision narrowed. Light escaped my path. I said no to the life Ron and Sheri birthed. No to the crumbs they handed me. No to being discarded. No to being forgotten. No to being unloved.

"No!" I screamed and ran toward the busy four-lane street. With intention. With purpose. With the hope of dying. Right then. Right there. As I crossed the first lane, my mental faculties collapsed. Colors suffocated my reason. Time lapsed. Cars passed and screeched. Drivers shrieked and honked.

Within minutes, someone scooped me into their arms and ran toward safety. Blue, white, and red lights blinked. Sirens penetrated. Faded. Then penetrated again. My legs and arms flailed. Uncontrollably. Without thought. Without care.

"What is your name? What is her name?" a voice asked while they slapped me.

"Layla," a guy answered from somewhere.

Two paramedics strapped me to the gurney.

"Layla, did you take something? Did you drink something? Layla?" another asked.

Random people answered. Some guys. Some girls. All young. All seemed to know me. But everything was a blur. While they gathered information, I fought for my death. With force. With reason. I begged them to leave. To go away. To stop. In mid-punch and kick, a needle penetrated my vein. I screamed and returned to black.

Groggy and exhausted, I woke feeling cold. I was in a bed. In a hospital. In white. A nurse checked my vitals.

"Where am I? Where's Chuck?"

She shushed me. I fell back asleep. In a twilight state, thoughts of Sheri flooded and flashed. Brown eyes. Bright smile. Brown skin. *I'm just like her. Oh, God, I'm crazy. I'm in the same hospital, for the same reason. Neither of us could pull it off. Both losers. Both insane. God, I don't want to be Sheri. I'm so sorry. Please, God, I don't want to be crazy. Oh, God, I'm just like her. Tell me I'm not her. Please let me die.*

Despite my efforts to leave Sheri behind, she was of me. Becoming me. Me. I pulled the covers over my head. I wailed until my body stopped. Weak. Embarrassed. Rotting with shame, I surrendered. I finally realized I was in too deep. It was too dark. I was too young. I was too damaged to save myself.

I needed support, resources, ropes, and people to pull me out of this hole. To keep me alive. To light my way. The hospital released me to Karen. I didn't fight. I didn't argue. I didn't want to. I didn't have the energy or the mental capacity.

My psychologist from my days with the Family called me, counseled me, and problem-solved with me. I told him I needed to rest. I needed time to think without any outside voices. Without any outside distractions. Without gossip. Without lies. Without problems. Lost in black, I craved my trailer's walls. Craved Snuggles's affection. Craved isolation. Craved sleep. I needed to hear my soul. I needed to hear.

After much debate, my psychologist admitted me to a psychiatric facility. For a week, I rested in my room. No roommates. No colors. No distractions. I attended counseling sessions if I felt like it. If I didn't, I wrote in my journal or met with my doctor.

For the first two days, Sheri and shame consumed me. Each carried debilitating weight. Each carried undeniable consequences. Each had a stranglehold on me. For the first time, following my own botched suicide attempt, I understood Sheri's embarrassment. Her recoiled demeanor. Her anger. Her brownness.

If life offered us suicide and we accepted, waking up to the same shit only prompted more thoughts of suicide. The ideations didn't dissipate. Rather, they intensified. They haunted and cradled me as a viable option. A family tradition. A coping mechanism passed from mother to daughter. But apparently, it was an impossibility in the hospital.

After forty-eight hours, I had failed to find one way to kill myself within those walls. Nurses were a constant. All eyes. All ears. All-knowing. All possible suicide techniques were foiled before a plan could be hatched. I contemplated drowning my head in the sink, but my sink failed to hold water. I brainstormed. Searched. Inspected. At some entry point, nurses confiscated all sharp or "dangerous" items. Fingernail clippers. Tweezers. Scissors. Shoelaces. Eyelash curlers. Medicines. Potions. And ultimately, my dignity.

Since I couldn't off myself, I turned to humor. Told jokes about suicide. About not wanting to live. About being alive. Apparently, my comedy wasn't welcome in a psych facility, so I wrote my material in my journal, saved it for PD, and then fell into a soothing sleep.

On the third morning, a nurse placed my long-lost suitcase on the bed. The suitcase I left at my dad's. After one look at it, I asked, "Hey, is my dad here? Does he want to see me?"

Kind and cautious, she sat beside me.

"He dropped your things off this morning. He declined to visit you."

Green splashed across my face. Melted my mind. Disappeared. My dad came and went. I fell back on the bed and sobbed.

How do I still have tears for this man? Why am I surprised? Why am I sad? You have to get over him! You have to stop! But I couldn't. I wanted his comfort. His love. His wisdom. His help. His hug. I wanted my fucking dad. As I laid there, I realized the Melendys were the only ones who called. The only ones who cared. Not Chuck. Not friends. Not Dad. No one.

After a pity-filled morning, I was sick of myself and decided to leave my room. I sat next to a handsome guy admitted for sex addiction. He convinced me to attend the morning group sessions.

"Shit, if you're going to be here, get something out of it. Though I don't know why you're here. Ya seem like the only normal one."

For the next four days, he was my buddy. My lifeline from hell. We attended sessions together. Ate together. Processed life together. He seemed wise beyond his experiences. Beyond his station in life. He led me to several enlightening counselors. Their words flowed down a direct path from God to my ears.

Finally, my behavior made sense. My feelings were validated. I learned about the effects of childhood trauma, abandonment, and parental mental illness. Apparently, I exhibited the symptoms: codependency, poor coping skills, anxiety, anger, depression, suicide attempts.

Within the sessions, within the white walls, I learned I wasn't mentally ill. Instead, I was physically exhausted from my life. I had had a mental breakdown—an inevitable, predictable breakdown due to trauma. Poor parenting. Non-parenting. In my attempts to understand my parents, I realized they were never parented themselves. I was born into a cycle of abuse. A cycle of trauma. A cycle I could perpetuate or end.

With psychology, I could identify, process, and release my childhood trauma. I could change my life. Oversee myself. Choose differently. Up to that point, psychiatrists felt wacky to me. Incompetent. Uncaring. Dismissive. I knew them only to diagnose bipolar disorder and prescribe Valium. In my experience, they failed miserably. This newfound psychology, however, offered me hope. Offered me another way of living. Of shifting. Of mending.

As the week progressed, I began to contemplate psychology as a career. It could be a way to heal myself through intense study. A way to remove the effects of Sheri from my future. From my children. From my bones.

On the fourth and fifth days, my doctor posed the same questions: "Where are you going to live? What is your plan?" These two simple but profound questions needed answers before they would release me. Initially, "I don't know" was the only phrase I could muster. Any option I had before my suicide attempt, I didn't like for one reason or another, or all of them. My mind was confused with colors that needed sorting—mostly browns, greens, and oranges. I no longer saw red or black. My anger and suicidal thoughts were tempered. Managed. Eased.

I still grappled with abandonment by those God deemed mine. Who should have been mine. *Why weren't they mine? Where did they go? What did I do? Why am I alone?* My brain knew abandonment wasn't my fault, but my heart kept up the ruse.

"People leave. They don't have to stick around. Get used to it," one counselor stated.

As I sorted and grappled, a nurse appeared.

"Layla, you have a phone call."

I walked briskly to the front desk with anticipation; colors performed and burst. I placed the receiver to my ear. A sweet voice came from the other end.

"How are you? This is Danette."

Another simple but profound question. Thankfully, my answer was "Better." As my lips moved, tears descended. I couldn't believe a new friend was calling. Concerned. I couldn't believe she was a friend. We talked about nothing. We laughed about everything. About the present. About being in a looney bin. About being homeless.

Thankfully, she got my sense of humor. Thankfully, I still knew how to laugh. After the call, I felt elevated. Normal. Happy. I'd been doused in purple.

On the sixth day, I woke with strength and focus. Ready to leave. Ready to resume my life. To stand alone. To decide for myself. To focus on my needs. My wants. My education. With pep and zest, I dressed. My doctor arrived in a hurried state.

"Tomorrow, we are meeting with your family. I have spoken with each one. I told them to show up if their home is an option for you. If they show, they will outline the guidelines you must follow while in their home. You can weigh your options. I think you will be pleasantly surprised. Take this seriously. I need a decision by tomorrow. I am releasing you," he said.

I heard him, but I failed to identify an emotion or an opinion. Some of my zest left. Within minutes, I identified shame. I did not want my family to see me in the hospital. I was unsure how to face them. Unsure of their thoughts about my attempt. Unsure of living with them. Unsure.

Who would show? What if no one shows? What if they all show? How do I choose one over the other? I don't want to hurt anyone's feelings. Shit.

I can't believe I'm here again. I stared into space while my doctor rambled. I tried to picture myself living with each family member. Tried to imagine life beyond the hospital. But nothing felt right.

"I think I need more time."

My doctor laughed. "No, you don't. It's time. I'll see you tomorrow."

I joined my final group sessions. Processed my decision with anyone who had ears. I said my goodbyes. Once again, I packed for an unknown home and an unknown life.

With my self-respect propped up by affirmations and hot air, I anxiously anticipated my family members' arrival. Within an hour, the doorknob turned. I jumped and immediately deflated. Like quiet, compliant schoolchildren, family members filed into my hospital room one by one. They sat awkwardly on the beds. Fumbled with their belongings.

I rehearsed my affirmations. Attempted to inflate. Karen rose. Asked for a hug. Aunt Rebecca and Mema followed suit. I comforted each of them. Focused on Mema. Loved on her. I took my seat. My heart jolted and flipped. My foot shook uncontrollably. I thanked God my dad and PD didn't show. I couldn't have survived their eyes. Their faces. Their discomfort.

For a fleeting second, as the women inspected me, I wanted to run. To scream. To burrow in my covers. To drown my head in the toilet. Instead, I yawned. Searched for oxygen. Felt sleepy. Finally, my doctor began.

"I asked each of you to outline your proposition for Layla. So let's take turns. Shirley, you go first."

Mema adjusted her purse and then addressed me.

"Pappa Dave and I love you very much. He didn't want to see you in here, but we both want you to live with us. You can go to Abilene Christian University. The Family has offered to pay. You can go and come as you please."

I listened and felt grateful for my grandparents. Grateful for college money. But I knew Abilene wasn't for me. Too far from home. Too far from civilization. I thanked Mema for the offer. Kissed her on the cheek. My doctor then nodded to Karen. She stood. Unfolded a piece of paper. Read aloud.

"You know we love you, and you know you can live with us. You can attend SFA or UTA. The Family will pay for either. But you must follow our rules."

One by one, she read each rule aloud. One by one, in the last four months, I had broken each one. I felt ashamed. Ungrateful. Small. I listened. Wanted to cry. I respected them and their home. But I knew that, at nineteen years old, I couldn't comply. I couldn't hurt her again. When she finished, I thanked her and hugged her.

"Your dad has also offered his home. And at the Family's expense, you can attend UTA or you can return to SFA . . ."

Before he was finished, all heads turned toward a knock at the door. My doctor answered. Whispered in the hallway. He returned irritated.

"Layla, a girl is here to see you. Keep it short."

Thankful for the break, I galloped away while my family conversed in their collective confusion. As I approached the hallway, there stood Danette in a blue-and-white denim short set. Long blonde hair. Big eyes. Pageant smile. We hugged.

"Hey, how are you? Is this a bad time?"

I laughed. Made light.

"Funny you should ask. My family and I are deciding where I should live. I'm being released today, but I don't have a clue where I'm going. Not sure what to do. But I have to pick one of them."

Danette further inquired, "You just need a place to stay? If that's all, I'll ask my mom. You can stay with me!"

I smiled, shocked. "Okay," I responded, half-hearted.

She walked toward the phone.

I peeked my head through the door. "I won't be much longer."

Within minutes, Danette returned. "My mom is fine with it." As strange as the situation was, it felt right. Felt natural. Felt destined. Felt purple. We entered the room. The adults glared at us. As I searched for words, Aunt Rebecca teared up. Mema waited for something, anything, to occur. My doctor sat, annoyed. I had no ability to say what needed to be said.

"I'm going to live with her," I blurted out.

All faces turned, shocked. All voices rose simultaneously. Some stood. Some adjusted.

"No offense, but who is she?" Aunt Rebecca queried.

Danette smiled. I fumbled for words. "She's a friend from high school. Her mom said I could stay with them."

Karen dropped her head. Shook it. Mema sat stunned. Needed a cigarette. My doctor tried to gain control.

"Is your mom good with this?"

"Yes! I just spoke with her," Danette said, flippant and fun.

Aunt Rebecca collected her purse.

"Well, okay. I guess we're done here."

She helped Mema to her feet. They introduced themselves to Danette.

My doctor slowed the goodbyes. "Hold on. What about college? The Family has offered to pay."

In a split second, with little consideration and my 0.7 GPA in mind, I had an answer. "In the fall, I'll go back to SFA and bring up my grades so I can transfer somewhere."

As I heard my own decision, I agreed with it. I looked at Danette. "All my stuff is at Karen's. I'll go home with her and call you. I need your number."

As the adults realized I hardly knew Danette and didn't even have her number, they shrank back in disbelief. Danette and I chuckled. After we exchanged information, I left the hospital, puffed up with purple.

14

Freed

No one outside ourselves can rule us inwardly.
When we know this, we become free.

—ATTRIBUTED TO GAUTAMA BUDDHA

Ocean sounds lulled Danette to sleep next to me. I lay wide awake in bed, pondering my life and praying, as I did almost every night.

God, thank you for this home. This friend lying next to me. This family. This experience. This. I wonder. God, I wonder. Who am I without Sheri? Without chaos? Without a brown straitjacket? Who am I to decide? To understand? To know the inner layers of my mind? Of my personality? Of my humanness? How are these layers affected by my experiences? Which experience makes one layer more salient than others? Which layer is me? Which layer is Sheri?

What if one layer was never realized? Would that layer shrivel and fall away? Would that Layla cease to exist? Would a new Layla emerge? The next Layla waiting in line, pushing past the old one? What if I had never met Danette or followed my gut? Where would I be? Who would I be? Would I be the sum of Sheri's secrets? Would I carry their depth and weight forever?

God, I've carried much more than I've shared. I've picked up much more than I've put down. I tempered my wants for Sheri. Harnessed my will. Quieted my goals. All this, so I could carry her. And to what end? For what purpose? Survival? Ignorance? Loyalty? God, may I stop carrying Sheri? May I set the weight of her down—or will she always be with me? At what point will I be free? Will I be me?

I know she is gone. Out of touch. Land and time stretch between us. At times, however, I still want to run toward her. Find her. Embrace her. But she is gone. And I am free.

I keep forgetting I am free! Why can't I remember to be free? Are all my layers already crushed under Sheri's weight, stained and soiled with brown? Do I have any salvageable layers left? God, please tell me these damaged layers are not me. My history is not me. Sheri is not me.

But then, who is me? Where does she end and I begin? Even more so, when will she end so I can begin? Who will win? I must begin. But, God, how?

Amen.

Oh, wait! God, are you still there?

A few more things: Thank you for placing the Bairds in my life and for lighting my path with purple. Please, God, bless Danette for sharing her family. And please give me the wisdom to know if I should stay or go.

Amen, again.

Returning for high school graduation felt like going backward toward my future—the one element out of place in a scene. I was the old, worn-out dude in a cap and gown. Regardless, Danette and I frantically sped to the chapel, late again and laughing.

As we parked, I saw Aunt Rebecca, who must have thought I was a no-show, leaving. At the sight of us, I saw her exhale with relief. We fastened our caps, ran to the chapel, and opened the door. The ceremony had already commenced. The music played and the audience stood. I

Layla and Danette

saw Lloyd Melendy. For a moment I flashed to Karen planning a graduation party for me, awaiting my return, and praying I chose her home over the Bairds. I stuffed the image. At the back of the church, Danette and I froze for a few seconds. Then we smiled and grabbed each other's hands, walking briskly to the front to stand with the seniors. The music stopped and our principal welcomed the crowd. Then he looked at us.

"Nice of you two to join us, Once-in-a-While-Mims and Late-la," he said with a smile.

After pomp, circumstance, and pictures, we were officially college students, and I was officially a college dropout and the one who broke Karen's heart. Despite it all, Danette and I partied for weeks after our graduation. We bonged beers and out-drank boys. I met Danette's friends, and she met mine. Since we both transferred to All Saints late in our high school careers, we had friends across several school districts. This allowed us to party-hop, friend-hop, barhop, and city-hop across the summer.

In the quiet moments, we delved into anything and everything. Boyfriends. Parents. College. Childhood. We joked about my stay in the psych institution. My suicide attempt. My homelessness. We mimicked our classmates' efforts to gauge my level of sanity.

"Are you okay in here?" she asked, tapping her finger to her temple. Our bursts of laughter through tears bonded us.

Our relationship grew more and more as we discovered our shared experiences. We both grew up as only children with single moms, no dads, and scattered siblings. We both adored our grandparents and handpicked friends as family. We knew country living with little money. We both loved sleeping and learning. We had bad tempers, but we laughed instead of cried.

In these moments with Danette, I let down my guard and backstroked in purple. I could be vulnerable. I was comfortable. I was safe.

In a hangover haze, the Bairds on Baird's Lane flowed in and out of my day. Danette introduced her family as they emerged with fresh faces and humble hearts. They were a family of beautiful, down-to-earth blondes. They were so welcoming, I felt as if they had been waiting years for my arrival.

The Bairds' compound, where most of Danette's family lived, comprised three homes nestled in the countryside of Mansfield, Texas. Just fifteen minutes from the Melendys and my old trailer park, Baird's Lane immediately felt like home. Danette lived there with her mother, Barbara—a good-looking, tall blonde with the bluest eyes—as well as Barbara's boyfriend and his oldest son.

Barbara was witty, honest, capable, and loyal. She was everything Sheri lacked or despised. She worked for her father, constantly baked bread, and kept a clean house. In one summer, she also broke my bad habit of throwing clean clothes in the laundry. I hated putting away clothes, so I would often throw them back in the laundry. However, within hours, they would reappear outside my room. Clean. Folded. Ready. Eventually, I felt bad, cut out the middleman, and hung up my shit.

Across the shared gravel driveway lived Danette's grandparents, Nana and Dada, and their adopted son, Jay. I adored all three, but Nana was the kind of character I liked to collect. Big glasses. Big hair. Big personality. She rivaled PD in attitude, style, and wit. She also possessed an honest tongue that cut through bullshit. With a few choice words and her own unique phrases, she could bring deserving individuals to their knees.

Multiple dogs roamed between the houses. Some were tiny. Some were large. Some were fatigued. All were welcome. Nana's two handymen, who were lazy and inefficient, lurked around the property, but both snapped to attention at the sound of her voice. Constantly and reluctantly, they loaded and unloaded her antiques—her side hustle, hobby, and focus.

"Everything is for sale except Jay and Danette," she often announced.

Barbara's younger brother and his daughter, both half-cocked and coming unraveled, lived in the third house on the property. Barbara's youngest sister lived with her husband and two daughters closer to town, up the road a piece—they proved to be the most entertaining. And the rest of the Baird crew often visited from San Antonio.

While getting to know everyone, I was often confused during family gossip. New characters always seemed to be getting introduced. Eventually, I requested a family tree so I could keep it straight. It was then I found out that each Baird had two interchangeable names: their name given at birth and the nickname Dada created.

"Why, there's ole Lyla!" Dada yelled from his recliner whenever I sauntered in the room. And with that name, I became a fixture on Baird's Lane. With my very own nickname, I became a Baird.

Under their roof, I experienced emotional and physical freedom I had never known. There were no strings. No hidden agendas. No secrets. No strict rules. No expectations. Adults acted like adults. Kids behaved like kids. All were allowed to discover their true selves.

Barbara treated Danette and me with respect and as equals. She loved us unconditionally. Provided us with a platform to develop. Blossom. Grow. Fail. Learn. I was punch-drunk on purple freedom, and I selfishly explored this new life.

Unconsciously, I tested their system. Tested them. Tested. I stayed out all night. Sometimes I stayed away for days with Jessie, Joey, or Chuck without a call or any other consideration. At some point, I would materialize tired, hungover, and ashamed. Barbara continued to provide a long rope. Compassion. Grace.

"Well, you're a regular curiosity, aren't ya?" Nana would say bluntly.

I sensed resentment in the air. The more I sensed it, the more I disappeared. My selfish behavior continued throughout the summer.

"The next time you stay out, you can sleep outside," Barbara's boyfriend barked one day after a late-night return.

As I complained to Danette about his rude comment, she listened and allowed me to vent.

"You know, you are being very selfish," Danette said simply.

My stomach turned. My mind tossed. My heart sank.

My trauma was triggered. This one sentence set into motion a deep-rooted concern with which I grappled for hours. For days. For weeks. At what point would Danette grow tired of me? Grow tired of sharing her home? Her family? Her kindness?

"Selfish? You can have all my clothes. All my money. I'll give you everything I own," I responded flippantly. But my insides felt differently. I worried. I analyzed. I crumbled.

I'm grateful for the Bairds. For the first time, I'm free without the burden of Sheri. Without the stress of the Family's expectations. Without the worry of shelter, money, or food. Without the fear of being beaten or sent away. Without the weight of another's responsibilities or problems. With the Bairds, I feel safe to explore. To run. To be free. To find me. But I don't want to hurt anyone, be a burden, or lose them.

Deep into the night, I realized that while my intentions were pure, my behavior was vulgar. Disrespectful. Out of line. Everyone had their limits, and the Bairds' kindness deserved respect. Gratitude. Consideration.

The fall semester approached with confidence and certainty, but I had neither. Insecure, I returned to SFA with my tail between my legs. However, I did return with a purpose. I intended to raise my grades and transfer in the spring. I had no clue where I was headed, but I knew had to go. I hated SFA, and I missed the Bairds. I missed being in the grips of purple. I missed my friend.

Danette wanted to leave her program at St. Edwards in Austin, too. Though both of us were able to maintain good grades, socially we were lost and lonely. Neither of us flourished on our respective campuses.

As I walked to class, memories washed over me. The old me. Chuck and me. The days I was blinded by his orange and suffocated by our dysfunction. But I couldn't let my memories become my reality. So, before my past kidnapped my present and I phoned Chuck, I made myself focus on purple. I conjured up thoughts of the Bairds and smiled at our experiences. I reveled in our summer until, without warning, those thoughts felt like a mirage. A dream. They were ideas I could not grasp. I was losing them.

But just when I feared they had forgotten me, a package arrived from Barbara—a Halloween package of small, painted pumpkins, goodies to eat, and words of encouragement. Treats to warm my soul. As I stuffed my face and grinned from ear to ear, Danette called. We sat on the phone for hours, investigating random topics and discussing our next weekend adventure.

With her, I explored my new life and freedom—my new self. We sifted through the phone book and searched for my new last name. We giggled at each prospect and dissected how the sound of each syllable might represent the new me. The found me. The future me. Little did she know Baird would have worked just fine.

Two weeks before Christmas, I planned to return to the Bairds for break. I packed some things, talked to myself, talked to Danette, and planned some more. I walked the campus lighter, brighter, and freer than the days before. As I locked up for the night, my answering machine blinked aggressively. Four messages screamed, *Listen to me now!*

I predicted one was from Nette, which I'd taken to calling my best friend. Hoped one was Chuck. Felt certain one was Karen. Had zero idea who the fourth could be. Maybe Barbara? With great enthusiasm, I pushed the button and plopped on my bed. Listened. Did. Not. Miss. A. Word.

One message after the other crept up my spine. My neck hairs stood on end. Each message was more desperate than the last. Sheri pleaded her case in each one. Begged for a return call. I lay paralyzed. Confused. Bewildered.

How did she find me? I contemplated. *Who gave her my number? Why is she calling? I thought we were done. Over. I thought I was free. I thought she was dead or locked up. How does she sound? Sick? Manic? Depressed? Close by? Of course, she isn't gone. Of course, I'm not free!*

I played the messages over and over. Tried to determine her mood. Her location. Her mental state. Listened for any clue. Wrote down the number. Didn't recognize the area code. Thankful it wasn't Texas. I paced. I tossed. I analyzed each conflicting thought and emotion muddying my brain. My heart. My world.

I desperately wished to tell Nette. I needed a sounding board. Needed advice. Needed purple to splash over brown. Needed. But it was too late. I was too deep inside a rabbit hole of anxiety and confusion.

I wallowed in the darkness throughout the night. In and out of sleep until lunch the following day, I missed classes. Missed reality.

Missed sanity. I anxiously waited for Nette to call when she returned to her room. I couldn't answer when the phone rang. I was terrified of the human who could be on the other end. However, as soon as I heard Nette's voice, I picked up. We analyzed the situation together from all angles. We decided I was in control. We believed one call couldn't hurt.

Sweating, shaking, and woozy on adrenaline and fear, I dialed the California number and promptly hung up. I paced. I processed. I procrastinated. With fingers trembling and heart pounding, I took a deep breath and dialed again.

With one hello, two states, and three and half years between us, Sheri transpired. Same voice. Same personality. Same color. She spoke calmly, bathed in her manipulative brown glory. Sweetly. Intentionally. Chose each word carefully. She recited well-rehearsed tales. Spoke of a grand life full of great adventure in California. A life adorned with mountains and marital bliss. A life full of hope with Mark, the hero.

Apparently, following my adoption, they married and left Texas. Left their victimhood. Left their mess. They promptly started a bed-and-breakfast and a BBQ restaurant in Amador County. Both businesses resided in the same building, and their life consisted of friends and customers. Fun and fanfare. They lived minutes from where I was born. Minutes from where my life started with Sheri and Ron. Minutes from where the chaos began.

I listened for hours. Answered questions. Offered little. Remained cautious. Concerned. But I was curious. Sheri concluded with a casual invitation.

"Come up for Christmas holiday or anytime you like. Come see where you were born," she said.

She knew I always wanted to see my birthplace. Experience California. Feel close to my parents. She knew how to persuade me. She knew.

Even the large mechanical Santa that greeted me at the Bairds couldn't erase brown from my mind. A beautifully adorned Christmas tree blinked hello over the colorful packages piled high under its branches. Nana's home smelled of fresh-baked pies, Christmas potpourri, and home-cooked cuisine. The Bairds were dressed in their Sunday best for the holiday. They dressed for the family photos and one another. Christmas with the Bairds felt like a warm blanket and a lavender bath. It was a true family holiday, and I soaked up each hug. Each bite. Each joke. Each drink. Each second of my three weeks with them.

I returned to SFA rejuvenated. Loved. Fulfilled. However, I returned to a full, insane answering machine. I listened as I unpacked. The first few messages were simple.

"Hey, Susie, it's Mom. Call me."

The middle few were longer. They verged on aggressive but were mostly excited. The last was a frantic run-on sentence without a single breath. Mixed with alcohol. Stirred with sarcasm. Laced with brown pain. I hit erase. Fell asleep.

Over the following weeks, I returned every fourth call from Sheri. Stayed in control. Didn't invite her in. Just cracked the door. But I caved. I agreed to visit on some undetermined date. Way in the future. Way past the present. I blamed school. Blamed my grades. Blamed. I gave myself ample time to analyze my feelings and determine a course of action.

Sometimes I enjoyed our conversations. Other times, her sharp tongue slapped me in the face. Too familiar. Too dark. It brought me back to reality for a moment, but I quickly forgot its sting. Confusion became my constant. Sheri and the new me were in a tug-of-war while the old me refereed. The game was lopsided. Unfair. Ridiculous. I was outnumbered. Out of my element. I couldn't fight them both. Even Mark chimed in periodically.

"Layla, you'll love it here. Come on. We'll buy your tickets."

Many thoughts swirled in my mind. *They seem happy. Almost normal. However, I know she hasn't changed. But I have! I'm not a child anymore with zero options. She can't hurt me now. And if she does, I'll just leave. Maybe we can have a great adult relationship. Maybe I can help her. What if she's better with some stability? What if she's on meds? What if I leave and can't return to the Bairds? What if they forget me? What if I don't finish college? What if?*

Barbara and I loaded my bags in her car. Nana waited in the passenger seat. Both had driven to Nacogdoches to bring me home.

"Is this all you have? Where is the rest of your stuff?"

As I closed the car door, tears stung my eyes as I choked back years of sadness. *The nightmare was over. SFA was my history.*

"I threw everything away that didn't fit in my suitcases," I said. Barbara gasped.

"You did what? In the trash? Are you crazy?" she asked.

Since she saved everything, and I do mean *everything*, Barbara never understood my need to travel lightly. As the highway moved beneath us, I mulled over my carefully laid plans. Nette and I arranged to meet at the compound, where we would hang out for a week and visit Terr and PD before flying to California.

I fought off an ugly cry for the next four hours while I attempted to answer Nana's questions about Sheri and California. I listened to their concerns and voiced my own. Barbara assured me I could return to her home. Tears rolled down my cheeks. Tears of joy over closing a chapter. Tears of fear over starting a new one. Tears of sadness over leaving Texas. The Bairds. Nette. Home.

I cherished my last week at the Bairds. I laughed louder and longer. Prayed for time to slow down. But secretly, as my departure date inched closer, my ulcers bled, and my nightmares began. A recurring childhood nightmare played out each night in black and white. Slow motion.

I stood over Sheri's coffin looking at her brown skin, black hair, and long lashes softly closed. As I marveled at how peaceful she appeared, how beautiful she was, she sat straight up. Arms outstretched, she strangled me. I woke up with a start. Shocked. Wet. Frightened. I hadn't experienced that dream since living with the Family. I feared my brain knew something my heart was denying. I feared I should stay home. I feared.

The innate need of a child to be with their mother pulled me to the airport. Pushed me on the red-eye. Propelled me into Sheri's arms at 2:00 a.m. But her hug made my skin crawl. Shockingly, I felt no attachment to her. No bond. Zero.

This was not the response I expected to have, though I wasn't sure what I expected. So I inspected her. Overall, she had changed minimally. A little bit meatier. A little less hair. A little less scary. Still beautiful. Still funny. Still dark. For an hour or so, I could hear her. But I couldn't make out her words. The sound of her voice became background noise. My anxiety morphed into the main character of the scene.

A stuffy, brownish air took over my chemistry. My head. My stomach. I couldn't focus on any one ailment for long. Just when nausea caught my attention, a headache pierced my focus. Then my hands began to sweat. My heart thumped. My feet tingled. My breathing became labored. All available light narrowed into a pinhole. I felt dizzy. I felt ten years old again. I felt out of reality. Out of control. Out of my body. I wanted out to get of the car. I wanted to get out of my past. I wanted to get back into my future. I wanted the Bairds. The Melendys. My dad.

"Susie? Hey? Did you hear me? Do you want something to eat?"

I shook my head. Flashed an awkward grin. Shifted in my seat. Blinked rapidly. Faked comfort until she closed the door on my new room. My body knew I was in the wrong place. With the wrong person. Sheri's presence alone triggered decades of trauma. Apparently, trauma is salient. Permanent. Delicate.

The nightmare played again as I slept.

When I rose in the morning, Sheri was black and manic. Lots of energy. Lots of movement. Lots of talking. Lots of everything. Her sentences flew by too quickly to catch, but I managed to grab the name "Judah." Instead of telling me her plan while I was still in Texas, she waited until I woke in California. Of course.

"Judah is on his way. Did I tell you we're talking?"

Her voice continued. But my ears stopped. The two sentences sprinted in circles around my brain. I froze and nodded. Old feelings only Sheri could summon welled up. And stayed. I was angry. Duped. Manipulated. Interrupted. Abused.

I also felt like a bitch. *What girl doesn't want her brother? Doesn't want to meet him? Hang out with him? Know him? Am I a monster? What is wrong with me?* I flipped through our conversations leading up to my visit. *I swear she never mentioned Judah. Never mentioned he was in her life. Never mentioned he was about to be in mine. She never, ever mentioned him.*

For ten years, I wasn't allowed to speak his name. Or think his name. Or want him. Or miss him. Or love him. I was made to believe he didn't exist. Made to believe he was a figment of my seven-year-old imagination. And now he was on his way. I didn't know what to do. Didn't know what to believe. Every cell in my body wanted to scream, *He is a stranger! You made my brother a stranger!*

I don't know what words left my mouth. My body reacted without my knowledge.

"She's uncomfortable with you. You remind her of y'all's dad," Sheri told Judah, based on whatever I'd said before his arrival.

This statement triggered more anger. There was no way I would say that because Judah didn't remind me of my dad. He reminded me of more childhood trauma. And unfortunately, after weeks together, he reminded me of Sheri. Same looks. Same behaviors. Same struggles. Same illness.

By day, I worked on the bottom floor, waiting tables in Mark's BBQ restaurant. By night, I lived on the second floor of the building, researching colleges, writing letters for grants and scholarships, and completing financial aid packets. Nette and I were planning to go to the same college in the fall, but we needed to get all our paperwork in order first.

For the spring semester, I saved every penny, and two nights a week, I took a social psychology course at National University. I kept to myself, studied, talked to Nette, or hung out with friends.

Judah worked somewhere, frequented bars, and hung out with barflies. We stayed in our respective orbits. When we shared space, I stared at him from across the room. Images of us as six- and seven-year-olds flashed across my mind. I saw us running around Taco Bell and eating our tacos the same way. I flashed to my mom decorating his room in blue cars, anticipating his arrival to our trailer. I flashed to never seeing him again. He'd vanished.

I couldn't reconcile that this tall, handsome man in front me was the same six-year-old boy behind me. I couldn't process this situation. This trauma. This so-called brother. And there was no one to help. My body still believed I couldn't speak of him. Couldn't tell our dirty secret. Couldn't be his big sister. I couldn't become emotionally available to him.

And I didn't. I stuffed everything and went inward. With each passing day, it became clearer that Judah and I were strangers in an inconceivable situation. Between us, there was too much unsaid. And too much that needed to be said. There was too much time apart. We were raised too differently to connect. There was too much trauma. We couldn't repair our parents' sins.

As the semester ended, Nette and I applied to Texas Wesleyan

University in Fort Worth. When we were both accepted, Nette registered us for the upcoming semester. Excited and homesick, I focused on my return.

As I planned, Sheri drank. Her personality dimmed. Her soul grew dark brown. Her vision of mothering her children slipped away. She witnessed the disconnect between Judah and me. Her and me. Judah and her. California and me. Palpable, it permeated every situation. While her attempts to mesh her family failed, so did the economy. The tourist dollars dried up. Their businesses couldn't pay bills. The electricity was cut off.

One evening as I returned from class, I witnessed Mark rigging the electrical wires. Methodically. Illegally. Secretly. We needed lights and a stove. We needed AC and a refrigerator. We needed the restaurant to make money. To function. To pay bills.

"Don't tell Sheri, okay?" Mark said. He was going to deal with it.

I started packing. A few nights later, after we closed, Mark and I ate a late dinner at the bar. When I inquired about Sheri and Judah's whereabouts, he acted nervous. Darted toward the kitchen. Weaseled out of the question. I shrugged. Focused on the TV. Finished my dinner.

Sheri and Judah burst through the door in a black, chaotic whirlwind. Drunk. Pompous. Secretive. Beers in hand. In a backwards baseball cap and ripped clothing covered in paint, Sheri flashed a satisfied grin to Mark and high-fived Judah. Both refused to meet my gaze.

"What's going on? Spill it," I asked. They laughed and refused to answer.

"They've been painting at the new house. They're just drunk," Mark interjected.

I inspected them. Wondered about the tin can I saw Sheri quickly hide upon their arrival. Confused and annoyed, I made for the exit.

"It's done," I heard Sheri say as soon as I was out of sight.

Two days later, Mark and Sheri shared some disturbing news, feigning shock. The new building they purchased before I arrived had burned to the ground. Along with it burned their dreams to remodel, plans for another B and B, and their ability to supplement their income.

As they recited their practiced script, anger washed over me. I wanted to bash their heads together and run. I knew Sheri and Judah had caused the fire. They lit the match and hid the evidence. I couldn't understand how three adults agreed to plan and execute a fire to commit insurance fraud. How they could choose prison over poverty. How they could be fueled by desperation over reason. How they could justify their actions and still sleep at night.

What angered me more than anything else, though, was their behavior that evening. Their arrogance. Their sense of entitlement. Their satisfaction with cheating the bank and insurance company. Their pride in pulling it off. When Mark concluded his rehearsed monologue, I said nothing. Went to my room. Called Nette. Moved up my departure date.

Grappling with the Three Stooges stunt, I envisioned buying a plane ticket and leaving in the middle of the night. Ditching the insanity. Vanishing without a trace. Instead, I settled on a road trip back to Texas. My boyfriend, who was visiting me in California, offered to drive me back. The long drive sounded exhilarating and healing. After I discussed the trip with Mark and Sheri, Judah asked if he could join us. Everything in my bones wanted to refuse. I couldn't imagine twenty hours in the car with him. I couldn't fathom that level of intimacy. However, I eventually agreed.

As we packed the car, my emotions were erratic. They ran across the spectrum and mutated every two minutes. Nothing made sense. Nothing felt right. Sheri attempted to calm me. Acted like a mom. Acted out of character. Explained to me what I was feeling, and why I was feeling it. She appeared rational and loving, which confused me more. We hugged a bit tighter. Exchanged last minute sentiments. Said goodbye to brown.

We set out on old Route 66 to take us home. I played the lyrics of "Route 66" by Depeche Mode backward in my head to determine the next city. For fifteen hours, our conversation was limited. The music blared. The tires rolled. We took turns driving. Sleeping. DJ-ing. Navigating. Paying.

A lover of road trips, I thoroughly enjoyed every second of the journey despite my strained non-relationship with Judah. That is, until we had a blowout in Texas. Our car came to a screeching, swerving stop in between Abilene and Merkel. We inspected the damage, called AAA, and waited. And waited. And waited. For hours. Since Judah lived in Merkel, he decided to walk to a pay phone and call his grandfather. Within minutes, his grandfather showed up to rescue him, and they left. Neither offered help. Neither offered concern. They left us on the side of the road for the rest of the evening—the rest of our lives, for all they knew. On that dark Texas highway, Judah and I locked eyes for the last time.

Finally back on Baird's Lane, I was immediately smothered in the smell of Dada's biscuits and lavender. Then Nette and I got busy living. Planning. Playing. Laughing.

As my first order of business, I divided up my saved money into six envelopes. Each envelope represented one month and contained four hundred-dollar bills. Each bill represented one week's spending. No more. No less. This gave me exactly six months to find employment.

The second order of business was to prepare for our road trip to Port Aransas, a small beach town off the Gulf of Mexico where Nette often visited her boyfriend. For weeks, we shopped for cute summer dresses under twenty dollars and created spa days at the house. With robes on and hair wrapped in towels, Barbara applied facials, highlighted our hair, made us snacks, and spoiled us rotten. While she cooked, Nette and I painted our nails, watched TV, and planned our evenings. I appreciated and cherished our spa days. They taught me how to color my hair and apply makeup. They showed me the importance of self-care and its effect on my self-esteem. I learned how to be feminine.

At night, we primped while we sang "Me and Bobby McGee." Dressed "in frocks," as Nana would say, we tried to look old enough that bartenders would look the other way and serve us. Some evenings we met up with boyfriends. Others, we bought a twelve-pack and drove around.

Our summer days were effortless. Each day leading up to our trip to Port Aransas flowed into the next. When the day of our departure arrived, my insides bubbled with excitement. My inner child danced freely. My body floated through the air.

Our trip to Port Aransas proved to be one of many firsts for me. Some of which I was aware on the morning we left, like my first vacation without adults. My first excursion with my best friend. My first conscious trip to the ocean. But some firsts I was unaware of. The first time I would smoke pot. The first time a pack of married, pregnant women would try to kill us. And unfortunately, the first time I went to jail. The experience was beyond comparison.

With cases of beer piled high and me squashed in the front seat, we set out on our adventure. We listened to The Doors and Yaz for eight hours. As soon as the smell of salt air saturated our car, we popped beers. We were hopeful. Happy. Heartened. When we arrived, Nette pulled up to the ocean. Caught up in being free and me, I jumped out of the car before the wheels stopped spinning and sprinted toward the water, where the moonlight danced on the waves.

"Your shoes! Take off your new suede shoes!" Nette yelled, stopping me just in time.

FREED

Port Aransas was all Texas. All freedom. All fun. Beach bums out-
fitted in bikinis and cutoffs covered the coast as far as the eye could see.
Beers tipped to lips. A parade of cars lined the sand. All types of music
drifted through the air.

Once we found the right spot, we parked. Drank. Joked. Swam. For
hours. For days. When we were sufficiently overserved and over-sunned,
we retired to the hotel, showered, napped, and then dressed for the
evening. Those clear Texas nights were magical. The ocean was our backdrop. Stars filled our eyes. The sound of crashing waves filled our ears.

"If you leave, you're going to jail!" my boyfriend yelled as I left the
hotel room.

Though all the bars were closed, and it was the middle of the night,
I was hungry. With Nette's keys and a girl I just met, I headed to Whataburger at 3:00 a.m. Determined. Starved. Drunk. As we ordered, a tall
rack of bun trays caught my eye. The rack, full of buns, was sitting outside in the elements. With the bugs. In the drive-thru. It was so weird
and gross, it was hilarious. It was also an opportunity.

Within seconds, I was stuffing large metal trays into Nette's car.
Hamburger buns flew onto the pavement and the floorboards. Laughing, we pulled up to the window to collect our food.

"Are those our trays? Oh, hell no! This girl has our buns in her car!
Hurry! Call the police!" the Whataburger employee screamed.

I peeled out and screeched onto the main drag, hauling ass toward
the hotel. As I escaped, my passenger threw a few trays out the window. Metal and buns sailed through the air. Police lights flashed. Sirens
blared. I pulled over and attempted to act normal, but the remaining
trays stuffed in the hatchback blew my cover.

The officer asked me to step out. As my feet touched the ground, my
terrible temper flared. My disdain for authority spewed. My inner Sheri
ranted. Accused. Argued. Alleged.

217

"Why are you worried about me? Focus on the girls who got raped today. I'm just having fun. You need more education to work with humans," I snapped.

He cuffed us, threw us in the cop car, and impounded Nette's ride. In my drunken stupor, I cracked jokes on the way to the police station. I requested breakfast taquitos, vogued for my mug shot and made light of the affair. As they locked us in the drunk tank, the policeman chuckled and shook his head. Unaffected, I slept. About five hours into our prison sentence, Nette's stepbrother and friend came to collect us. However, they told the police to keep us a little longer and left. After fourteen hours, we were set free. Barbara's boyfriend had all the charges dropped, and Nette's car was released.

With brown paper bags in hand, we stepped out of the jailhouse and directly onto the beach. Everyone watched. Pointed. Giggled. It was a small town. Word travels fast, especially when the jail backs up to the tourist attractions. Thus, for the remainder of our vacation, we were heralded with quips like "What kinda bird don't fly?" On the ride home, though we joked about my prison stint, much of me felt ashamed. Felt scared. Felt wrong.

For the second time, I felt like Sheri.

———

Texas Wesleyan was a breath of fresh air. A fresh start. A fresh take on college. The classes were small, the students were diverse, and the professors were caring. Barbara acted as our alarm clock.

"Time to get up," she yelled as she flipped on the light each morning, right on cue.

Since neither Nette nor I was a morning person, neither of us obeyed. Nette would turn off the light and hop back in bed. Within minutes, Barbara would return and flip on the light again.

"Girls, get up!"

I rolled over. Turned off the breaker. Went back to sleep. Eventually, Barbara won.

Nette and I rose and dressed. We commuted to campus together, attended classes together, and studied together. And on beautiful, sunny days, we skipped school and went to happy hour together. Life was simple. Predictable. Achievable. In this environment, I could exhale. Flourish. Excel.

Well into the semester, Sheri called. She wanted to visit. Wanted to meet the Bairds. I became possessive of Nette and Barbara. I didn't want Sheri to meet them. Didn't want to mix brown with purple. Didn't want to mix my pretend family with my real family.

If Sheri appeared, my illusion and reality would intersect. Collide. Crash. And possibly collapse. I liked Sheri in California away from Texas. Away from the Bairds. Away from me. Our relationship worked over the phone. It was too complicated in person. In my experience, she wreaked havoc on all things normal. All things human. All things me. However, reluctantly, with great trepidation, and after much debate, we decided to invite Sheri for lunch, dinner, and a one-night sleepover. I promptly began to prepare the Bairds.

When Sheri stepped onto the porch, I wanted to vomit. To run away. To call it off. I mimicked Barbara and Nette instead. They were as cool as cucumbers—lighthearted, classy, welcoming, and inclusive. As we ate lunch, Sheri looked scared, insecure, and out of place. I felt her uneasiness, and my anxiety heightened. I braced for something dark and unexplainable. I braced for odd behaviors and hurt feelings. I braced for the unknown. I braced for black.

As Barbara's niece ran around the table, Sheri glanced at the toddler.

"I don't like kids," she announced, a comment that baffled us all.

No one knew how to respond. Our eyes darted back and forth. My

219

heart pounded. My foot shook uncontrollably. My finger scratched the same spot over and over, but Sheri continued to eat. She thought nothing of her comment. My mind flipped.

Why would she say that to Barbara about her niece? Why would she say that to someone taking care of her daughter? Why would she say that, period? Is this meet and greet too hard for Sheri? Too overwhelming? Shit, we still have ten hours of this. I don't think I'll make it. I can't do this. Hopefully, Barbara isn't offended. Will she kick me out? Shit, should I kick Sheri out? Should I ask her to leave? Breathe, Layla. Breathe.

After an awkward silence, we moved on. Pretended the comment didn't occur. Pretended Sheri wasn't offensive. Pretended. As we cleaned up the dishes, Nette showed Sheri to her room, where she could store her belongings and freshen up. Apparently, it was also a space where she could hide. Sheri went into the room and did not return. She isolated herself until the next morning. Until she was dressed. Until she left. As she drove away, we all exhaled. Decompressed. And then we went about living.

With Sheri's gaffe and the Bairds' subsequent grace, I felt a thick, brown fog lift. Felt the grips of anxiety loosen. I felt my past inch away. But mostly, I felt firmly planted in the Baird family.

My self-perception as a pitiful, damaged girl began to fade. In that moment, I realized my past and my mom didn't scare them. Didn't intimidate them. Didn't disrupt their lives. Didn't define me in their eyes. For the first time, Sheri's wake didn't drown anyone. Not even me.

With that epiphany, confidence soaked my body. I celebrated the holidays a little stronger. A little freer. A little more secure. On Christmas Eve as a family, we bonded over a shared cocktail of familial ties and a festive drunkenness. I expressed how amazing I felt by singing "Fancy" by Reba McEntire on repeat at the top of my lungs until I blacked out. Purpled out, really. They may not have known it, but the Bairds set me free. I was no longer lost in the mix, frightened by my reality, or spooked by my family. Instead, I found me. Not Sheri's me. Not broken me. But my me.

15

Married

Most people would have found it grotesque, but when you're in love
nothing is so abstract or horrible that it can't be thought of as cute.

—DAVID SEDARIS, "APRIL AND PARIS"

Lipstick. High heels. Short skirt. Flannel shirt. "Over-21" wrist-
band. I sauntered into the Aardvark, a local Fort Worth bar.
Cigarette smoke and grunge tunes billowed out the door. I was with
three Texas girls, four Texas guys, and zero concern beyond my next
drink, bathroom break, or smoke. An incestuous bunch, over the
years, each of us was attracted to the others. This led to various pair-
ings within our group. Sleeping together. Then cheating. I blamed our
behavior on a drug-induced coma and youthful, fucked-up principles.
We were inseparable, immoral, good-looking, and high.

The girls squashed in the booth while the guys stood and hung over
our backs. We were all graduating from college soon, looking for a good
time, and feeling old and cynical. As the live band howled our generational
grunge, our conversation centered on the future. Stuffed in the corner
and barely paying attention, I heard every third word. A few were leaving
for Europe. Others were taking jobs in far-off cities. Some were returning
home. I was working on applications to graduate schools.

The serious talk ended as quickly as it started. The guys turned sarcastic and playful. We girls smiled, swayed, and smoked. The night continued undeterred. The band played uninterrupted. The guys delivered drinks to us nonstop, the ashtrays overflowed, and the jokes landed. The guy I was sleeping with, Ned, looked hotter and hotter, but we were nothing serious. Two weeks prior, Ned lost me and a twelve-pack of beer in a game of poker to a random student at a party. But tonight, all was copacetic.

As I downed my drink, a young guy appeared. He stood still and stared at me.

"Layla. Layla?"

For some reason, I felt embarrassed. I tried to play it off and attempted to nonchalantly ignore him. The girl to my left elbowed me.

"Walter's talking to you."

I engaged. I focused. He was Ned's younger fraternity brother. Another SAE. Another Texas boy. As I lazily connected the blurry dots, the two groups greeted one another and exchanged niceties.

"Layla? If you give me a chance, I'll make you the happiest girl for the rest of your life," Walter was saying.

I looked at him. Everyone stared at me. Stunned. We all waited for the punchline. Instead, he repeated himself, but just a bit louder.

"If you give me a chance, I'll make you the happiest girl for the rest of your life."

I turned into a statue. Eked out a smile. I may have nodded. Walter spoke to Ned briefly and then walked away. Within hours, I was yelling Walter's name through the second-story window of his fraternity house.

It was not love at first sight. Not at second sight. Or third sight. Our initial encounters were fuzzy and forgotten, through no fault of Walter's. It took years for me to notice anyone besides Chuck. I traveled through an orange fog, intentionally and continuously running to Chuck at any opportunity. Though I slept with other people and even maintained long relationships with some, I could not seem to shake Chuck. I even cheated on everyone with him.

At my first encounter with Walter, Nette and I had just returned from celebrating with a bachelor at a party in Las Vegas, where I'd hooked up and fallen in love with the groom. While detailing this experience to my friend, Ned and Walter jumped into my car for a lift home. I remembered the encounter, but only because I was sleeping with Ned, my friend's boyfriend, and I was a bit nervous having them both in my car. I had no memory, however, that the tall blonde with Ned was Walter.

Our second encounter was the following weekend. As I basked in the sun at the Holiday Inn pool, a friend pulled up and yelled, "Quarter pitchers at Aardvark for an hour!" I hopped up, slipped on my flip-flops, grabbed my belongings, and hauled ass to the bar, bikini on and quarters in hand. Quite thirsty, I ordered a few pitchers while the owner, a friend from Burleson, laughed at my lack of attire. Somewhere between ordering and drinking, Walter came and talked to me. Still wrapped up in the groom and Chuck, the only thing I remembered about our conversation was that I was wearing a bikini in a bar.

The next Thursday at Aardvark, we had our third encounter. Same friends present. Same grunge music blaring. Different booth. Well into the evening, Walter complimented my boots and continued with small talk. I vaguely recalled the moment. I also liked my boots.

Days later, Walter semi-proposed to me that night at the Aardvark. That time, I remembered him. That time, I noticed. That time, I bought his bullshit. Three weeks later, Walter had already moved in with me and become part of our crew. A full rainbow of colors and light descended on my apartment. On my life. On my heart.

Bird Man. Wally Bird. Wally. He answered to any name we spouted. To any name we branded him with. Each alias described a different personality, physical feature, or color. He was a tall, gangly, bowlegged, longhaired, bearded, feathery fellow: a Bird Man. He walked the campus and bars in PJ bottoms, a V-neck tee, a beaded necklace, and Moses sandals: a Wally Bird. Without warning, he burst into song, busted out dance moves, or begot poetry: a Wally. His character, his mood, his behavior incorporated all the colors with ease and chaos. He was a cross between Scott Weiland and Willie Nelson. A character. Thankfully, he was my character. My poet. My rainbow.

The early days were a whirlwind; the mood was fast and frantic. It set the tone for our relationship. I integrated into his friend group and he into mine. We comingled laundry and bills. We were serious before I even knew Walter's age—a fact Ned enjoyed.

"Do you even know how old he is?"

As he spoke, I searched the dark interiors of my brain for Walter's age. Puzzled, I felt stupid and feared the answer.

"He's eighteen," Ned said, smirking.

As the number escaped his lips, I almost swallowed my tongue and choked. Speechless. Shocked.

"Walter uses someone else's ID to get into bars and buy alcohol," Ned happily continued.

My mind raced with humiliation. Confusion. Anger. *Damn it! He uses the ID to have access to us. To infiltrate our crowd. To fucking impersonate a twenty-two-year-old. What the hell? What have I done? What else don't I know? I can't tell people he's eighteen! I'm a fool! The only way to make this okay is if I marry him, I think.*

After the initial shock and embarrassment, I decided to embrace Walter as if his age did not bother me, the four-year gap was normal, and I knew all along.

We became one. Enmeshed. Entangled. Embroiled. En-love. We moved from apartment to apartment to house to house. Along the way, we made a home and a family. We acquired a dog named Skinner, my old friend and current roommate Jessie, and a crew of six guys and one girl. We found favorite spots, made memories, and on occasion, like colorful confetti, Walt threw proposals. I laughed, blushed, and declined. Walt skipped away, vivid and bright.

"I'm excited you're meeting Walt. You'll love him. He has a great family. He's very funny. Super smart. Huge partier. And he's eighteen," I told Joey casually the night he was going to meet Walt.

Joey heard nothing but "eighteen" and busted into a belly laugh. I flushed. Joey was one of my oldest friends, and I needed his blessing almost like he was my dad.

"He's a kid, Lulu!"

I heard him, but I did not listen to him, even as he jabbed and jibed until Walt arrived. When all the colors appeared, I flashed Joey a stern look. Their initial introductions were civil. Light. Fun. After a brief period of typical guy talk, a little bravado surfaced, and a lot of territorial marking ensued. Too much whiskey disappeared and just enough wrestling occurred to create a testosterone tragedy.

"Stop! Stop, now!" I yelled.

But they continued. Ignored. Escalated. Since booze, boys, and brawling always ends in fists flying, I grabbed my keys and headed for the door.

"I'll meet y'all at the bar. I'm not watching this."

Walt grabbed my arm,

"Don't leave. We'll stop!"

With laser focus, Joey saw Walt's hand on my arm. He saw red. He picked Walter off the ground and slammed him down in milliseconds. His knee was on Walt's neck.

"Joey, let him go!" I screamed.

As I pleaded, their skin turned black as fire ants crawled up Joey's knee and Walt's face. Their faces were red from rage.

"Apologize for grabbing her arm! Apologize, motherfucker!" Joey growled.

A scared "Sorry" filled the night air. They wiped off their ants, anger, ego, and arrogance. With a hug, they became brothers for years.

Walt and I integrated all aspects of our lives and families. The Reeses, the Melendys, the Bairds, and the Sheri all embraced Walt and our relationship. They embraced the ride—and what a ride it was.

With Walt's hyperactivity and my lethargy, we navigated life as best friends and lovers. We were high and sober, vertical and horizontal, stable and chaotic. Our oneness was twisted, pulsating, inspiring, and all-consuming. We bordered on the ridiculous and absurd, but we had a consistent heartbeat and a definite future.

As undergraduates, we held odd jobs and shared funds. When we were unemployed and broke, we ate at Taco Bell, laid low, gambled, and played the lottery. One time, we won three hundred dollars and blew it in two days.

Walt had an odd relationship with money. He never cared about it but always had it. To my shock and horror, he happily spent his last buck on rings, bracelets, books, and excursions for me. After he gave me gifts, I lectured him on the value of money. But somehow and from somewhere, money appeared again. I, on the other hand, worked, saved, and hoarded. I always felt poor. When I was not working, I studied, researched, and wrote. I focused my energy on graduating and graduate school, while Walt did anything but study. He sold his books, played golf, and played with Skinner or any available friend. Played.

On weekends, though, we were sympatico. Inseparable. In sync. We may even have been a little out of control. This worried those on the fringe and invigorated those in the circle. It also terrified his parents and, oddly, Sheri.

My approaching graduation was an unprecedented event. No family member, on either side of my family, had ever graduated from college. I understood the significance and felt the gravity. The weight. The anxiety.

My ulcers bled. Walt tried to process with me and understand, but he came from a long line of college graduates—a Harvard legacy, a pristine pedigree. I appreciated his empathy and pride; I felt his support and love. But I clung to Sheri. I needed my bloodline to validate my success and witness my accomplishment. I also, of course, craved my dad's attendance and adoration. But green had left long ago, so I settled for brown.

Every morning, Sheri and I sat on the phone. We discussed. We brainstormed. We planned my graduation party. Proud, Sheri insisted on hosting the event, and I acquiesced, although I remained cautious. Terrified.

I was intentional with my guest list. I wanted all my families present. I wanted to be surrounded by everyone I loved: Terr, Joey, Danette, Barbara, PD and Mema, Karen and Lloyd, Robby, Jamye, and Keisha. The numbers and stimuli had to be limited to minimize the drama.

Sheri had long since severed ties with the Reeses and the Melendys. She also refused to socialize with the Bairds. I didn't know why or care—these long-held grudges were made of spite, jealousy, stupid arguments, and a distorted, bipolar reality. Reluctantly, I chose Sheri's presence over others. I broke their hearts and bit my tongue.

Before the festivities, I received an acceptance into Texas Christian University's (TCU's) doctoral program in experimental psychology. I bubbled with joy and puffed up with pride. Sheri and Mark gave me a laptop and diamond earrings to celebrate. Both lovely. Both unexpected.

On December 20, 1996, I graduated from college with a BS in psychology. Walt, friends, and Sheri were present. With dignity, I crossed the stage toward what I now knew was my destiny. I heard Sheri's screams and cheers. I heard my ancestors' cries and hopes. I heard my offspring's giggles and songs. I bonded with Sheri over our mutual elation. And maybe, just maybe, our mutual achievement.

At the party, Sheri proved delightful. Brown and beautiful. Hopeful and helpful. Gathered up presents and paper as I unwrapped. She offered to frame a poster from Mark's sister—an image of an aboriginal girl surrounded by indigenous animals from Australia. It was a beautiful print, a kind gesture, and my favorite gift of the evening. At the conclusion, Sheri graciously thanked everyone for coming. She hugged. Smiled. Once alone, she promptly tore up the poster. Threw it in the garbage. Believed it to be demonized.

When the new semester started, I learned that confidence is fleeting and quite fragile. One moment, I floated into TCU on my accomplishments. I decorated my office, organized my desk, and met my fellow students. The next moment, I shriveled into a heap of idiocy inside the classroom walls. I was lonely. Lowly. Lost.

Danette had warned me about TCU's graduate programs after she tried the year before. She felt the same disillusionment I was feeling now, so she transferred. I heard her, but I did not listen to her. I thought I would succeed. I thought it would be different for me because I picked a different topic of study. I had a different major professor. It was a different year.

But by the third day of graduate school, the competition was palpable. Both the professors and students were cutthroat. I lost my stride.

I lost my balance. I lost my motivation. Still, I pressed on. Studied. Researched. Wrote. Taught. I lived and breathed psychology 24/7.

After each assignment, the professors posted rankings. I never made the top ten. Instead of motivating me, the rankings mutilated my confidence. I felt hollow. Incompetent. Out of place. Trashy. Cruel thoughts haunted me when I woke and as I fell asleep. *What are you doing in a PhD program? Who said you could be a psychologist? You're from a trailer. You're born of mental illness. Born of poverty. Born of ignorance. You have no business being here. You failed the eighth grade. They know you're a fraud. You need to quit.*

But I couldn't quit. Couldn't let go. I failed at failing. For five years, I'd prepared for a doctoral program. I didn't have a plan B. I wanted to be a psychologist, so I pressed on. While I labored, Walt and our crew partied. They made memories. They had inside jokes. They had a life outside of me.

Walt often voiced his loneliness and frustration. He begged me to hang out. To come home. To stop the insanity. I heard him, but I didn't listen to him. I barely noticed his affection. The proposals vanished; his songs and poetry in my honor ceased. His light and rainbow faded.

After the first semester, I still loved psychology but not my program. The idea of researching, experimenting, publishing, and filing my work away isn't what I wanted. I wanted to use my knowledge and apply research. I wanted to help people. But I was terrified to quit. I was terrified another program wouldn't accept me. Wouldn't give me a chance. Wouldn't see my capabilities. To add more anxiety on top of anxiety, I refused to tell anyone. I wanted advice, but I was too scared to ask. I couldn't face the humiliation.

During the semester break, I decided to rest. I needed to engage and reconnect with Walt. I wanted to party with friends. Walt and Jessie heard that Tripping Daisy were playing under a fake name in Denton,

Texas. I wasn't much of a Denton fan since I associated the city with Terr's time at Texas Tech and his dumb idea to enlist in the army. Regardless, I needed to escape and forget TCU for a night. I needed to be with Walt, Jessie, and Jamye, who was going to join us. We loaded up the car and headed to our destination, where we danced and sang all night. We killed all our brain cells and poured fun on top of fun.

At 2:00 a.m., we walked through the parking lot. A police officer was standing at Walt's car. We traded our silly drunk gait for a fake sober walk.

"Which one of you is Walter Salek?"

Walt raised his hand.

"Turn around," the officer said. "You have the right to remain silent . . ."

While we danced, the police ran license plates in the parking lot, and Walt had warrants out for unpaid tickets. As the police discussed the situation with Walt, another cop asked us to sit in our car. We complied. I positioned myself in the driver's seat. Five minutes later, an officer appeared at my window, knocking on the glass with his pinky ring. As the window retreated, my temper rose, and I vomited cuss words, accusations, and advice.

"Listen. Y'all need more education to deal with people. This is entrapment. Not to mention bullshit!" I ranted.

A quiet, scared voice from behind yanked my attention.

"Layla, stop. I have a warrant," Jamye whispered.

"I have a warrant, too," Jessie chimed in softly.

I heard them, but I didn't listen to them. I continued on my entitled tirade. Mid-bark, the cop angrily and abruptly walked away to talk to another officer. He pointed at me. I rolled up my window. Breathed deeply. Other cars were leaving the parking lot. Walt laughed with the officer.

"Layla, drugs are in this car. Lots of weed. Lots of mushrooms. And a case of beer. Please calm down," Jamye begged frantically.

My heart sank. My future disappeared. My offspring cried from the trailer. Inside the car, the air grew thick. Still. Tense. We all fixed our eyes on the cop as he walked toward us. He knocked on my window. I hated his pinky ring. His presence. His face. I rolled down the window once again.

"Yes, sir?"

He ignored my newfound respect.

"Ma'am, step out of the car!"

On pure instinct, sheer fear, and adrenaline, I slammed the car in reverse. Pushed the pedal to the floor. It accelerated beyond expectation, and I peeled out of the parking lot. Turned down the street.

"Stop!" the cop screamed as he ran to his car.

"Oh, shit!" Jamye yelled and fell back in his seat.

"You're going the wrong way on a one-way!" Jessie screamed.

I did a U-turn in the middle of the street and again passed the police, who were starting their cars. I passed Walt in handcuffs. I passed the point of no return. Jessie knew Denton because her sister lived there, so she took charge of directions.

"In three streets, turn to the right. One . . . two . . . *three*!"

I turned. The police lights disappeared, but the sirens grew closer.

"When I say, turn right down the alley and turn off your lights. Wait . . . wait . . . wait . . . *now*!"

I turned on her command. Shut off the lights. Shut off the car. We lay back in our seats. Didn't move. Didn't talk. Barely breathed. Lights and sirens came and went. After an hour—or maybe an eternity—we crawled out of the car and slithered into the house. We smoked pot while we decided our next move.

In between puffing and hysterically laughing, we determined a few things. We were wanted humans with a wanted car. We couldn't afford bail. We couldn't show our faces at the police station. We couldn't drive down the street. And we couldn't leave the house.

We lit another joint and popped a few more beers. We decided Walt's parents needed to be involved. Jamye and Jessie voted me to be the one to call them. I paced. I pleaded. And then I dialed. The phone rang. His dad answered. With a crackly voice and my friends snickering in the background, I halfway explained the situation, leaving out several important, criminal details. Walt's dad called back with his flight information and specific instructions less than forty-five minutes later.

By morning, Walt sat in the passenger seat of the wanted car. Walt's dad drove us back to Fort Worth while Jamye, Jessie, and I sat in the back, drugs unknowingly in tow. Jessie and I laughed nervously and uncontrollably the entire way.

We hated the situation, and Walt's dad hated us. This mishap damaged my relationship with Walt's parents and Walt's relationship with Sheri. Without knowing all the details, the situation stoked Sheri's now-unchecked paranoia, fueling her erratic emotions about Walter's age, intentions, and everything else Walter.

I tried to make light of it all, but Sheri failed to see the humor and couldn't let it go. Her continued paranoia made me suspect that she might be in a manic episode. However, I didn't ask about her cycles. Her meds. Her doctors. After I fled at fifteen, I lost the right to that information, and to even ask felt intrusive and wrong. Instead, I managed the situation and tried to shield Walt from her madness. This worked until Sheri left screaming messages on our machine. Black reverberated through our airwaves.

Amid this chaos, I returned to graduate school for the spring semester. I'd decided to propose a project to my major professor: the chance to apply his life's research at Union Pacific and see if his experimental findings yielded the same results in the field. His research centered around competition, cooperation, and intrinsic motivation. It was perfect for Corporate America.

He loved the idea, so we met with Union Pacific's attorneys, and they signed on. However, the chair of the Experimental Psychology program squashed the project and with it, my life raft and my sanity. Deflated and pouting in my office, a fellow student popped in.

"I just saw Walter. He got in the car with some girl," she said.

The oxygen evaporated from the room. My lungs. My heart. I sped home. I waited for Walt.

"Who were you with today?" I asked as soon as he arrived.

At first, he attempted to lie, but I found out the truth. He left. All colors disappeared but red. All feelings vanished but rage. I threw his belongings into the garage and rearranged the furniture as if he had never been. As my abandonment issues surfaced, I cried for hours. Slept for days. Stayed drunk for a week. Resumed grad school as a shell. Each day all my families offered love. My guy friends offered support and then some. Sheri seemed pleased Walt was gone. She stopped screaming. Stopped accusing. Stopped calling Walt's family "damn Yankees!" She blinked back to brown from black.

A week later, while I lay in bed, I replayed the last two weeks and realized I had zero notion of where Walt hung out or with whom. I was completely clueless. I only recalled an endless experience of classrooms. Assignments. Books. I lay in the dark and took stock of my life. Listened to my inner voice.

"I'll finish this PhD and then get a PhD in what I want," I heard myself say. *How ridiculously stupid. How ridiculously stubborn. Stop the insanity. Finish the semester, and then quit the program and find the right area of psychology for you.*

After this epiphany, a calm befell me. In prayer, I vowed to finish the semester. To stop worrying about grad school. About Walt. About Sheri. I rose from bed and blasted "The Rain Song" by Led Zeppelin. Smoking a joint, I was calm and open. My younger self appeared before me. White hair. Ratty ponytail. White nightgown. Roni Rabbit in hand. We stared at each other. We tried to recognize and understand each other. We both teared up.

"You'll be okay. I promise. Stop crying. We'll be fine. I won't let us down," I told her.

A few days later, Sheri asked me to testify for her to validate her mental illness and corroborate her inability to maintain employment. In other words, she needed my help to prove why she needed Supplemental Security Income (SSI). I agreed and informed my professors.

Jessie and I drove to Austin. We stayed at Sheri and Mark's apartment, where we laughed and drank until bedtime. I slept until anxiety crept in. As we ate Mark's breakfast, Sheri cracked jokes and Jessie slept. I sat silently while my ulcers bled. As we inched closer to the courthouse, Sheri's behavior turned erratic. She was easily irritated. Quickly angered. Worried about her bald spot and weight. Without warning, she turned hilarious. Then back to angry. Back to black.

Upon our arrival at the courthouse, her attorney placed me in the witness room. I read a book for school. Sheri's wail pierced through the walls at random times. Wail. Then nothing. Wail. Then silence. Another wail. Quiet. I felt sorry for her attorney. Pressure and accountability never mixed well with her and often shocked the shit out of those trying to help her. After an hour or so, the door opened, and Sheri's attorney motioned for me.

"How's it going? Is she okay? I can hear her," I asked nervously.

He laughed and shrugged his shoulders, looking defeated.

"She needs you in there."

As I entered the courtroom, eight people stared at me. All annoyed.

Possibly traumatized. Sheri smiled. The bailiff pointed to my seat. The judge introduced himself. He gave both Sheri and me a few instructions.

"Ma'am, if you continue with your outbursts, you will be removed. Do you understand?"

She flashed a gap-toothed smile and nodded. Her brownness pulsated nervously but beautifully. I sweated uncontrollably as both attorneys inquired about my childhood. About life with Sheri. About her incompetence. Her fights with employers. Her neglect. Her abuse. Her son. Her episodes. Her suicide attempts. I took sips of water in between questions. I answered. Succinctly. Honestly. Tensely.

It felt weird, as though the sequence of events was out of order. Sheri and I had never discussed these topics before. Not between us. Not with a counselor present. Not with a mediator. Not with a friend.

In that moment, I realized Sheri and I never discussed anything of substance. Nothing to heal us. Nothing to rebuild us. Instead, we lived in survival mode. Shifted between dark colors, chaotic episodes, and hurt feelings. Rested in between highs and lows. Buried the trauma and the past.

As the judge spoke to the attorneys privately, I went inward. *Somewhere, at some point, a psychologist should've worked with us. Should've helped us. Should've navigated mental illness and trauma with us. Instead, doctors drugged her and ignored me.* As the attorneys resumed, I wanted to stop the proceedings. Stop the questioning. I wanted to speak with Sheri alone. Without an audience. Without strangers. Without judges and attorneys. I wanted to yell, *This is not right! It's out of order! It's all wrong!*

Instead, questions persisted. One question after another. One attorney after another. My focus waned and divided into thirds: the voice in my head, the attorney's voice, and my speaking voice. All were distant and faint. All struggled for attention. After each question, I vaguely heard myself recount gruesome details.

The voice in my head rambled as I heard myself speak. *I can't believe I survived. That I'm upright. That I'm okay. And that I'm helping Sheri. My abuser. My neglecter. My mom.* When the attorney referenced the Family and me leaving at fifteen, Sheri wailed. I snapped back to reality. My focus narrowed in on her cry. Her dark demeanor. The dark brown heap.

The judge asked the attorney to repeat the question. He repeated it. I took my last sip of water. As my answer materialized, Sheri wailed again and physically broke down. The judge called a recess. Told everyone to leave. Demanded the bailiff to walk Sheri to the witness room. He asked me to remain seated. Sheri laughed uncomfortably while she exited, but her brown film remained. I felt light-headed. I asked for more water. The judge moved closer.

"How are you this put-together? I'm listening to your answers and at the same time looking at you. I can't reconcile your past with your present. I have many questions. Are you a student?"

I answered his questions as best I could, detailing my course of study and my present path. To my surprise and Sheri's luck, he was an alumnus of TCU.

"This shouldn't come as a shock, but I'm not a fan of your mother's. I don't like how she conducts herself in and out of my courtroom. However, I am a fan of yours. I'm going out of town right now. I'll write my decision next week. Thank you for your honesty and courage. Good luck with your future," he said.

We shook hands. He disappeared. As our tires propelled us home, Sheri giggled like a little girl. Apologized. Wiped tears from her tan cheeks. A month later, she received her first SSI check.

Depleted but enlightened, I returned home to a remorseful Walt.

A single Walt. An eager Walt. However, I was a skeptical Layla. A distant Layla. A prickly, burned Layla.

I focused on moving and found an apartment all my own. It was a perfect size. I perfectly decorated it. I loved the feeling of living alone. Of waking alone. Of adulting alone. However, I did not like being alone. I missed Walt. Missed our life. Missed his charm. Missed all the bright colors.

I wanted to go back to the beginning. Back to the days when Walt showed unexpectedly at my apartment and found me high, unshowered, and on the couch listening to "Summertime Rolls" by Jane's Addiction. Back to the days when he would whisk me off to an Italian restaurant, a movie, and then some unexpected adventure.

I wanted to go back to those days, but my past paralyzed my present. I knew I needed to forgive not just Walt, but my dad, my mom, the Family, and Chuck. I needed to let go of my heavy baggage. Of the feelings that I deserved to be abandoned. Deserved to be cheated on. Deserved to be painted black and discarded. Deserved to be alone.

I knew my past had caused these warped feelings, but I had no clue how to heal. Where could I start? To whom could I turn? In the absence of answers, I chose the only thing in my power. I chose to forgive Walt and see his love. I chose to see his youth and the humanness of his mistakes. Sheri, however, viewed Walt's indiscretions as a major character flaw and an indication of how he handled relationships—a sign of his future self. I heard her, but I didn't listen to her.

After much thought, consideration, and multiple conversations, Walt and I resumed dating but not living together. Without the pressure of pseudo-married life, our relationship felt light. Manageable. Age-appropriate. While he finished up his undergraduate degree, I completed a year of graduate school. Then I left TCU and started teaching children with disabilities—a job I loved and a population I adored.

While teaching these children, I witnessed their struggles, their strengths, and their accomplishments. I witnessed the work their parents and teachers did behind the scenes. I witnessed the importance of a support system. Of a team. Of help.

Am I helping Sheri enough? Could I do more? What does she need? I wondered.

When we talked, I began to inquire about her doctors, insurance, income, medication, and cycles. I inquired about everything but her bowel movements. She was forthcoming. Appreciative. She informed me that the only help she received was the SSI check, so I diligently researched doctors, funding, and recommended treatments. I discovered that, because of her Native American heritage and tribal card, she qualified for free mental healthcare.

With a bit more digging, I found a Native American psychiatrist in Dallas and made her an appointment. I drove Sheri to see him, and after the introduction, they met alone. I scanned his tribal memorabilia. Viewed his art collection. Felt at home in his office. Read a magazine. I waited. In under an hour, Sheri exited his office. Red-faced. Puffy-eyed. Deflated. The doctor followed close behind.

"Your mother needs consistent medication and treatment. However, she lives too far from me. This is like opening a can of worms I cannot ethically open knowing she can't see me regularly," he said.

I asked for referrals in Austin. Asked for any suggestions. He had none. We returned to square one.

In fall 1998, Walt planned a dinner at our favorite pizza restaurant in Dallas. When the pizza arrived, I noticed a gold box in the center. Before my synapses registered what was happening, Walt was kneeling on one knee and proposing. The gold box, which I first presumed to be Parmesan, held a beautiful pearl-and-sapphire engagement ring. After many years, more proposals, one breakup, and a makeup, I accepted. I leapt. I cried. As we drove back to Fort Worth, we stopped along the highway and used a pay phone to spread the news.

Within weeks, we set the date and busied ourselves with planning. On weekends, Walt and I trekked to Houston to discuss details with his parents and then trekked to Austin to discuss details with Sheri. Wrapped in our engagement bliss, we were blindsided by the problems that arose from all sides. Everyone had an opinion, a request, or a complaint, each of which was indignantly, rightfully based in family tradition. Family religion. Family finances. Family dysfunction.

From the beginning, Sheri and I were outnumbered. Out-financed. Out-argued. Outranked. Out-traditioned. With no money to fund a large wedding, Sheri and I explored outdoor options, small venues, and weddings on a budget. When Walt's parents offered to finance the event, we happily accepted. But with that one decision, our wedding became about their choices. Their wishes. Their traditions. Their church. Theirs.

Like a wave, their decisions rolled over me. Options came and went. They were planning alongside me but without me. Sheri and I felt deserted, discarded, and stripped of our expression. Our moment. Not wanting to appear ungrateful or demanding, I did not voice my concerns to his parents. Instead, Walt and I acquiesced.

However, the more I rolled over, the more enraged and aggressive Sheri became. She left screaming messages on my answering machine. Over and over. Louder and louder. My ulcers bled. I tried to calm her. Tried to explain. Tried to navigate all the colors. All the shades. All the tones.

"I love him. I want to be a part of his family. I don't want to cause any problems. Let's just get through this wedding," I explained during one of her meltdowns.

But she continued to yell. Loudly. Inaudibly.

"I love you. I love you. I love you!" I repeated louder and louder.

Nothing worked. The more Sheri pushed, the crazier she appeared to everyone. Except me. For the first time, I did not label her reactions as mentally ill, out of line, or irrational. I understood her position. It was mine as well. She expressed our collective disgust. Our collective grievances. I approached Walt with the idea of elopement. He agreed and broached the topic with his parents. They dismissed the idea with bribery.

"You will get more cash gifts if you have a wedding," they said.

Apparently, bribery worked. We rode the wave and left Sheri drowning in a brown wake. The wedding inertia moved on with force and intention. We had a deadline. Each decision, regardless of its significance, resulted in hurting the people I loved. They were excluded. Offended. Walt, being all of twenty-two, failed to mitigate the disaster, as did I at the ripe old age of twenty-six.

Three decisions caused significant damage and pain to my families. For one, Walt's parents insisted the wedding occur in their Episcopal church. Since my families were Jehovah's Witnesses, attending a church service of any kind was not an option. Therefore, the Melendys were out, as were Sheri and Mark. After the venue was solidified, Walt and I focused on the guest list and wedding party. During this time, I received a call from PD. Mema had colon cancer. She could not leave her home or doctors. They were out. I was devastated.

I turned to my dad. I craved his attendance, his approval, his validation. At the very least, he needed to meet Walt. I found my dad and set a date to see him, and Walt accompanied me. After formal introductions between Walt, my dad, my six-year-old sister and me, it turned into an odd encounter. None of us knew how to act or what to say. In a quiet moment, I slipped my dad the tuxedo information and wedding details.

"So, who's giving you away?" he asked.

"Joey, my best friend from the third grade," I answered, blushing.

His face fell. His color dimmed. His conversations turned light. Quick. Stupid. After promises and hugs, we left.

Days later, Sheri offered to pay for my wedding dress. I exhaled. Thanked her. I welcomed the chance to civilly discuss some part of the wedding. As we flipped through magazines and discussed styles over the phone, Sheri casually asked about my wedding colors.

"Since I have three groomsmen and two bridesmaids on my side, I decided the girls should wear long black dresses to match the black tuxedos," I explained.

Once the word "black" left my tongue, every emotion and every shade of brown spilled out of Sheri.

"What are you doing? Where is your fucking brain? Why are you letting these people control you? Does Walt have an opinion? Does he care that your family won't be there? Does he care about you? Do you care about your family? What are y'all saying to his parents? Whose wedding is this? Wake the fuck up! If you can't stand up to them, y'all don't need to be married! Walt is too young anyway," she berated.

I struggled to interject. Struggled to answer the questions. Struggled to defend Walt and myself. But I had no defense. She was right. Everything she said was right. In my pause, she continued. But with more black rage. More volume. More venom. More illness.

"You're telling these people they can walk all over you. That your feelings don't matter. That your family doesn't matter. Why? For a fucking wedding? A wedding in a church! Have I taught you nothing? Layla, you know that church is of Satan! Your ceremony will be of Satan! Those fucking black dresses are of Satan! My God. What are you doing?" she raged.

I hung up without a goodbye. I heard her, but I didn't listen to her, though I wish I had. That was our last conversation. Ever. In my anger, in my shame, in my retelling of the tale, I wrote her off as crazy, irrational, mentally ill. Others followed suit.

I abandoned her. I treated her poorly. And it was at a time when she was trying to be my mom. Like so many in her life before me, I abandoned her. For Walt. For a chance at a legitimate family. For a shot at a functional future.

———◆———

On May 29, 1999, Mr. and Mrs. Walter Salek married at St. Martin's Episcopal Church. A poem created by the groom for the bride was printed on linen wedding invitations:

> Kneeling in front of these pages, I write about love.
> Never will the oceans know the depth from which I speak.
> Nor the sunshine so bright as to shed light on this passion.
> For what is bestowed upon me is divine.
> Keeping her in my rapture shall not prove but isolation.
> But without her, I tremble with fear that there is no beauty
>   as hers.
> No peace shall beset upon my walls,
> All anger and greed encompassing,
> Because I have seen divine perfection in this world and above.

The groom's family and friends were present. A few of the bride's family and friends attended. The father and mother of the bride did not. Following the ceremony, the couple moved to Houston, Texas, where they sold their souls for a down payment on a house and fifteen hundred dollars cash.

16

Duped

Never let the truth get in the way of a good story!

—MY FRIEND TIFFANY SMITH

Hairspray. Cologne. Cigarette smoke. Laughter bellowed about. Love burst about the moment. Full and complete. Easy and comfortable. PD and Mema had arrived for a visit with their grand-children. Fort Worth was a pit stop on their way to Vegas, their favorite destination and pastime. And if they were in town, I was present with friends or Walt in tow.

I loved to show off my grandparents. Loved to show off PD. Loved the stories. Loved the show. On cue, the curtains opened, and PD dominated the stage. He performed with one of his instruments: his guitar or his wit. After a few pleasantries, PD hyper-focused on Aunt Rebecca's black Christmas tree with its disco ball ornaments.

"Well, that's straight out of Borneo. Deep Africa. That's some voo-doo right there, kids," he said.

As we laughed, he picked up the guitar and strummed for a bit. Then he spun tales of breaking out of and back into prison. Of fighting off an anaconda with a knife. Of touring with country legends. With each concluding sentence, Mema smiled and reveled in our reaction.

I particularly loved the new stories, especially the ones he wrote down and intended to publish. My favorite was "Jumpy the Frog," a children's story of a purple, polka-dotted frog with no friends or redeeming qualities. Initially, I believed PD wrote the story to encourage children to include everyone regardless of difference or disability. But as I read the manuscript, I quickly realized I was off the mark. It was a tale about avoiding those with differences. Steering clear of them to protect yourself. Before I could voice my concerns and to my horror, PD lashed out at the Japanese.

"I sent my manuscript to Japan to be published, but they stole it and never gave me money for it," he complained.

Thankfully, it was never printed. Never read. However, "Jumpy the Frog" became legend in our family—another tale that left us satisfied with aching cheeks, side stitches, and stories to recount for years. As PD and Mema left Fort Worth, their love and presence lingered and never left.

In 2001, I was deep into my master's degree when I received word that Mema's colon cancer had progressed. She needed surgery. The whole family reunited at the hospital. All her daughters arrived. All the grandchildren. Some brought friends, boyfriends, or spouses; others just brought their personalities.

As the new, unsuspecting audience introduced themselves, PD pounced. Since the fresh meat was not versed in his stories, he performed in the waiting room. As he spun and weaved, his grandchildren engaged in their own sideshows. Terr and Walt rapped lyrics from Dr. Dre's new album. Terr's brother and I visited empty hospital rooms. Answered phones. Told callers their loved ones had passed away. It was a typical Reese gathering.

After several hours of surgery, Mema rested. We congregated in her room and hovered around her bed. We took turns sitting next to her, rubbed her hands, and offered her water.

"This is the strangest thing I've ever seen since I landed on the moon," PD quietly said to Terr's brother as we all doted on Mema. Then he stood silent and somber. Withdrawn. Serious. After ten or fifteen minutes, he looked around at all of us, his family. Met our eyes.

"Did y'all know that your great-grandmother, my mom, was an Olympian?" he asked.

The grandchildren's eyes darted back and forth as they shook their heads and smiled with excitement and anticipation.

"She competed in the Olympics in Warsaw as an ice-skater," he continued. "For practice, she raced beside the trains on ice. Isn't that something? What do you think about that?"

We smiled. PD smiled wide and watched his grandchildren as our small talk grew to big talk. We were intrigued and thrilled by the idea that an Olympian's blood might course through our veins.

Mema shook her head and tried to open her eyes, no longer able to hide the truth. Honesty, or possibly anesthesia, took over in her moment of weakness. She shook her head, her eyes half-closed.

"The only truth in that story, kids, is that your Pappa Dave had a mom. None of his stories are true," she quipped in a soft, raspy voice.

On November 29, 2003, a few years after this day in the hospital, the *Abilene Reporter*, a newspaper in Abilene, Texas, wrote a story about Pappa Dave in a Life section piece titled "He Puts a Song in Their Hearts." The article highlighted how PD combined guitar playing with volunteering. Each weekend, PD found a captive audience at the state hospital. It talked about how his love of strumming and entertaining filled his time and how he never missed a show or missed a beat.

The photo attached to the article illustrated one patient's sheer joy listening to PD perform his favorite beer-drinking songs, often beginning with an original he wrote and recorded called "Good Old Drinking Song." Years ago, they said, it even reached number one in Merkel, Texas.

As grandchildren, we beamed with pride and anticipated the publication, excited for his ten seconds of fame. Our family's fame. Our fame. As with all gossip, the article disseminated with lighting speed and little precision. Terr called and directed me to check my email. I stopped everything to read the article. My eyes rapidly scanned the pages. With each sentence, with each story, my mouth dropped. At the end of the article, I sat still and stunned for minutes.

At the start, the piece focused on why and how PD came to volunteer in this manner. However, after sitting with PD, the reporter quickly realized he lived a fascinating life, so the final cut outlined his younger days. It talked about his "colorful life" touring with "Gary Jones, Merle Haggard, and Buck Owens." It shared that throughout his life, he learned "the words to five hundred songs" and "people stop and listen" as he plays "on the street corners." I erupted into laughter. Not one story about his early life in the article was true.

When I had gently asked PD about the *Abilene Reporter* years after and his tales of days with country legends, he'd replied, "I was on track to be a country star, but it was derailed by Jack Daniels," which was, of course, also untrue.

But on September 6, 2010, the curtain closed. Mema, the heart of our family, passed away.

17

Birthed

The question, O me! so sad, recurring—What good amid these,
O me, O life? Answer. That you are here—that life exists and identity,
That the powerful play goes on, and you may contribute a verse.

—WALT WHITMAN, "O ME! O LIFE!"

Waiting. Nesting. Planning. Growing. Bed resting. The anticipation alone prompted immense introspection and contemplation within me. Intense giddiness and nervousness coursed through me.

With each knock and kick from inside my belly, I dreamed of her hair. Her voice. Her eyes. Her nose. I prayed she had Walt's sister's hair. Long. Brown. Straight. Thick. I prayed she had my nose. Small. Pug. Feminine. I wanted her to be tall like her dad. Like my dad. She would be able to hold her own. Command respect. Walk as an equal among giants.

I prayed for life. For health. For twenty digits. For four limbs. For strong lungs. For big eyes. For a typical birth. For a brain free of mental illness. The news of a pending girl rather than just a pending baby incited fright in me. I felt pause. I had some sleepless nights. The what-ifs of a mother-daughter relationship swirled around my head.

What if I'm not good at mothering? What if a motherless daughter can't mother a daughter? What if Sheri taught me nothing but fear and trauma? What if I have nothing to offer? In Sheri's absence, I did have good role models: Mema, Karen, and Barbara. Those relationships were loving. Successful. Fulfilling. They will help me. Teach me. Guide me. I'm not alone in this uncertain, unstable world. Is the world truly unstable? Or just my world? Or my perception of the world? Am I foolish to bring a child into my world? How will my trauma affect her?

As I attempted to process my feelings, an all-too-familiar tug at my heart caught my attention. I wanted my mom or dad to answer these questions. To reassure me. To calm me. To hug me. Sorrow pulled on me with strength. The weight and my anger about mental illness pushed on me.

Then I felt a kick. A smile grew on my face. Gratitude filled my space. I fell asleep with Walt by my side, Skinner at my feet, and life flourishing in my belly. I dreamed of carrying my baby. Gently. Proudly. Securely. As I walked down the street, I softly bounced her in my arms. Stared at her puckered lips. Her pink cheeks. Her long eyelashes. Bounced until my baby folded into a purse. Transformed. Disappeared. Frantically, I tried to open the purse. Tried to push a button. Tried to undo what had been done. Tried to find my baby.

As I screamed, no one turned to help. Instead, everyone continued to walk. My mouth was open, but my screams were silenced. I couldn't produce any sound. Couldn't open the purse. Couldn't find my baby.

I woke. Frightened. Heart pounding. Hair soaked. Mind panicked. *Oh, shit, what if I lose my child? What if I forget her in a store or in my car? What if I hurt her? What am I doing? I can't be a mom. I don't know how.* My brain and my anxiety generated more and more what-ifs. Some reasonable. Some ridiculous. All day. All night.

Then, on the evening of May 6, 2003, after two botched IVs,

cramping, contracting, pushing, and pulling, I heard her cries. Her innocent, delightful sounds wiped away all the uncertainties. All the what-ifs. I reached for her, my arms outstretched, and my heart widened with anticipation as her tiny body collapsed on mine. And for the first time, I experienced yellow. My yellow. My sunshine. Our tears rose and rolled. Our bodies shuddered and shivered. I met my daughter, and I realized this most perfect being was mine. Truly mine. All mine. Created from my body. From all God's chemistry.

From thin air, a perfect, bright light materialized. A perfect Heris Oliva Salek emerged. In that instant, I transformed. I entered the hospital as one person and exited as a completely different one. I exited a mom. With Heris as my daughter, I would contribute my own verse to the tangled history of life.

Our decision to have Heris was intentional, and her birth in May was meticulously planned. By the time she arrived, I had completed my first year in the Educational Psychology PhD program at the University of Houston with an emphasis on behavior psychology. With this timing, I had an entire summer to be with Heris uninterrupted.

The hospital days were a blur. My training as a behaviorist kicked in. I instructed the nurses on a specific sleeping and feeding schedule I had predetermined. I slept when Heris slept and leapt with joy when my yellow woke hungry. Then my instincts as a mother lion took over. I did not want anyone to hold her. To look at her. To breathe on her. She was small and beautiful. Vulnerable and innocent. Dependent and mine.

Without a thought, my body became hers. I was no longer mine or Walt's. I no longer had an autonomous or sexual body. Rather, I was a feeding machine. A protective shelter. From the first touch, we were in sync. Inseparable. One. She latched immediately, not only to my breast but to my heart. To my life. To my every decision. We spent hours feeding, sleeping, and cooing.

But the more we gazed at each other, the less I understood my parents. I often hoped having a child would bring me closer to them. Help me grasp their decisions. However, it did the opposite, which I had not anticipated.

How could they experience me as a helpless child and abandon me? Did Sheri's mothering instincts never awaken? Is bipolar stronger than a mother's love? How could Sheri look at her own flesh and reject it? How could she leave me anywhere, at any time, away from her? Why? Did she not want me? Could she not deal with me? Did she want me at first and then slowly started hating me? Was I not enough to make her seek help? Or want to live? What was my dad's excuse? What was he feeling? Anything? Even before Heris was a thought, I knew I needed to break generational curses. All my major decisions were for her. So, why?

My line of internal questioning was harshly punctuated by a phone call to my hospital room. Walt and I looked at each other, shocked. The phone had sat silent for our entire stay. Not a peep. Walt reached for the receiver. A millisecond after bringing it to his ear, Walt's face transformed with anger. Sheri's screams pushed through the phone. Her black bravado reverberated the room. My heart pounded and sank to my feet. I pulled my yellow closer.

"I want to see my grandchild! You can't keep her from me! Do you hear me?" Sheri and her unchecked bipolar cried out with desperation, screaming as if she were in mid-argument.

Walt hung up and demanded the front desk hold all future calls. I knew then brown would absorb yellow. The two could never mix. Once we got home, our loved ones came to meet Heris Bean, the nickname Walt aptly coined. I struggled having people around her. I made up excuses to exit for a feeding. I only felt comfortable with Barbara or Walt holding her.

For the first week or so, Barbara, now Honey, stayed with me. She watched Heris in the evenings, helped around the house, and lightened my load. It was a loving gesture, especially considering Danette was home with a two-month-old. Honey made motherhood look easy and made my job easier. I could not fathom life without her.

When Honey left, I broke down. Walt calmed me. Reassured me. Helped me. He proved to be an attentive father. With each silly sound or airplane ride, Heris adored him more. She smiled wide at his colorful presence and stared at his every movement with her big green eyes. She took quickly to the men in her life, as if she realized they were characters. Fun. Unique. Humorous.

PD was the biggest character of them all. Heris laughed and swayed as he serenaded her with guitar and song. She seemed at ease with all her admirers and the world. She never cried or whined. She never caused problems. She smiled often, ate on cue, stayed on a schedule, slept through the night, and explored effortlessly throughout the day.

On the other hand, my brain, infected with anxiety, was morphing me into a mess. During any activity with Heris, the worst-case scenario flashed across my mind. I pictured her death several times a day. I saw her neck break, eyes poked out, legs bent in half, and skin severed. I cringed. My fists clenched. Eyes squeezed. Jaw tightened.

In the evenings, as she slept, I rested my hand on her belly. I needed to feel her body inhale and exhale. Needed to ensure life and breath. Needed to ward off disaster and death. When I was away from her or in public, I noticed peculiar behaviors in myself. I could only last about five minutes in crowds before I felt impending doom. Then I fled. In small groups at school, I completed my tasks, but it required constant self-talk. *You're fine. Heris is fine. Class is almost over. You got this.* Once I arrived home, I could relax. Breathe. Reset. But only for a moment. If the doorbell rang, I panicked. Scurried. Hid. I could not bear to see people. I could not visit. I could not make small talk.

Danette advised me to hang a robe by the front door and throw it on before answering, looking groggy and disheveled. The plan worked beautifully but only solved one issue. My social issues, all deeply rooted in fears over Heris, spun out of control. The fear of me losing her. The fear of her losing me. The fear or unforeseen circumstances. A mass shooting. A building collapsing. A plane crashing. A tornado forming. A car wrecking. A bird pecking my brain. The more I conjured up freak disasters, the more my body responded in sheer terror until I bolted and returned to yellow.

As her tiny feet mobilized and her babbles morphed into words, I felt an overwhelming urge to engage Heris in grand conversations about music. About animal behavior. Space exploration. Comedy. My thirty-year journey. Her parents' adventures. PD's stories.

Most importantly, though, I wanted to talk with her about the multiple topics Sheri failed to convey to me. Boys, first loves, friendships, enemies, hygiene, fashion, makeup. Girl stuff. Basic life lessons. I wanted our conversations to last for hours and encompass any and all tangents. I wanted it to be the opposite of Sheri's three-minute advice, only doled out while she dressed, walked out the door, or drove away.

"Don't sleep on your face. You'll get wrinkles."

"If something happens to me, check my pockets for money."

"Never depend on a man."

Whether or not Heris could grasp the topics at hand, I needed to have these conversations so she would never feel confused. Embarrassed. Alienated. A motherless child, I wanted to mother. Before a sentence left Heris's lips, I propped her up and discussed these grand ideas. I talked to her like an adult. Explained the movements of the smallest bugs. The patterns of the sun. The journey of a sea turtle. The importance of kindness.

At first, she responded with a weird, Mandarin-like language of her own. Her responses lasted thirty seconds. Her eyes blinked and her hands waved. However, before long, her pseudo-Mandarin transformed into complete English sentences spoken with a confident voice.

She had such a curious brain. For any comment or topic, Heris asked, "Why?" There were so many whys. On the flipside, Aunt Danette introduced, "Why not?" which opened Heris's mind to more possibilities. To more questions. To more subjects.

When we lunched in public, strangers marveled at her language skills. They watched, and I grew anxious over their stares and whispers. When they ventured to our table, I began to sweat.

"How old is she? Her language is impressive," they asked.

When I smiled awkwardly and answered, "Two," they inevitably looked amazed. I asked for the check, grabbed my child, and scampered home.

When Heris turned three, the next logical transition was imminent. I needed to work. She needed preschool. Our days of leisure, exploration, and observation were over. Thankfully, Heris was accepted into our first and only choice, the Awty International School. Upon our initial visit, the guide informed us that since the school taught second and third languages via immersion, students were required to attend until 3:00 p.m. I understood, but it felt as though they were tearing my child from my loins, kidnapping her, and dragging her into adulthood. I cried and ran out of the school.

Slowly and reluctantly, I shared my yellow. Returned to work. Continued chipping away at my PhD. Whatever I learned in my evening classes, I applied to my client base the next day. My studies and work life were intertwined by design.

I consulted for children with severe behavior disorders. I wrote behavior plans. Consulted and taught behavior. Trained staff and parents. I passionately used behavior psychology to change each child's way in the world, transform family dynamics, and alter their futures. With each success story, I imagined I was saving my mom. Saving someone's future parent. Saving someone's future childhood.

I often wondered how different Sheri would be, or I would be, if her family would have or could have intervened. *Would she have owned a franchise of housecleaning services? Or been a dancer like she dreamed? Would she have maintained a loving marriage with my dad? Or be best friends with me? What type of mom would she be? Attentive, strict, funny, compassionate? Who would I be? An astronaut, the president, or someone loved and normal?*

I vowed to help as many children as possible as I simultaneously vowed to ignore my own issues. My increased weight. My heightened anxiety. My decreased libido. My infected brain.

Instead of looking inward, I focused on carpooling. Seeing my yellow. Hearing her experiences. Marveling at her insights. When she entered the car, I always asked, "Did you teach them something today?" To which she either responded with details of her lessons or with my favorite response, "Well, I tried."

"I not know what they say," she said, sitting in her car seat with big tears in her eyes after her first day of Spanish immersion. When we got home, she clung to my side, we popped in a movie, and we napped for hours. We completed homework after naptime, both hers and mine. We ate dinner as a family and then collapsed in our sheets.

By kindergarten, most days Heris woke herself when the sun rose, made her bed and breakfast, and then dressed herself. When she appeared in my room, she asked for either a big ponytail or a small ponytail. I followed her directions as she outlined her day. For the final touches, she clipped a huge, colorful bow to her head. Then she kissed me goodbye, donned a backpack larger than her personality, and disappeared into the garage with her dad.

At 3:00 p.m., she reappeared in the carpool line with a crazy story or adorable sentence, like "My now is now!" which was her motto for kindergarten. Each day, she promptly set out to rule her world. With a unique bent on the twists and turns of her little life, her mind operated like a little adult—possibly a little dictator. Heris observed all and laid down the law.

"You're the boss! Not Heris!" I often reminded her nanny.

However, the dictator vanished, and the child materialized when words like "bookini" (bikini) and "re-memory" (memory) slipped from her lips. Pronunciations that, because of the cuteness, we purposefully did not correct for years. As she developed, Heris became more and more independent. And when she was age seven, I cried because I realized she no longer needed me.

While my yellow grew, I discovered ways to isolate myself. I stayed mostly with Walt and Heris during the week and the Bairds on the weekends. When I was home and not studying, photography became my creative outlet. It gave me the chance to forget childhood trauma, both my clients' and my own.

With Heris as my muse, I spent hours teaching myself film and digital photography. Macro and portrait. I spent more hours writing my dissertation and creating behavior plans. For my remaining hours, I swam in yellow.

Although each attempt to insulate myself from society was understandable, they also reinforced my social anxiety. Unconsciously, I modeled my maladaptive behaviors for Heris. When the doorbell rang, Heris and I both darted. Peeked out the window. Stood silent. When the phone rang, she and I looked at each other, laughed, and continued our activity. When the mail arrived, we sorted out bills and threw out the social invitations. When night fell and Walt was out of town, we shared a bed, scared. When a storm formed, we panicked.

I embraced fear and hid from life. The unknown. Old and new friends. "You went underground," Danette would say later. Walt participated in playdates with the Awty moms. He attended children's birthday parties and maintained our social calendar. In moments of bravery, I dressed for a cocktail party, kissed Heris goodbye, and held Walt's hand in the car. But inevitably, my bravery disappeared while waiting for valet. As we inched closer, my anxiety spiked.

"Walt, I can't do this! You can go, and I'll take a cab home," I blurted before the valet opened my door.

Quickly and thankfully, Walt returned us to yellow. While he was patient with my behavior, he drew the line when I decided to no longer fly on planes. Not for vacation. Not for an emergency. Not for any reason. I also refused to fly without Heris.

"What if we crash? She'll be parentless!"

Walt appeared puzzled but listened.

"You need to talk with someone. Your anxiety is out of control. You've stopped socializing. You've stopped sex. And now, you've stopped our vacations. We are too young for this," he said gently.

As he outlined my problems, I thought to myself, *And I've stopped living. I relentlessly think about suicide.* The idea of killing myself was a constant. A possibility. A solution. A way out. Once Sheri planted the seed and modeled it, suicidal thoughts and plans formed routinely. Unconsciously. Automatically. Sometimes in the face of a problem. Sometimes just for kicks. Potential ways to die tumbled about in my mind. All possibilities became possible. Once I settled on a specific possibility, I wondered if it would actually kill me, and if it did, I wondered what people would say. Would they harp, "Of course she committed suicide. What else was her fate?" Should my chosen method just maim me and leave me soaked in shame, would they say, "I told you so, and how pathetic!"

Usually, the ideations floated by like storm clouds. Colorless. Emotionless. I noticed them. Used humor to deal with them. Then watched them dissipate in the distance. If they hovered and swelled into an actual plan rather than just a possibility, I confided in Walt or a friend. The very sound of my voice, the shame in my gut, and the look on their faces dissolved the matter, at least until the next problem arose. Until the next storm blew in.

Either way, I believed I had it under control. I had no intention of leaving my rainbow or my yellow alone. Also, I didn't want Heris to know. I didn't want to transfer this burden or this dysfunctional coping skill to her. She was my reason to live. She was my reason to be.

With this in mind, I shielded her from my suicidal tendencies and agreed to seek help. My issues were interfering with all aspects of my life. In the evenings, I researched anxiety and suicide with urgency. I studied the latest research and techniques. Then, as if I were a client, I wrote myself an anxiety behavior plan. I created a suicide safety plan. I promised myself to follow both consistently.

I journaled two times a day, worked out three times a week with a trainer, and adhered to an individualized meal plan. Through the process of desensitization and positive self-talk, I participated in social events for a designated period, beginning with Heris's social calendar and then tackling mine. Once I could tolerate the set number of minutes, I systemically increased the time period I required of myself until I was able to enjoy the entire event.

With these interventions, my social anxiety slowly receded. My weight decreased. My libido increased. My colors brightened. My suicidal thoughts remained in the distance. All came together just in time for my dissertation defense.

Full of preparation, perseverance, and controlled panic, I stood in front of my four hand-selected dissertation committee members. As they engaged in small talk, a favorite lyric from Pink Floyd's "Fearless" repeated over and over in my brain: I was the idiot facing the crowd. I could think of nothing else.

"Layla, you may start," one of the members said, interrupting my loop.

Promptly, I smiled, cleared my throat, and recited my research. My method. My findings. As I spoke, their faces flattened. Their bodies adjusted. They frantically scribbled. No committee member offered any glimpse of hope or gesture of approval. As I concluded my presentation, each professor inquired about my methodology, statistical approach, and the future implications of my findings.

After my defense, they each thanked me and motioned me to the bench in the hallway, where I sat, sweaty and silent, ruminating over my defense. The inspiring high points, the humiliating low points. As the clock ticked, I contemplated escaping to my car and fleeing to Mexico. Instead, I engaged in positive self-talk. Paced. Called Walt. Waited. Tortured myself. My major professor opened the door. I rose to my feet. As I entered the room, each professor greeted me with a handshake and my new title. "Congratulations, Dr. Salek."

I floated home. Called Walt and Terr. Informed Danette and Honey. Planned my graduation. Dedicated my dissertation: *To my yellow: I trust that my achievements teach you that anything is possible, regardless of life's obstacles or criticisms. I dedicate this degree to you.*

In May 2007, I walked the stage in full regalia. After being presented with my degree, I faked a stomachache, exited backstage, and left the auditorium. Walking around the building, I threw my cap into the air and twirled in a private Mary Tyler Moore moment. Also in that moment, I craved my parents. I craved parental recognition and adoration.

But in their absence, in my hunger, I had an epiphany. In that instant, I understood what a miracle it is to be me. Statistically, I am an outlier. An anomaly. A deviation. A trailer-park, throwaway child who transformed into a success story. Into a successful behaviorist. Into a competent mother. I healed so my yellow could soar. Could do anything. Could be in love with everything. Tears wet my cheeks. My smile touched my ears. Every cell in my body bathed in my accomplishment.

As usual, the Texas sun melted our summer plans. However, throughout elementary and early middle school, I turned the hottest weeks of the year into "Mom Camp"—an at-home camp where Heris and I followed a self-created syllabus and schedule. In the mornings, we focused on exploring various topics, from the blues and rap to the scientific method and reproduction, to cinema, fiction, and nonfiction. We completed scavenger hunts, collected specimens, and evaluated them under the microscope. We turned our home into a lab. We questioned all our surroundings and life's mysteries, known and unknown. After lunch and a nap, we rode bikes, created pottery, planted flowers, and attended tennis or horseback riding lessons. Our days were busy with expanding Heris's world. Solidifying our bond. Understanding her mind.

Heris proved to be black and white, rule- and routine-oriented, bossy, and confident. She was wickedly and unapologetically smart. Proficient in piano and languages, she was an expert in Taylor Swift and Johnny Cash. She was so easy to parent and fun to be around, I almost felt sorry for other parents until, one day, I was faced with one of my deepest fears.

One day during Mom Camp, Heris awoke from her nap, dropped to the carpet, walked to her window, and urinated on the floor. The first day it happened, I cleaned up everything, processed the situation with her, and moved on. When the same behavior occurred the next day, fear seeped into my consciousness. After Heris and I cleaned, I analyzed all the stimuli. I discussed her behaviors with Walt. On the third day, I panicked. Cleaned. Cried.

I curled into a ball. For hours, I felt the fear. *What is wrong with her? Is she mentally ill? Is this how it starts? Have I caused this? Is Sheri manifesting in her? What do I do? How do I fix this? I fucking hate mental illness! Should I suffocate us both?* Once my tears and anxiety turned into honesty and humor, I created a behavior plan. Interrupting Heris's routine, I placed her in my bed for naps. When she woke, I immediately walked her to my bathroom. The urinating on the floor stopped.

However, her odd behavior didn't. Randomly, in the middle of the night while I slept soundly, my brain detected someone staring at me. As my consciousness pulled me from slumber, my eyes fluttered open to a face just inches from my own. Instinctively, I screamed and jumped. Walt yelled. Heris cried. After the fourth time, I realized these bizarre behaviors were not signs of mental illness, but rather symptoms of sleepwalking. I exhaled for a moment.

As yellow dictated our world, we stepped in line with the American ideal. Two working parents. Two-car garage. Two fluffy pets. Two vacations a year. With Honey in tow, we set out to create memories in St. Martin, Belize, Lake Tahoe, and Europe. At any destination, at any age, Heris tirelessly played with Honey. Nipped at her heels. Copied her. I took great pleasure in observing them—their easy movement and conversation, their certainty of each other's love and reciprocation.

As sand and water flowed in and out of their fingers and toes, I thanked God for Honey and her presence in my life. For her love in Heris's life. Mid-prayer, my mind turned to Sheri. To her existence. To her state. To her absence. I began analyzing society's role, my role, and Sheri's role in bipolar's destructive hold. I tried to picture Sheri and Heris swimming in the ocean. Laughing in the breeze.

Heris and Honey

Walking hand in hand on the beach. But the imagery felt wrong. Felt forced. Felt fake.

Why can't I imagine Sheri with Heris? Would she play with her grand-daughter, or would she hide in her room, angry and sulking? Would Sheri scare her or make her laugh? Would Heris even like her, or would she still prefer Honey as her grandmother? As Heris ages, will she cry because she did not know her, or will Heris understand my decisions? Understand that I tried to help her, or will she hate me for keeping them apart? Maybe, just maybe, my yellow would brighten Sheri's dark world. Inspire well-ness. Inspire good choices. Maybe I am wrong.

As I stuffed Sheri deep into my bones, middle school approached. I braced myself for hormonal chaos. For emotional outbursts. For broken rules. But to her parents' delight, Heris continued to be consistent and predictable. She embraced the challenges brought on by puberty. Mean girls. Boyfriends. Academics.

Surprisingly, however, bees, needles, mascots, and tests rattled her. Caused anxiety. Caused concerning behaviors. When I witnessed these fears, I found strategies to help her. I booked hypnotherapy sessions to eliminate the phobias, but hypnosis did nothing. Her mind was resistant to hypnosis. Peer pressure. Suggestions of any kind. She was unshakable. Immovable. Impermeable. Stood her ground. Stayed the course.

When her future goals changed from becoming a detective to forging a path as a spy, it made complete sense. Heris listened and observed more than she spoke. She maintained a constant poker face. She never disclosed personal information. When she bought a new phone, she turned in her old one to be erased. Wiped clean. Destroyed. She even hid her money in picture frames hanging on the wall.

If there was an incident at school with friends or teachers, we were forced to use psychological tactics to gain information. When we asked questions backward and forward, Heris turned into a statue. Said nothing. Stared in space. Short of waterboarding her for answers, it took time and energy to break her down.

Before our eyes, she morphed into a personal investigator. She bought gadgets and apps to aid her quest research into anything and anyone. She noticed the nuances in people's behaviors and patterns. She relied on and tested her gut instincts. She practiced playing dead in the pool "just in case it is ever needed."

Not only were her psychological skills impressive, but she was a perfect shot. The first time Walt took her to the gun range, he texted me a picture of the target. All her shots hit the heart and head. Shock and awe dissipated my worry and concern when we realized Heris could take care of herself and possibly rule the world.

Once again, I wished I could tell my parents about Heris's proclivities. I wanted to see Sheri smile. I wanted to hear my dad recount Heris's tales to his friends. While trial and error told me my dad was not an option, I tortured myself about Sheri. I tried to determine if she could handle a relationship with me. With Walt. With Heris.

Maybe society has assisted Sheri at this point. Maybe someone has taken some responsibility and acknowledged the humanness in her mental illness. Offered aid. If not, with no meds, no intervention, no psychological help, is it selfish of me to bring Sheri around my new family? Around Walt's family? Around an innocent child free of trauma? But if I decide to keep her away, will Sheri ever know her granddaughter? Ever know how intelligent she is, or how much Heris looks like her? Or that Heris's name is spelled in her honor? Will she ever know that with one movement of the letter S, Sheri becomes Heris? If she knew, would it change anything? Would Sheri run to me and hug me? Would she want me? With Heris as her granddaughter, do I have enough to offer?

As I wrestled with a mother's guilt and a mother's love, I decided to be transparent about my childhood with Heris. One summer afternoon, with gentleness and intentionality, I had the conversation with Heris. All ears and all eyes, my yellow absorbed the tales of her blood family and not-so-blood families. She heard of those who adopted me, and those I adopted. I concluded our talk with her genetic predispositions, her Native American heritage, and her Irish lineage. Silence settled in, and anxiety waned.

"I don't ever want to be around anyone that hurt you. Honey is my grandmother," Heris said.

And with that, my yellow dissipated the confusion. The darkness. The storm clouds.

18

Polarized

My identity constantly shifted because of her,
oscillating between two halves of me—the one that was
trying to please her and the one that was trying to live.

—FARIHA RÓISÍN, "LIVING WITH
MY MOTHER'S MENTAL ILLNESS"

In defense of being raised by a bipolar mother, I possess the ability
to bob and weave throughout all aspects of life. I can bob in and
out of different families. I can weave with any education level. I can be
alongside those from all walks of life. Deep within my being, I inhabit
the extremes and everything in between. I draw and pull whatever personality traits, behavior, and skills are best suited for the scene at hand.
I can be seedy. Mainstream. Classical.

I can be whatever is ordered because I am:

An orphan of four families
An only child with five siblings
A motherless child with three mothers
One person with several aliases
Homeless with multiple homes
An academic failure with a PhD

A trauma victim healing others' trauma

Alone with many friends

An insecure child with boundless confidence

A girl who prefers boys as friends

Suicidal while loving life

White trash in high society

Affluent but still feels poor

Voiceless with a respected voice

A motherless daughter mothering a daughter

A teen with bad behavior teaching behavior to teens

A psychologist who distrusts psychiatrists

An expert who feels like an amateur

A person who creates order from chaos

Serious with a wicked sense of humor

Scared but fearless

A childlike adult

Anxious but laid-back

A person with an active mind and a lazy body

A person who lusts for consistency but has a taste for chaos

Repelled by mental illness but attracted to pain

A problem becoming a solution

A victim of trauma but never a victim

Born out of darkness into a rainbow

A daughter who abandoned her mother but craves her
    mother's love

19

Reattached

Love is that condition in the healing spirit
so profound that it allows us to forgive.

—MAYA ANGELOU, *OPRAH'S SUPER SOUL SUNDAY*

In the winter dark, we passed through Arlington, Texas, in Terr's truck. Street after street. House after house. Car after car. People tended to their lives. Their struggles. Their triumphs. Their chores. My hyper-awareness spiked as we inched closer to an unknown address. Closer to an unknown family. Terr drove. Jessie sat in the back. I stared out the window from the passenger seat.

The moment felt right but surreal. Like a familiar dream. Like a glimpse of something I craved but could not grasp. At the core of the unreal-ness, a heavy reality grounded me in its true reality. In how truly profound the experience was. In how important it was for me to soak up each second of this event. This encounter. This long-awaited meeting. I needed to feel how this meeting, the first in fifteen years, could possibly be the last. And I had to do it alone. No Terr. No Jessie. They could not continue with me past the drop-off.

"Call when you're finished. We'll be close," Terr stated, looking worried.

I closed the door. Stood paralyzed. I was having too many thoughts to latch on to just one. Too many emotions to sense just one. I caught my breath. Felt my heart. Walked toward the front door. In the pause after I rang the doorbell, I caught a thought. *Wow, he lives here. All these years, he's lived right here. Only fifteen minutes from the Bairds.*

The door unlocked. The handle turned. My stepmom, Priscilla, appeared. We hugged and made small talk while we moved through their house. Moved in the direction of Ron. I was unprepared to come upon a man lying on a couch. He was frail. Sick. Bald. Skinny. Pale. My dad was dying of bone cancer.

"Dad keeps asking for you. He would like to see you. He wants me to update you on his condition," one of my sisters had informed me two months prior.

After years of therapy, I was at peace with him. I needed nothing from him. Once I chose to believe my dad loved me, I released all pain and attachment. I possessed no desire to go in reverse. To depend on him again. To want him again. To be abandoned again. I was primed to release him. But my sister kept calling.

"He stopped breathing for a period. A priest is about to read his last rites," she said.

The information hurt my heart but didn't alter my position until a conversation I had with Danette's husband.

"You may not need anything from him, but what if he needs something from you before he dies?" he asked.

I listened. I shifted. I wrote my dad a letter. I spewed my guts and organs onto the page. Detailed my life with and without him. Outlined my innermost grievances and realizations about him. I recounted my depth of despair over losing him. Meticulously, I related a firstborn's admiration, almost idolization, of him as my hero. As my best friend. As my father. With each sentence, I let honesty dictate our relationship moving forward. No matter how brief. No matter how significant.

Somewhere between leaving the hospital, returning home, and receiving a stem cell transplant, my dad read the letter. Still, he requested my presence. And now, here we were. Face-to-face. Smile to smile. Father to daughter.

My breath caught. His body on the couch. His facial expression. They stumped me. Shocked me. Soothed me. He looked relieved. Excited. Ready. He looked as if he was waiting for me all these years. Waiting for me to walk through the door. Pull up a chair. Join him for a drink. My green was waiting for my return.

In that moment, his absence felt like a blink. A snap. A ripple. Time collapsed. Grievances dissipated. As he labored to speak, the man on the couch materialized into my dad. I recognized his tone and inflection. His handsome features. His beautiful smile. His spark. His wit. Within minutes, I was hooked. Back in love. Absorbed in green.

I cried all the way home. Relief and release.

A month later, at my dad's request, I returned. Unsure of his physical and mental state, I dropped all my appointments to spend a day with him. As my plane slid along the icy runway, I spied a tall, healthy blonde standing in the waiting area. Tears came and my smile swelled. Once off the plane, I ran to him. We hugged. He told me he beat bone cancer.

And now, I have a dad. My very own dad. My dad. Just saying the word "dad" felt satisfying. Fulfilling. Warming. Felt green. Our conversation over lunch and a beer in his favorite Mexican restaurant was more than I could absorb. Energy jolted and pulsated throughout my body. I became giddy. Smiley. Dare I say, happy. *This is my dad! He's going to live! We are fine!* I wanted to yell at all the customers. Instead, we played catch-up.

He inquired about his granddaughter, Walt, and my career. I learned about his, Priscilla's, and my three siblings' lives. Priscilla ran marathons, and my dad still found her beautiful. We discussed how one of my sisters and I reconnected randomly one evening at a bar, and how she lived with her boyfriend of many years. My brother graduated from Texas Tech. He loved acting, the ladies, and being a personal trainer. My youngest sister looked like Heris and me. She attended the University of Texas at Arlington and waited tables. I reveled in each bit of information until it was time to board my plane. Then I returned home as a daughter grounded in the presence of her father. Grounded in green. I'd released this feeling and belief so long ago but was so thankful for its return.

In relaying my day of bliss to Walt, I realized my husband was unfocused. It felt like a narrator interrupted our lives with "And now the role of Walter Salek is being played by . . ." He was drunk. Uninterested. Possibly not even living in reality. It wasn't him. The man looked like him and sounded like him but didn't act like him. His eyes were black. Hollow. Remote. His being was disconnected from reality. He was nestled in some place I couldn't reach. Couldn't penetrate. I couldn't pull him back. No colors. No light.

From that night on, I began to hyper-focus on his behaviors. I replayed the last two weeks in my mind. I examined. Inspected. Probed. He denied. Gaslit. Squirmed his way out of the interrogation. But I continued in my pursuit to find clues. Details. Information. Anything to explain his strange behavior.

As friends and family swapped stories, we realized each household in our orbit had a bottle of vodka in their freezer for Walt. Each time he visited, he returned to the freezer over and over for shots. Walt was drinking too much. Gone too much. Protested too much when I asked. One morning, I started counting his drinks. As he downed his thirtieth drink of the day, my heart sank. My world toppled. My Walt spiraled.

During my pursuit of answers, Walt took a hunting trip with friends. I snooped through his belongings. Acquired his text messages. Questioned his friends and colleagues. Lost myself. Lost my dignity. Lost my mind. I didn't recognize either of us. I despised the sneaking and spying wife I was becoming, but I despised a dishonest husband even more. I couldn't trust Walt. Not his words. Not his behavior. Nothing added up. Nothing made sense. He barely called home from the trip. When he did, his stories sounded like tales. Tall fictitious, outlandish tales.

"Sorry, I haven't called. My phone fell into the AC vent. It took days for workers to retrieve it," he'd say.

After a week, Walt returned home with two friends from the hunt and, intentionally, I inquired about their adventure. I knew his friends were lying. Immediately. Their words fumbled. Eyes darted. Feet shuffled. Stories crumbled. At the first opportunity, they escaped and left Walt behind. As the front door closed, I asked Walt to join me in our room. Walt sat. I stood. I spoke and held a sealed envelope.

"Do you want to be married?" I asked. Simmering.

"Yes, of course."

"Do you want to be married to me?" I pressed.

"Of course!" he answered again. "Where are you going with this?"

I stared at him for a moment. Penetrated his dark eyes. His colorless soul.

After some silent seconds, I continued.

"In this envelope is everything I discovered about you and your travels. I consulted a private investigator, our family, and friends. Is there anything you would like to tell me?"

Walt's head dropped. I braced myself. The space between us expanded exponentially. His remaining colors dimmed. He felt foreign. Ill. Guilty. As a couple, we felt fragile. Broken. Over. But what fell out of his mouth floored me. Devastated me. Shook me to my core. I could hardly process his words. I only understood fragments. No details. No complete sentences. Random words such as "stripper," "New Orleans," "drugs," and "thousands of dollars" broke through, then muted. Red filled my vision. I threw him out. As I held the door open, Heris appeared. Pleaded for us to hug. Physically pushed us together. We complied coldly and then parted. Bag in hand and headed for the car, his tall stature looked diminished. His ego deflated. Gray. Dim.

I held my yellow while she broke into pieces. As we rocked in silence, old feelings flooded my senses. Memories of wanting and begging for my dad sat heavy on my heart. I knew how Heris felt. I hated that she, too, was experiencing the loss of her father. I wanted to shield her from the pain of abandonment. Shield her from the confusion and loneliness of divorce.

While swimming in my sorrows, the doorbell rang. To my surprise, but apparently at Heris's request, it was a close friend and neighbor. We talked for hours.

"We'll be fine. Please don't worry. Go home to your family," I reassured her.

But I was lying. Nothing was fine. Far from fine. I needed to be alone with my daughter. Alone with my thoughts. Alone in my home. Once Heris slept, I craved my trailer. Craved something I understood. Craved warmth and companionship.

But who do I call? Who do I disrupt? Who do I involve in this bullshit? Once again, my life is filled with drama. And now, Heris's life is shattered! I'm so ashamed. But why? I did nothing wrong.

I fought the moment. Resisted. Collapsed. Heard my familiar suicidal script. Slept. Woke crying. Suffered. Resisted. Then accepted. Not necessarily in that order. Not that quickly.

Throughout my history, during any crisis, the sunrise saddened me.

Small Layla hated waking to a fresh day. A fresh start. A fresh look at life continuing without me. *Doesn't the sun know I'm in pain? I can't move. I can't regroup that fast. Life must stop so I can think. Cry. Sleep. I need time. I need space! I need help!*

Amid the loss and chaos, amidst the cleanup and process, I wanted my dad. Needed his wisdom. Yearned for his support. But I couldn't involve him with us just newly reunited and him newly healthy. I couldn't insert my drama into his world. Couldn't harm him. Couldn't drive him away.

I screamed at God instead. Fell to my knees. Buckled. Surrendered. My throat burned. Tears and snot wet my face. I couldn't believe God's plan. How could He return my father and simultaneously remove my husband? How could He replace one male figure for the next? Did He replace one family for the other to ease the abandonment? To lessen the heartache?

After I pushed myself from the floor and pulled myself upright, I informed my family: Danette, Honey, and Walt's immediate family. Danette drove to Houston. Honey called several times a day. But to my surprise, Walt's parents offered no help. No support. Because of their own shame, their own dysfunction, they couldn't or wouldn't extend an ounce of kindness to any of us. Walt's brother, however, proved himself the family ambassador and helped when he could. Once I secured our family support system, I informed a few close friends, who responded with compassion. I leaned in and built a cocoon around Heris and me. I licked our wounds. Focused on answers and solutions. Convinced Walt to meet with a psychiatrist.

The following week, Walt and I met at the doctor's office. A silent elevator ride to the fourth floor preceded a silent stay in the waiting room. Words weren't necessary. Sufficient. Supportive. By that point, we had said too much. Some things hurtful. Most things unhelpful.

We had sunk to the dark depths of relationship hell and were actively clawing our way back through silence through grief with intention.

When Dr. Cambor opened the door, we both jumped. We followed the little elderly man as he shuffled to his seat. On cue, Walt and I took turns outlining the problem. As we each saw it. As we each experienced it. When our stories concluded, Dr. Cambor shook his head and shuffled back through his door and returned with two surveys. Asked Walt to complete the survey from his perspective regarding his behaviors. Then asked me to complete the survey from my perspective regarding Walt's behaviors.

When we finished, Dr. Cambor collected our assessments. He scored and analyzed them while we watched. We waited. We anticipated. After an eternity, Dr. Cambor looked up at Walt.

"Walter, you have bipolar disorder. You received twelve out of twelve on both of the Goldberg Bipolar Spectrum Questionnaires," he stated matter-of-factly.

I quivered. My head fell. Images of Walt's odd behaviors throughout the years glitched in my brain. His struggle with drugs and alcohol. With money management and transitions. With honesty and relationships. His colors fading. His lights flickering.

How did I miss this? Why didn't I know? What kind of psychologist am I? What kind of wife am I? How ignorant can I be? Oh shit, what if Heris is bipolar? How in the hell did I marry someone bipolar? Am I attracted to mental illness? Attracted to pain? Will I ever be free? What have I done? Am I being punished? Is it my karma for abandoning Sheri? Will Sheri always follow me? Is she of me and living within my dysfunction, living within my marriage, living within me?

A mental image of me as a ringleader formed in my mind. I stood in the middle of a circus on a tall, round stage in a red-and-white tent. I was directing everyone with mental illness. Young and old. Known and unknown. Clients and family. Managing the chaos as vibrant colors flew through the air. As their talents and beauty were on display. As they twirled. Sang. Painted. Danced. Cried. Risked. I watched in awe but felt no peace. I attempted to keep us all upright. Functioning. Living. I attempted.

The cheers turned to jeers, and I felt my anxiety rise. My heart raced. I started losing control. I needed more arms. More hands. More eyes. More tools to juggle the mayhem. But no matter my efforts, the performers crashed and fled. The colors fell to the floor. Fell to my feet and left me far behind. Empty. Depleted.

As my energy drained, I felt the presence of Walt and Dr. Cambor again. I sensed my body in my chair. While pushing through profound confusion, a deep, primal sigh left my body. Once again, words failed me. I sat defeated. Triggered. Swallowed whole. Walt observed my reaction.

"Layla will divorce me now," he said.

But I couldn't. With every bone in my body begging me to bolt, I couldn't. With my inner child screaming at my adult self, I couldn't. With loved ones validating and encouraging me to divorce, I couldn't. With all the embarrassment and humiliation surrounding our name, I couldn't. With one look at Heris, I couldn't leave her without a dad or leave her dad ill. With one thought of Sheri, I couldn't abandon Walt.

Ultimately, my decision to leave my mom failed us both. It failed to cure her bipolar. Failed to bring about peace. Failed to mend our relationship. Failed to solve any of my childhood problems. To my mind, leaving a loved one to battle mental illness alone fails us all. The patient. The spouse. The child. The family. The friends. The community. No one wins. No one heals. Everyone remains in the dark.

So I stayed and vowed to fight bipolar. Vowed to fight for Walt. Our family. Our reputation. Our sanity. I accepted my role. I placed my

Layla, Walt, and Heris

top hat on my head, buttoned my coat, straightened my tails, tied my black boots, and stepped onto the stage. I got to work. Immediately and meticulously, we followed Dr. Cambor's plan. Even though it was expensive and time-consuming, his plan was our only hope.

Walt completed an outpatient drug and alcohol rehab program. Took his medications. He attended individual counseling. We attended marriage counseling. With Heris and me as his cheerleaders, Walt worked hard to take control of his life. With each step, his rainbow returned. The universe rewarded us all. Our family unit slowly functioned with a modicum of trust and comfort. We always operated from a place of love.

After months in the trenches, my dad texted me. Green tinted the moment.

Come into town tomorrow. Let's talk about your horrible parents, he wrote.

Any other topics? I replied.

Why you're a Democrat? he quipped. He had wit for days.

Never mind, I shot back with a smile emoji, *let's talk about my horrible parents. See you tomorrow for happy hour.*

I drove one hundred miles per hour to Arlington in pursuit of more time with my dad. More conversations. More answers. More more-ness. We threw back a few beers at his house and then headed to a dive bar. Whether in the house, in the car, or in the bar, his words were intentional. They embodied years' worth of his thoughts. In between and over songs, he shared questions and comments about himself or Sheri in relation to me.

"You can call me any time of the night, even three in the morning, and yell at me. Cuss me out. I'll take it."

I felt his parental guilt and boyish shame. Felt his fatherly love and profound sincerity. Each statement hung in the air with compassion and healing intentions. I matched his energy and purpose.

"Dad, I'm not angry. I was never angry. I was just so sad. I just missed you."

He listened and fumbled with the radio.

"I would understand your anger. I deserve it. What kind of father signs over parental rights to strangers?" he asked after a few quiet moments.

And there it was—the reason my green stayed away. The reason he didn't attend my wedding. The reason for so many of his behaviors I never understood and struggled with for twenty-five years. Those behaviors for which I blamed God. Blamed myself. Blamed Sheri.

I reflected on all the years we wasted. All the lost moments. All the hurt caused. I fought tears. I wanted to grab his hand. Wanted to comfort us both. Wanted to squeeze away the pain. Instead, I offered clarity and accidentally added to his guilt.

"Dad, I asked you to sign over your rights. I was fifteen. I didn't realize what I was asking you. I just couldn't live with my mom anymore, and I didn't want to burden you," I said.

"Well, that's horrible, too," he said as soon as the word "burden" stepped into our atmosphere. By the end of the evening, however, we joked about tough topics in typical Reese style. Flung one-liners. Made light of trauma. Frolicked in green.

"I went through three stages with your mom," my dad said. "First stage, I was madly in love with her. Second stage, I was mad as hell at her. And third stage, I was scared to death of her."

We laughed and laughed at Sheri's expense because we both experienced those three stages. We had earned that right. We genuinely knew her. And at one point, we both deeply loved her. Through boozy sarcasm, we cleared the air, aligned ourselves, and moved on.

I visited my dad and siblings often, sometimes bringing Heris and Walt for a weekend. It was a welcomed, albeit delicate, juggle to spend time with all my loved ones. I stayed with Danette and her family, shared a long, loving lunch with the Melendys, and chilled with my dad for happy hour and an evening of fun. Heris put it best.

"Mom, you have too many families," she said on more than one occasion.

I always nodded and smiled in response. I thanked God for answering my childhood prayers. For placing these families in my path. For returning my dad. For filling my life with love.

With each visit, I focused on gratitude and deepened my relationships. To my delight, I realized how much my dad and I are alike. As a child, I only knew our features favored each other, but as an adult, I learned we possessed parallel personalities. We were both hypochondriacs. Both laid-back with a temper if pushed. Both tend to be socially anxious. We possessed similar senses of humor, like mannerisms, and the same taste in music and movies. With each unearthed similarity, I reveled in knowing where my traits originated. Knowing where I was rooted. Knowing where I belonged.

But after each long, loving weekend, trust issues seeped into my consciousness as we pulled away from Arlington. Butterflies danced in my stomach. Negative thoughts bounced around and multiplied. *What if that's the last time I see my dad? What if I offended him? What if he changes his number? Or moves without telling me? What if cancer returns and he dies? What if . . .* I mentally and emotionally tortured myself for hours. Sometimes days.

One negative thought gave birth to another. Often, disruptive thoughts of my dad morphed into fearful thoughts about Walt. *What if Walt stops taking his meds? What if Walt leaves Heris and me? What if he decides treatment isn't worth it? What if he ruins his career or hurts our loved ones? What if he commits suicide? What if I commit suicide?* Even with Walt working on his treatment plan, even with my dad proving dependable and healthy, the same unfortunate pattern repeated.

I consulted with my psychologist in an attempt to process the effects of my childhood trauma and identify my current triggers.

"The juxtaposition of Walt's crisis and diagnosis along with your dad's return and near-death experience triggered abandonment issues causing extreme anxiety," she stated after a few sessions.

With this in mind, she administered a measure to assess the level of childhood trauma I experienced. The results floored me. Out of ten possible childhood traumas a person can experience within the immediate household—verbal abuse, physical abuse, sexual abuse, no family support, neglect, divorce, spousal abuse, drug abuse, mental illness, or parent in prison—I experienced eight. The only two I escaped were sexual abuse and a parent in prison.

As she discussed the findings, I ruminated. *How can I function as a successful adult and mom with all this trauma? How am I able to help others? How am I upright and relatively happy? How did I ever leave the trailer? My God, how did I survive childhood?* Eventually, I voiced my concerns, and we analyzed them over and over. Back and forth. This way and that. The following session, my psychologist administered the Resilience Questionnaire from the Trauma Informed Care Project. Out of a possible fourteen, I yielded a score of thirteen.

"Because of the access you had to loving people such as your grandparents, the Melendys, the Bairds, and even Snuggles, resilience developed and thrived within you. This enabled you to survive intense trauma," she explained.

Regardless of the hurt inflicted on me, I believed I was loved. Worthy of love. Capable of love. Therefore, I did not internalize the abuse or identify with it. I refused to believe that poverty, abuse, neglect, and abandonment were my fault. A part of me. Me. As a child, I placed the blame squarely on Sheri. As an adult, I rightly and easily placed the blame on Sheri's mental illness and her incompetent doctors.

In counseling, I continued to explore. In life, I delved further with family and friends. To my surprise, Karen proved the most helpful.

"Ron loved you very much. He got you whenever he could. I would go over to see if he wanted help or needed a break, but he wouldn't let me. He tried to get you, but the courts wouldn't let him," she matter-of-factly stated when we were discussing my dad.

I was floored. I had zero clue my dad wanted custody of me. Zero clue he fought for me. Through research, I discovered that judges in the 1970s rarely awarded the father custody. Even with an unfit, mentally ill mother, my dad never had a chance. More and more, I understood that society's safety nets failed our broken family: the justice system, the public school system, the mental health system, and Child Protective Services. My mom never had a chance either.

Thanks to all my families, my survival was not dependent on these systems. I had a chance. A parachute. A future. Families. Siblings. And a father. I wanted for nothing. With my newfound knowledge, my inner child calmed down and played in colors.

With each visit, each text message, each phone call with my dad, I experienced healing from within and, as a result, without. As I healed, the little girl within danced and smiled. Loved and rested. I became rooted in my family. Rooted in belonging. Confidently rooted in my being.

I was no longer the little girl in the window, looking out with longing. Waiting. Dying. I was no longer gazing into another family's window either. Wanting. Begging. My nose was no longer pressed to the glass while my breath fogged the pane, leaving imprints of my nose, forehead, and fingerprints behind. My indescribable longing healed over time.

As I solidified my new roles and new relationships and created space in my life for my dad and siblings, Hurricane Harvey hit Houston. Devastated our city. Paralyzed our way of life. Our house was spared, but many lost everything. Nearby neighborhoods banded together to rebuild through the suffering. We all cleaned up together. Protected one another.

After days of home isolation and wading through water, I received several messages from Sheri's husband, pleading for me to return his call. I didn't. Then Keisha called. Judah had died in a motorcycle accident on August 26, 2017, she told me. As the news crawled through the phone, I felt nothing a sister should feel over a brother's death. No grief. No sadness. No loss. While I experienced some empathy for Sheri over losing her son again, I felt nothing for Judah.

Guilt about my lack of feeling lingered and weighed heavily on me. I tried to conjure up images of Judah when we first met at Taco Bell or last met in California. I tried to feel something, anything, other than guilt. But nothing occurred. I had no tears to spare. No tears for Judah. No tears for Sheri. Both were relative strangers to me. They were tragic figures in my life. Distant and foreign. Ill and lost. I wasn't sure who I felt sorrier for while I juggled these thoughts in my mind. I wasn't sure who I felt guiltier about leaving.

As Judah's funeral inched closer, Sheri left multiple hysterical messages on my phone. The ones I listened to were inaudible. I deleted the others.

Sheri hurt, and I understood her pain. I was a mother, too. She wanted me to hurt, too, but I couldn't do that to myself. I had long since stopped our pattern of suffering. When the funeral commenced, I was in Scotland with my family. I was a no-show, and so was my dad.

I wanted to have a conversation with him about the moment. About Judah's death. About his life. Why was he left as an infant? Why all the secrecy? Why? But Judah was an unspoken, forbidden topic. My dad never broached the subject, and Judah's name never left his lips in my presence. Never. Ever. More than most, I also understood the deep need to put your spouse's mistakes behind you, fix the problem, and move on. I understand this need especially when the spouse is mentally ill.

I was not even certain my dad knew of Judah's death, unsure if anyone told him. With my newfound understanding of my dad's love for his children and grandchildren and how he fought for me, it made me wonder if Judah was not my father's son. I don't think I will ever know. It will remain unspoken. Buried in Merkel, Texas, at the age of forty-four. Buried in my parents' past.

Weeks after the funeral, someone sent me Judah's obituary. His birthdate, which I never knew, was August 21, 1973. One day before Danette's. Once again, I marveled at the brilliant way God restored loss in my life.

Finally, tears fell.

20

Untethered

No one ever told me grief felt so like fear.

—C. S. LEWIS, *A GRIEF OBSERVED*

Call me when you can talk, Keisha texted.

It was 8:00 p.m. in Round Top, Texas, on October 1, 2019. I called within fifteen minutes. Her words carried a pain-filled message. A sucker punch. A blow. As the blood rushed to my face, before my brain understood the meaning, I knew. Motherfucker, I knew.

"Your mom died on Wednesday. I wanted to confirm it before telling you. It's all been oddly kept quiet," she said.

I heard myself respond. I saw my body absorb the news. I watched Layla process the death of Sheri. I saw shock. I saw sadness. I saw brown. I saw myself break in two. But my tone and words sounded professional and appropriate. Sounded like Dr. Salek. I immediately cared for Keisha.

"Thank you for telling me. I know it's always hard delivering my bad news," I said.

The call ended. *My mom died*, I texted. One to Terr. One to my dad. One to Walt. One to Danette. Simple. No emotion. Terr called. He informed me his mom had been visiting mine for months. *Seriously? What the fuck?* I broke into more pieces. Three separate people. One who observed. One who held the phone. And one little girl in the corner spinning. Hurting. Shattering. But I didn't allow her to surface. Not yet. Not time.

I kept dialing. Texting. Talking. Moving. Reacting. Possibly breathing. For an hour, I talked to my dear friend Riley, who was with me. I spoke of history. A troubled life. An ill woman. A dark color. I talked to my friend, but I was actually talking to the little girl in the corner. I processed the news for my younger self. My words were clear and gentle. Deliberate and motherly. After a hazy, purposeful conversation, I retreated to my room, and Riley moved to hers.

As soon as I crawled between the sheets, I curled into a ball. I melted. I cried. I shook. I wrote. I wanted my mom. I wanted her to ease the abandonment. Ease a lifetime of shame. A lifetime of need. A lifetime of loneliness. As I rocked in a ball, swaddled in brown, I felt my trailer. Felt Snuggles's fur. Felt my mom's embrace. Felt it all. I wrote a poem to her that night:

> Somehow, your death bookends my life.
> Beginnings and endings rise and fall.
> I feel relief.
> I prayed for decades for peace in your soul.
>
> But I cannot change a lifetime of sadness and lack.
> I chose to save me, Mom.
> Save our lineage.
> Save my child, Mom.
>
> You taught me the sidelines were safe
> And life with you was made of lace.
> I sincerely apologize for sacrificing you,
> I didn't mean to.

Rest now.
Feel your best now.
Leave the contemplation to me
Now.

Know I'm confused; know I'm off.
Don't you see me shaking, writhing, and lost?
Did you think I wouldn't miss you?
Did you believe I wouldn't care?

Well, Mom, I am untethered now,
Spinning uncontrollably
In the fetal position through space now.
Alone. Scared. Trying to find you.

Trying to connect,
Trying to reattach now.
Where do I belong?
Where do I land?

I swear I feel your energy;
I feel every part of you.
I reach for your heel,
Grasp on to your leg.

But I cannot clamp down.
My fingers fail to hold.
Your movement has purpose,
And it's away from me.

Again? Are we here again?
Abandonment, Mom?
At forty-seven, the all-too-familiar feeling of wanting you,
Looking for you, begging for you.

This feeling is like an old friend knocking.
I refuse to answer.
Instead, I reach for you.
My body falls; my breath escapes.

Sorry you can't stay.
Sorry I stayed away.
Sorry we got askew.
What do I do?

Mom, answer me!
This is the wrong ending.
No goodbyes? No apologies?
You can't leave yet; I need you to take it all back.

Mom, take it back!
I need you to stay. Please stay.
I can't take this.
This will definitely break us.

You went out with a whimper,
But I was waiting for a bang,
One big bang.
I would have followed the bang.

I would have run and sat by your side.
Who knows you better than I?
Who knows us?
No one, Mom.

Denying me the chance
To say goodbye feels immoral,
Feels too final,
Feels wrong.

I now know you were asleep,
Unconscious, unaware.
So, come back, Mom!
Let's wake together and be reborn, Mom.

I meant to be there; I promise I did.
I wanted to take you to the edge,
I wanted to lead you home.
Only I can tell God you didn't mean it.

God, you made her ill.
Now, cradle her; don't punish her.
Let her rest; give her peace.
I beg you for peace.

The next day was a blur. Every thought led to Sheri. Led to her last days. Led to all her days. Her beauty. Her smile. Her hate. Her illness. Us wrestling. Us laughing. Us yelling. Each thought birthed a new thought which bred even more thoughts. My emotions tangled in brown. My gut ached. My heart crumbled. My brain hurt.

With each step, I retraced the steps of our complicated path. Searched for her. Looked for me. Probed for answers. Deep in my journey, the painful, historical, too-familiar sensation of being left behind consumed me. Suffocated me. Compressed my body. The realization of her death and its finality were more than I could digest.

"I am unprepared for this," I said over and over.

Hidden in grief, I stumbled upon the smallest Catholic church. I stepped in. Prayed. Experienced the moment. But comfort escaped me. As I sat with God, more and more people from my mom's past contacted me. Reached out in love. Reached out because they were equally shocked. No one knew why my mom chose to die without me. Without her siblings. Without her dear friends. Explanations were offered. None sufficed. I needed to hear her voice. Her words. Her meaning. For the first time in decades, but like in every other moment of my life, I needed my mom.

My inner little girl kicked and tantrumed until sleep took her soul. But even in sleep I found no relief. No comfort. No rest. With a blonde ponytail and blue dress, I searched for my mom. Wanted to collect my belongings. Wanted to bring her home. I searched in the thick darkness. Searched under rocks. Behind trees. In holes. I searched. I called. Suddenly, I found her. Through the mist, in the cold, she lay. Long black hair. Petite. Tan. I lifted her in my arms. Her limbs synced with my movement. Her white dress whispered on my legs.

Just when I could no longer carry her weight, our trailer materialized. The single-wide glowed in the moonlight. Snuggles waited by the trees. Showed me the way in the familiar scene. Welcomed me. Unfolded me. Told me I was home. I followed Snuggles to the backyard. To the silent woods. The woods where Snuggles and I played. The woods where Snuggles perished. I laid my mom on a bed of wet leaves. My arms tired. My will exhausted. But I dug. Soil stuck under my nails and between my toes. My dress tore. My knees bled.

Once I finished, I gave her back to the earth. Back to God. I collapsed next to her. With Snuggles at my feet, I contemplated going with her. Imagined her wanting me. Imagined finally being hers. Finally having a mom. Suicide tugged at my heart. I romanticized us being mother and daughter. Best friends. Confidants.

But I knew she must pass alone. In this moment, there was no choice. In this moment, I was not in control. I had to go. As I covered her peaceful body, I jolted to my senses. I woke to sadness. I woke to stillness and sweat. I woke motherless and brown-less.

At 4:00 a.m., I frantically searched the internet for her obituary. Frantically attempted to find her funeral service. I needed actual evidence of her death. I needed physical confirmation. I needed to know. I texted Terr. Texted Keisha. Left the bed. Found my favorite chair. Sat in the dark. Terr responded. Offered to ask his mom. By sunrise, Lloyd called everyone who might know. By lunch, it was confirmed. She was gone.

Her current husband requested no service. No obituary. My mind raced. *Were those her wishes? Or his wishes? She had a life. She deserved recognition. She deserved to be honored.* Lloyd sent me her husband's cell number. I called. I left messages. I texted. I begged. No response. *Why? What am I missing? I think I have the right to ask. The right to know. Do I, Mom? Were we not connected? Was I not your daughter?*

I didn't care for the feelings of being a motherless child. I hated them, actually. Too familiar. Too wrong. Too painful. Walt called funeral homes in Fort Worth. Searched. *Once again, I am searching for you, Mom. I don't like this. I'm unprepared.* With his second call, Walt found her. Finally. Thankfully. When he asked if I could say goodbye, the lady responded, "She was cremated immediately at her husband's request."

"May her daughter have a moment with her ashes to say goodbye? Or may she have some of her ashes?" Walt offered as an alternative.

I paced. I held my breath. I felt close to her for the first time in several days. Possibly in several years. But as I grasped at her heel, she ascended.

"We cannot allow it without her husband's permission. Her legal next of kin."

My heart fell. Anger swelled. *Legal next of kin? I wanted to scream. I am her daughter! I am her next of kin! That's my mom! Give me my mom! My ponytail swung. Blue dress swayed. I searched in the dark. Stomped and huffed in the night.* I pulled myself back. I texted her husband. Asked for permission. No response. I didn't exist. I didn't have the right.

And like that, I remembered a letter my mom wrote years after Heris's birth. One plea was embedded in her sentences: *Layla, don't punish me for the rest of my life.* A rush of truth hit me.

"I did just that," cut from my lips, a whisper. "I did exactly that."

I put distance and time between us. I froze our relationship in 1999. I'd had enough suffering. I'd been hurt by her enough. Waited long enough for her to change. To get help. To be different. Be healthy. Be loving. Be golden brown instead of dead black.

Because of me, she died daughterless. Grandchild-less. On the verge of being trapped in sadness, trapped in consequences, I stepped away from my muddled emotions. I deliberately conjured up memories of why I left. Why I could not stay. Memories of darkness. Memories of illness. Memories of us at odds. Unable to coexist. Unable to live in peace.

As my memories developed and dispersed, people from all points in our past continued to call. Continued condolences. They dropped bits of love. Offered support. Poured compassion. I switched to gratitude. Because of my mom, I have many families. Many angels. Because of her, God sent others to nurture, protect, and guide me.

Amid this realization, one of my angels offered me a chance at closure. Shared the idea to have a service for my mother without her body or ashes present. *Yes, I can honor my mom. Yes, she existed. Yes, I am her daughter. My legs skipped. My ponytail leapt.*

The week before the service, I walked within gratitude but stepped in and out of confusion. In the absence of answers, speculation filled the gap. Many wondered about my mom's decision to die alone. Die without friends or family. Die without an obituary or funeral service.

Some felt it was her last act of meanness. Her last chance to stick it to us all. To die with her middle finger erect and high. Others believed my mom felt undeserving of a funeral. Underserving of a place in history. Unworthy of typical human traditions. Typical rites of passage. Others thought maybe she believed no one would show for the ceremony. Show for the send-off. Show for the show.

I chose to believe differently. To me, and only me, it felt like her last act of motherly love. Her last gift to me. By not contacting me, not causing drama, not departing with a bang, she spared me the emotional turmoil of the end. Spared me the decision of whether to show. Spared me the pain and distress of watching my estranged mother suffer and die. A conscious decision, a motherly decision, to finally let me go.

I handpicked the guests for her service. I chose to invite those who truly loved my mom, even if their love was brief. I chose those who missed their chance to say goodbye. Those who would come with forgiving hearts. Those who understood their hearts were not broken by her, but by mental illness. Our sweet service included Aunt Lottie and her daughters, as well as Winona's son and her grandchildren. The Melendys attended, of course, as did Honey, Danette, and a few of my mom's dear friends. I spoke first. Fighting tears, I tried to ease everyone's confused hearts, including my own.

I spoke of things I knew for certain after life with my mom.

"First, my mom loved each one of you," I began, "and I know you loved her. Second, my mom did the best with the hand she was dealt. With the unspeakable circumstances of her childhood, with a debilitating illness, she truly tried her best. Third, God put each of you in her life to guide and love us. Without question, you rose to the occasion. Finally, and with complete certainty, I know forgiveness is the most powerful act of love. I wish she would have experienced your forgiveness and love in her final days."

While trembling, I closed with thanking the Melendys for being her best friends and my most loving parents. I thanked Honey for treating Heris and me as her very own, even though this was a role she did not seek.

The service concluded with one of my mom's dear friends retelling endearing tales. Each painted a picture of her sense of humor. Misplaced emotions. Untamed spunk. With each sentence, I could see her gorgeous smile. The gap in her teeth. Her brown eyes twinkling. Her long black eyelashes fluttering. I could hear her voice. Feel her presence.

As Lloyd gave the final prayer and each word ascended to God, my mom kissed my forehead. Gently pulled the ribbon from my ponytail. For one last time, I experienced her beauty and free spirit. My hair fell free.

Epilogue

Goodbye? Oh no, please. Can't we go back
to page one and do it all over again?

—WINNIE THE POOH
(PRINTED ON THE FUNERAL SERVICE PROGRAM,
BECAUSE NO "MOTHER" POEM WOULD DO)

Following the funeral service, guests gathered at the Melendys for food and fellowship. In my conversations with Aunt Lottie, her daughters, and Winona's son, I discussed this book and recounted a few stories. We laughed over the family reunion that ended with fists flying. I asked about her story of Pat trying to kill my mom, to which she only responded, "I probably shouldn't have told you that. Well, not at that age anyway."

Before they left, we exchanged numbers. In the years following my mother's death, I have spoken with Lottie's oldest daughter numerous times, and each phone call has been enlightening. Being four years older than me with a relatively sane mother, she was able to offer some truths regarding our Native American heritage, as well as clarify a story or two housed within this book. In fact, she informed me that my mother's tale of how her own mother died may have been inaccurate.

"Lena Mae didn't die by suicide. But she did die in a car accident and may have been decapitated. She was drinking and driving fast on an old country road," she shared.

We questioned my mother's motives to twist the event into something horrid, but my cousin's version makes more sense. Now I understand why no other family member recounted the same tale.

After Keisha and Karen read a few chapters, they asked why I had not written about my mother's only suicide attempt, of which they were aware. I was stunned. As they recounted the event, I had zero memory of it. Regardless, I felt it was important to include since it was a part of my mother's and my history and directly speaks of her mental illness.

This attempt is recounted in the chapter "Failed" within the correct timeline; however, the words and details are from Karen and Keisha. Even after we discussed the attempt at length and I was present for it, I still had no memory of the incident. As far as I know, this is the only memory I have ever repressed. This repression of such a serious moment is quite shocking to me, even as a psychologist.

I clearly remember the hospital visit of the first attempt outlined in "Displaced," but I don't remember who took me to and from the hospital; nor do I remember any conversations about the attempt following the incident. I was also shocked to learn that Karen thought my mother and I both stayed with the Garcias for that year. For her last known attempt detailed in "Isolated," I clearly remember all the specifics before and during but not after, or so I think.

Other than the aforementioned story about my mother outlined by Karen and Keisha, every other story is written from my memory. No matter how faulty. No matter how distorted. No matter how ugly or beautiful.

I am now more than ever aware that trauma is stored in our brains differently than any other event or information. So I completely understand that my account could be jumbled and misplaced along the timeline. I welcome conversations with other people in this book or others who simply knew my mother. I welcome the chance to complete the puzzle of my story and relationship with her.

I want to thank my cousins on both sides for their validation of my stories and their support. We have all carried trauma and lived in chaos because of the abuse our parents endured. Once we knew better, we behaved better.

For an update on my family members, Walt, Heris, and I are doing well. Heris successfully transitioned to Boston University, which was harder on us than her. In the midst of moving across states, Walt experienced another manic episode with significant fallout.

After he stabilized, I began writing my next book, *Dear Caregiver*, which is a diary of sorts to help other caregivers of spouses with mental illness. As with this text, I hope to help others like me, or at least provide some insight or comfort. Thankfully, we have multiple loving families who support us. Honey, Danette, my siblings, my father, Terr, and the Melendys are a constant source of love and compassion. And all are thriving. To our surprise and delight, my father is still in remission and is a constant in our lives.

On a sad note, Pappa Dave died on September 8, 2020. His death shook my foundation. He died alone as a result of COVID-19 protocol, and we were not allowed by his side, a fact that still haunts me at night. I firmly believe the strict pandemic regulations killed PD. They broke his spirit. Clipped his wings. Since the nursing home was on lockdown and required the residents to stay in their rooms, PD could no longer entertain or socialize.

After the news of his death, I collected myself and wrote on social media:

> He was hands down the greatest comedian of all time.
> As Terr said, "His brain was clocked differently." He
> weaved story after story to his family or anyone with
> ears. As children, we believed everything he told us,

regardless of how insane it sounded. The last story he told Heris and me was, "Publishers told me they won't print and sell my memoir because my life is too close to *Rambo*."

Rest in peace; I am so sorry you died alone. You will forever be with me. You are my heart and my funny bone. I would have loved to have heard your stories one last time. I wonder what your crazy, half-true story about death would be. I cannot wait to hear it! At least you have new material now!

At the start of 2021, I sunk into a depression about PD. Since I did not attend the funeral, I had no closure. His life, his memory, and our love weighed heavily on me. I spent long periods of time recounting stories and staring at his photos. Tears followed. Walt was concerned.

Layla, in Groucho Marx glasses,
and PD just before the pandemic

On February 11, 2021, I received a long text message from my brother's wife. It was odd, since neither she nor my brother ever met PD. When I first scanned the text, I fled the table where we sat at a restaurant. Went outside. Caught my breath. I read and reread the following:

> Your grandfather says hello. He loves and misses you.
> He is so proud of your daughter. Also, he says you keep
> looking at a certain photo of him. He is watching over
> y'all. He is a funny man yet serious. I don't know which
> photo. It looks like an older one. However, he is showing
> me one of him walking with someone in his arms either
> holding hands or holding hips. I can't tell. Anyway, it's
> cute. I thought I would pass along the message. If you
> haven't found it, it is a picture of when he was younger,
> and he keeps showing it to me. He wants you to know
> that he is okay. He said he is in your dreams and to pay
> attention.

Obviously, Walt and I were shocked. Walt was the only person who knew I stared at his photos and cried. When we arrived home from lunch, I sent her my cherished photos. She responded.

> Lord, that seriously gave me chills. That first picture!
> That's it! Man! That's insane! Well, just know I felt so
> much love he had for you. He was so happy to show
> me you. It was like he was gloating. Seemed as if he
> was telling me a story. Which is weird cause normally
> when they come through, they just show me images and
> they're done. But not him. It was like he was making

them into stories. I know that makes no sense, but it's how it felt. I know I didn't know him, but I would have loved to.

It all made perfect sense.

A final word on Sheri: I initially wrote these stories for her and me to read and, I hoped, discuss. My intention was for us to finally have the hard conversations we'd never had. About a year into writing, I received word that she had passed. With that news, I had an ending to the book, but my purpose and intention switched. I focused on healing myself and others through our stories. I have felt closer to her while writing this book and following her death than I ever have in my life. I take great comfort in knowing she is no longer suffering. I think of her daily. I can hear her voice. See her smile. Feel her at peace. Breathe in her brown. Laugh at our hilarious and absurd moments.

Since her death, I have studied Eckhart Tolle every morning for one or two hours. His teachings have allowed me the space to let go of a traumatic childhood and reside in the present moment while living grounded in my being and gratitude. One of his quotes stands out over all the others, offering me the space to forgive my mother:

> If her past were your past, her pain your pain, her level of consciousness your level of consciousness, you would think and act exactly as she does. With this realization comes forgiveness, compassion, and peace.[1]

With forgiveness, I no longer carry the weight of our stories. Chaos has calmed. Only captivating colors remain.

---

1 Eckhart Tolle, *Stillness Speaks* (Novato, CA: New World Library, 2003), 92.

About the Author

R. LAYLA SALEK, PhD, is retired from a twenty-year private practice. She trained professionals and parents in behavior psychology techniques to help children with behavioral disorders (see www.drsalek.com). She sits on multiple boards and is the founder of Susie Bean Gives (www.susiebean.org). She is also a travel photographer and writer and is working on her second book, *Dear Caregiver.*